Edgar Rice Burroughs and Tarzan

Edgar Rice Burroughs and Tarzan

A Biography of the Author and His Creation

ROBERT W. FENTON

McFarland & Company, Inc., Publishers
Jefferson, North Carolina, and London

To Rick, Heidi and Todd
and to Duff

Frontispiece: Edgar Rice Burroughs on his favorite horse, "Colonel," at Tarzana Ranch, 1928. As lord of the manor, ERB rode every morning before breakfast to survey his holdings. (Photograph copyright © Edgar Rice Burroughs, Inc., 1975)

The present work is a reprint of the illustrated case bound edition of Edgar Rice Burroughs and Tarzan: A Biography of the Author and His Creation, *first published in 2003 by McFarland. That edition was a republication of* The Big Swingers *(Prentice-Hall, 1967) but with new photographs and a new foreword.*

LIBRARY OF CONGRESS CATALOGUING-IN-PUBLICATION DATA

Fenton, Robert W.
Edgar Rice Burroughs and Tarzan : a biography
of the author and his creation / Robert W. Fenton.
p. cm.
Includes bibliographical references and index.
ISBN 978-0-7864-4908-8
softcover : 50# alkaline paper

1. Burroughs, Edgar Rice, 1875–1950.
2. Novelists, American, 20th century — Biography.
3. Adventures stories, American — History and criticism.
4. Tarzan (Fictitious character)   5. Africa — In literature.
I. Title.
PS3503.U687Z664   2010   813'.52 — dc21   2002015980

British Library cataloguing data are available

©2003 Marie Fenton Griffing. All rights reserved

No part of this book may be reproduced or transmitted in any form or by any means, electronic or mechanical, including photocopying or recording, or by any information storage and retrieval system, without permission in writing from the publisher.

On the cover: Denny Miller in *Tarzan the Ape Man,* 1959;
Edgar Rice Burroughs on the set of *Tarzan's Revenge,* 1938.
Background image ©2010 PhotoSpin

Manufactured in the United States of America

McFarland & Company, Inc., Publishers
Box 611, Jefferson, North Carolina 28640
www.mcfarlandpub.com

Acknowledgments

For personal information about Edgar Rice Burroughs, I am indebted to his daughter, Mrs. Joan Burroughs Pierce; his nieces, Mrs. Evelyn B. McKenzie, Mrs. Katherine Moss Konkle and his nephew, George Tyler Burroughs III. Also, to Cyril Ralph Rothmund and Mrs. Mildred B. Jensen of Edgar Rice Burroughs, Incorporated; and to Burroughs' second wife, the former Florence Gilbert.

For information on the publishing activities of Burroughs, I am *most* appreciative for the wholesome "open-door" policy and kind assistance of the A. C. McClurg & Company, Chicago; its executive vice president, Morton P. Weisman and to Mrs. Anne Wengerd.

I am thankful to Sol Lesser, veteran movie producer, for taking the time to fill me in on Tarzan (and Burroughs) in Hollywood; also for the cooperation of Hank Fine, formerly Mr. Lesser's director of publicity; to Rex Maxon, who helped uncover the comic strip Tarzan; and to Jim Freeman and Albert Moody of United Features Syndicate.

For World War II reminiscences, I thank these gentlemen: former Brigadier General Kendall J. Fielder, General (Ret.) Truman H. "Ted" Landon, and former Air Force Captain Oliver R. Franklin. For Hawaiian atmosphere and names, Miss Maye E. Biven. I also am indebted to Thurston Twigg-Smith, president and publisher of the Advertising Publishing Company, Honolulu, Hawaii, through whose courtesy and cooperation I was able to uncover and reprint for the first time Burroughs' war-time columns which originally appeared in the *Honolulu Advertiser*. Thanks also to Mrs. Jane Arita.

For taking me back to the late nineteenth and early twentieth centuries in Chicago, I would have been at a loss without the noble assistance of Mrs. Roberta B. Sutton, chief reference librarian, Chicago Public Library. Thank you, Mrs. Sutton, for bearing with me. Other librarians and researchers were most helpful (and always so patient). Particularly, Mrs. Lillian N. Schwartz, Academy of Motion Picture Arts and Sciences, Hollywood, California, and Mrs. Joanne Godbout, Museum of Modern Art in New York. Also, Mrs. Judith A. Schiff, historical manuscripts, Yale University, and a special thanks to Mrs. Juliet R. Kellogg, Phillips Academy, who, I know, exerted considerable effort in sorting through early Academy records.

The Burton Historical Collection of the Detroit Public Library was the source for material concerning the Michigan Military Academy at Orchard Lake, Michigan; as was the village of Orchard Lake, Michigan. The New York Public Library proved a reference mine of information, as well as providing work space. The Los Angeles Public Library unearthed pertinent information.

I am also indebted to the Archives and History Section, U.S. Military Academy, West Point. In Washington, D.C., to the Library of Congress; to Major General J. C. Lambert, the Adjutant General; to Victor Gondos Jr. and to Elmer Parker, Army and Navy Branch of the National Archives and Records Service. Thanks also to Pare McTaggart Lorentz, who proved to be a one-man research center in the nation's capital.

Also thanks to Philip Lewis, Research and Special Projects Director for the Chicago's Board of Education; and to George B. Vidal, National Publicity Director, Sears, Roebuck and Co.

To the Burroughs' Bibliophiles: A big thanks to Henry Hardy Heins, (author of *A Golden Anniversary Bibliography of Edgar Rice Burroughs*), who proofread my manuscript and made the necessary corrections; to Vernell Coriell, founder of the "Bibliophiles" and publisher-editor of three different fan periodicals, and to Camille Cazedessus, Jr., publisher-editor of another fanzine. Like Vern, "Caz" came to my rescue with last minute and sorely needed photographs and facts; also, thanks to D. Peter Ogden, third of the major fanzine publishers.

Lawrence S. Fanning, editorial director of the Publishers Newspaper Syndicate, voluntarily supplied me with clips from the *Chicago Times* and the *Chicago Daily News*. I also thank the editors of *The New York Times* and the *Los Angeles Times* for allowing me to rummage through their "morgues." The management of *Popular Publications* kindly allowed me to look through the early ERB stories, originally published in *Argosy Magazine* and *All-Story Weekly*. The editors of the McCall Corporation allowed me access to early issues of *Red Book* and *Blue Book Magazines*.

For permission to quote copyright passages I am also indebted to the following: Macmillan & Co., Ltd., London, England, Doubleday & Co., Inc., New York, for extracts from *Rudyard Kipling, His Life and Work*, by Charles Carrington; Mrs. George Bambridge, the Macmillan Co. of Canada Ltd., and Macmillan & Co., Ltd., London, England, for quotations from Kipling's *The Jungle Books*; the stanza from "The Ladies," by Rudyard Kipling, is reprinted with the permission of the current copyright holder, Macmillan & Co., Ltd., London, England, Mrs. George Bambridge, the Macmillan Co. of Canada Ltd., and Methuen & Co., Ltd., London England; Harvard University Press for extracts from *Sleuthing in the Stacks*, by Rudolph Altrocchi; Charles T. Branford Co., for extracts from *Comics and Their Creators*, by Martin Sheridan; *Los Angeles Times*, for its editorial on the death of Edgar Rice Burroughs; publishers of *The*

Burroughs Bulletin, ERB-dom, and *ERBANIA* for permission to reproduce pages of their respective "fanzines."

There are others who supplied me with anecdotes and personal information and, as well, with "arms and legs." Included in this group are: Mrs. Patrick Duffy, Sr., Jack and Ruth Alpert, Edward Clarke, Ralph Dorn and for extra effort, Bernice Fenton. Thanks to Dorothy and Harry Davis for their valuable contribution. To Robert Meisner of Radio/Television/Films Inc., with whom I am associated, for being a friend indeed. Pete Myers, of radio station WNEW, New York, suggested the title of the book.

And by no means least, to the "regulars" of the *S.L.S.N.P.P.* (*Sneden's Landing Saturday Night Poker Players*)—who, throughout this writing, so nobly maintained me with light heart (and lighter pocket) for the forthcoming week.

—*R.W.F. (1967)*

Contents

Acknowledgments v
Foreword by George T. McWhorter 1
Preface 5

	Prologue 9
I	Formative Years 1875–1897 15
II	Search for Adventure 1898–1904 27
III	A Lord's Trial 1905–1911 35
IV	Like Ulysses… 41
V	The Ape-man Cometh 1912 43
VI	Breakthrough 1913 49
VII	Tarzan and Friend 55
VIII	Those Crazy Moving Pictures 1913–1918 63
IX	On to the City of Gold 1918 77
X	Tarzan bei den Affen 1919–1932 81
XI	King of the Serials 1919–1925 87
XII	*The Girl from Hollywood* and Other Romances 1916–1922 95

Contents

Between pages 102 and 103 are 16 pages containing 27 photographs

XIII	Tarzan Swings 1920–1929	103
XIV	Tarzan of the World 1920–1929	109
XV	The Mid-Rancho Period 1922–1929	113
XVI	The Comic Strip 1928–	123
XVII	Two Women 1931–1933	127
XVIII	The One and Only 1932–1943	135
XIX	On Location in Africa 1933–1934	143
XX	New Adventures 1934–1938	147
XXI	Monkey Business 1935–1950	153
XXII	Search for the Fountain of Youth 1935–1937	161

Between pages 166 and 167 are 16 pages containing 38 photographs

XXIII	Pre–Pearl Harbor 1938–1941	167
XXIV	The Great Adventure 1941–1945	175
XXV	Last Years 1946–1950	181
	Epilogue	183

Appendices

    A   Chapter Notes   187
    B   99 Days   191
    C   War Correspondent   193
    D   Proposal for a National Reserve Army   199
    E   Novels of Edgar Rice Burroughs   201
    F   Edgar Rice Burroughs' Ape-English Dictionary   205

Index   209

Foreword
by George T. McWhorter

Edgar Rice Burroughs and Tarzan—first published in 1967 as *The Big Swingers*—holds the distinction of being the first commercially published biography of Edgar Rice Burroughs. Out of print for more than thirty years, Robert W. Fenton's book emerges today as an excellent source of information and entertainment for a new generation of readers. The Burroughs world has not stood still since Robert Fenton and his wife Marie purchased the former Burroughs home in Tarzana, California, where Fenton was inspired to compile his biography. Since 1967, the expanding Burroughs universe has grown to include five new books by Burroughs himself, a dozen major literary studies, nine feature Tarzan films and two non–Tarzan films, and the continued daily and Sunday Tarzan strips in the newspapers, the comic books, and more than a dozen fan publications which have sprung up in the USA and abroad.

Since Fenton's day, nine Tarzan movies have been made, starring (in order of their appearance) Mike Henry (1967–1968; two movies), Ron Ely (1970; two movies), Miles O'Keeffe (1981), Christopher Lambert (1984), Joe Lara (1989), Casper Van Dien (1998) and the voice of Tony Goldwyn in the animated feature "Disney's Tarzan" (1999). The first TV-Tarzan series ran from 1966 to 1968 and starred Ron Ely with such first-rate supporting stars as Julie Harris and The Supremes. A second series began in 1989 starring Joe Lara for two years and continuing with Wolf Larson until 1993, after which it enjoyed reruns in Canada, Australia, France and Germany. An animated Tarzan series appeared during the 1970s entitled "Tarzan Lord of the Jungle," and a second animated series was debuted by the Disney Studios in 2001. David Fury's *Kings of the Jungle* (McFarland, 1996) is an excellent filmography which gives more specific details.

The Tarzan Sunday "funnies" that began in May 1931 have enjoyed a continuous publishing run by the United Features Syndicate in American newspapers for over seventy years. For eleven years, 1968–1979, the Tarzan strips were drawn by Russ Manning, considered one of the "big three" Tarzan illustrators along with his predecessors, Hal Foster and Burne Hogarth. Gil Kane (originally from Latvia) drew the strip 1979–1981; Mike Grell, 1981–1983; and Gray Morrow, 1983–2001. Morrow (who died in November 2001) held the longevity record of eighteen years at the drawing board and will be sorely missed by his legion of comic strip fans.

On the comic book scene, the Gold Key comics of Fenton's time continued the Tarzan comics under the DC label until 1977. The Marvel Comics Group stepped up to bat from 1977 to 1979, followed by a hiatus of fourteen years when the only Tarzan comics to be found were in foreign markets, notably France, Italy and the Baltic countries. Semic International and Malibu Comics brought Tarzan back to the USA in 1992, followed by Dark Horse Comics in 1995. Before leaving the comics scene, it should be noted that Burne Hogarth, the "Michelangelo of the Comic Strip," came out of retirement to illustrate two new Tarzan books for Watson-Guptill: *Tarzan of the Apes* (1972) and *Jungle Tales of Tarzan* (1976).

The best news for Burroughs buffs came during the last decade of the 20th century with a sudden flurry of hitherto unpublished works of Edgar Rice Burroughs. The first, published in December 1995 by Dark Horse Books, was an unfinished Tarzan fragment of eighty-three typewritten pages, completed by Jose Lansdale and titled *Tarzan: The Lost Adventure*. Dark Horse followed this with a 1998 first printing of a 1906 fairy tale Burroughs had written when living in Minidoka County, Idaho, in his gold dredging days along the Snake River. He called it "Minidoka: 937th Earl of One Mile, Series M." The publishers included some of Burroughs' own drawings as well as those of artist Michael Kaluta. In 1999, Donald M. Grant, Inc., gave us the long awaited premiere publication of a 1924 novel entitled *Marcia of the Doorstep*, illustrated by Ned Dameron, in tandem with Burroughs' only play, *You Lucky Girl!* which he wrote in 1927 as a vehicle for his daughter's budding stage career. The play was given its premiere stage performance in the spring of 1997 at the Palmdale Playhouse in Palmdale, California. In 2001, Grant publishers reissued its scholarly 1964 *Golden Anniversary Bibliography of Edgar Rice Burroughs* by Henry Hardy Heins, to which Heins contributed an updated epilogue. Finally, *Forgotten Tales of Love and Murder* (2001) is a compilation of the author's shorter, mostly unpublished pieces, edited and privately published by John Guidry and Pat Adkins in an illustrated hardback first edition. As far as we know, *Forgotten Tales* squeezes the orange dry, and those clamoring for more and more stories by Edgar Rice Burroughs will have to be content with the occasional pastiches or the unabated pleasure of rereading his standard classics.

Major contributions to the Burroughs legend have taken their places on the shelf next to *The Big Swingers* since 1967. The 1975 centennial biography by Irwin Porges, *Edgar Rice Burroughs: The Man Who Created Tarzan*, represents more than three years of intensive research and can never be duplicated for its voluminous information. Erling B. Holtsmark, a professor of classics at the University of Iowa, produced two important books of literary criticism: *Tarzan and Tradition* (Greenwood, 1981) and *Edgar Rice Burroughs* (Twayne, 1986). Robert B. Zeuschner's *Edgar Rice Burroughs: The Exhaustive Scholar's and Collector's Descriptive Bibliography* (McFarland, 1996) filled a large gap after the Heins bibliography went out of print. The most recent biography to be published is the work of former *Newsweek* editor John Taliaferro: *Tarzan Forever* (Scribner, 1999). I have seen it referenced and quoted in many book and magazine articles after the critics gave it a "thumbs up" vote of confidence.

I close out my remarks by saying that *The Big Swingers* has never gathered dust on my shelf. I have pasted up some of its book charts and appendices over my desk for many years, and still refer to them when answering telephone questions about Edgar Rice Burroughs. It has proved to be a useful book, and I'm glad that latecomers to the scene will now have a chance to own a copy.

Mr. McWhorter is Curator of the Burroughs Memorial Collection and Editor of the Burroughs Bulletin.

Preface

Back in those good, old days of the mid and late 1930s, I shared with millions of other readers and movie-goers, the grand adventures of *Tarzan*, the mighty ape-man. As far as I was concerned, the Big Swinger was a combination of Hercules, Marco Polo and Tom Mix — solidly packed in one bronzed, sinewy body. I was enthralled by the fantastic sweep of Burroughs' imagination ... his complete knowledge (and mastery) of jungle lore ... the bizarre peoples and pre (sic) pre-historic monsters of his "lost civilizations" and, too, there was none of that boy-girl nonsense. Sex (except for several early lapses by the ape-man) lay only in the foul minds of foul and swarthy villains. That's how long ago it was. I stopped reading Burroughs at about age thirteen and ceased going to *Tarzan* movies at sixteen. By 1939 — and I was right — *Tarzan* was dead.

It was not until 1955 that the swaying boughs of the jungle forest lured me back. With my wife and children, I had returned to Southern California from a five and one-half year working séjour in Europe and we decided to make the San Fernando Valley our home. One day's safari led us through the underbrush to Tarzana, where the old office of Edgar Rice Burroughs lay hidden behind a weatherbeaten grapestake fence amidst an overgrowth of Eucalypti, Pine and Pepper trees, and clumps of bamboo and papyrus plants. The house itself had been vacant for several years after a long occupancy by Jack, the author's youngest son and illustrator of many of his father's stories. We negotiated and eventually purchased the place from ERB, Inc.

As a free-lance writer, it was quite natural that the thought occurred to me of doing a story on Burroughs and the Tarzan mystique. But, first, I might again read several of the author's stories to re-familiarize myself with the underbrush. The local branch public library, however, did not carry one volume of Burroughs'. "His works are not considered to be of sufficient literary merit," I was told. But I did locate some of the author's works at a second-hand book store and then Ralph Rothmund, general manager of ERB, Inc., presented me with a dozen of Burroughs' later novels. I searched for and then read his non-jungle stories as well—of Mars, Venus, Pellucidar, western, Indian tales and other adventures, including several "modern romances." Here might not be an author of great literary merit, but here, *obviously*, was one of the greatest storytellers of all time. But—what about the *man*?

Although I had never set eyes upon the author, after re-reading the stories, his works seemed to suggest that Burroughs' life might closely parallel the thoughts, philosophy and experiences of his creation, *Tarzan*. Rothmund allowed me to look through some [but not all] of Burroughs' files, letters and press-clipping books. What would I discover? Was Burroughs an intrepid adventurer of the Fran Buck "Bring-'em-back-alive" school? Was he brought up in Africa, perhaps the son of missionaries or traders? Was he, too, an Englishman of noble ancestry—counterpart of Lord Greystoke, also known as John Clayton and *Tarzan of the Apes?* This was mine to uncover since no recognizable biography of Burroughs had ever been written. This was mine to discover since the biography would be "unauthorized"—sans blessing of the Burroughs' heirs.

To find the *man*, it has taken me awhile to find the few who knew the author well, and to locate others whose letters and papers have proved to be invaluable source material. It has been a long but pleasant hunt.

ROBERT W. FENTON
Sneden's Landing, New York
September, 1966

...I do not know how old I am. I recall no childhood. I have always appeared to be about thirty years old. I still do.... Perhaps I am the materialization of some long dead warrior of another age. Who knows?
                                            The City of Mummies, 1941*

---

*First published in the March 1941 issue of *Amazing Stories*; subsequently in the novel, *Llana of Gathol*, published by ERB, Inc., March 1948.

Prologue

Every artist writes his own autobiography. Even Shakespeare's works contain a life of himself for those who know how to read it.

Havelock Ellis
The New Spirit, 1890

To millions of readers and cinema fans the world over, Tarzan was for roughly twenty-five years (1914–1939) simple, strong, heroic, free, clean, honest, brave, courageous, just, handsome, virile and noble. In all probability, no fictional character has had greater impact on so many people. By 1940, the twenty-three* Tarzan novels of Edgar Rice Burroughs had been printed in thirty-one languages and dialects, including Danish, Italian, Urdu, Icelandic, Hebrew, Esperanto and Russian. Sixteen† Tarzan movies had been made to an estimated gross of more than $100 million. The fictional mine of the author was a waterfall of gold emptying into a constant running stream.

But another kind of drama unfolded in the forties and millions of American boys reluctantly set aside their Tarzan adventures for those of an equally cruel but nonfictional world. By 1961, Tarzan and the

---

*Three other Tarzan novels subsequently were published. (See Appendix for complete listing.)
†Plus twenty-two additional Tarzan films from 1946 to 1966.

empire created by ERB were in a long drought.

The final Tarzan novel, *Tarzan and "The Foreign Legion,"* had been published in 1947, three years before Burroughs' death. But save for the revenue from leasing title rights for an annual Tarzan motion picture (plus some income from a declining comic strip market), the lord's once-leafy jungle was still as an elephant's graveyard. Where Wappi, the antelope, once roamed, $40,000 tract houses cluttered the hills of Tarzana,* back to the tinder-dry Santa Monica mountains. Where Ara, the lightning, once flashed and Pand, the thunder, once rumbled, the only movement in the desert air of the Valley was the smog—relentlessly creeping north and west from downtown Los Angeles.

The three Burroughs heirs—comprising Edgar Rice Burroughs, Inc.—were living unpretentiously in the San Fernando Valley, near the site of the 540-acre "Rancho Tarzana" that Ed had purchased in 1919: daughter Joan, married to real-estate developer and one-time movie Tarzan (*Tarzan and the Golden Lion*, 1927) James Pierce; son Hulbert, who dabbled in photography; and John, an artist and illustrator of his father's books. The corporation itself had been masterminded since 1940 by general manager Cyril Ralph Rothmund, an astute and taciturn Scotsman, who thought Burroughs was the business machine company of the same name when he answered an advertisement for "secretary wanted" in 1927.

Southern California is a land of extremes with conditions that defy normal barometric reading, so it was only fitting that Los Angeles be the port of call when the deluge hit—ending a drought which had withered the jungle nigh over a quarter-century. Rothmund was negotiating with Western Printing for publication of a comic book, based on *Tarzan of the Apes*, when the sluice gates, ironically, were opened by a schoolteacher from Downey, a suburb of Los Angeles. It was reported she withdrew two Tarzan books from the shelf of the school "donated" library after a parent had complained that Tarzan and Jane not only were *unmarried* but, mercy, they had a son!

Editors immediately sniffed a story. (*Ah, what was that? The shadow of a sound had come to those keen ears. There was but the suggestion of a breeze, but what there was moved.*)[1]

December 27, 1961
Los Angeles Mirror
"Tarzan" Banned in Downey School
Ape Man and Jane Never Married

December 28
Baton Rouge (Louisiana)
Morning Advocate
Tarzan Book Ban Protested

December 28
Santa Ana (California) Register
(Associated Press Story)
Tarzan Fans Say Ape Man
IS Married

December 30
Long Beach (California) Independent
Right There on Page 313
Tarzan, Jane Wed Way Back in 1915

January 2, 1962
Pittsburgh Post-Gazette
Me Tarzan, Me Banned

Stung into action, the legion of Tarzan admirers poured forth to support their

---

*An unincorporated community in Los Angeles' San Fernando Valley, about twenty miles northwest of city hall. (There is also a Tarzan, Texas.)

great *Tarmangani*.*I (*A shower of missiles fell upon them, and then Tarzan called on his followers to charge. Roaring and growling, the Bolgani* and the Gomangani* leaped forward to the attack.*)² In the *Gridley Wave*, a nonprofit amateur "fanzine," published by Vernell Coriell (the House of Greystoke, Kansas City, Missouri), Burroughs bibliophile John Harwood listed no less than five hundred passages to indicate that Tarzan and Jane were indeed married.

It was all nonsense,† of course, for in the second Tarzan novel (*Return of Tarzan*, 1915) Tarzan and Jane were married by her father, Professor Porter, an ordained minister, in the very cabin where Tarzan had been born. But the stampede was on—for fathers to rediscover and their sons to discover the adventures of the mighty apeman. However, Tarzan books were almost impossible to obtain. The publishing house of Grosset & Dunlap, which had reprinted Burroughs' novels since 1918, was at the tail-end of a three-year contract (negotiated in December 1959), and although they moved quickly to meet the new demand the few books that remained of their current lot proved no more than a twig in the vast jungle.

New York booksellers Jack Biblo and Jack Tannen found themselves swamped with requests for Tarzan books. "We had written Burroughs, Inc. several times but never received a reply, so we decided to initiate a survey of copyright clearance by the Library of Congress."³ Messrs. Biblo and Tannen said they were flabbergasted to discover that, in their opinion, the Burroughs corporation had neglected to renew the precious copyright on at least half the ERB's total output (U.S. Copyright expires in twenty-eight years unless renewed before the end of that period. A new copyright law, expected to be enacted by Congress in 1967, would extend the term of a copyright to the life of the author and 50 years after his death).

There has been much confusion on the copyright status of some of Burroughs' early works. Are they or are they not in the public domain? In an article published July 14, 1963, in the *New York Herald Tribune*, when asked who in the organization had blundered in failing to renew the copyrights, Hulbert Burroughs was quoted: "Just say that it was carelessness." When asked, in the same article, whether the heirs were dismayed upon learning they might not be receiving royalties on some of their father's works, Hulbert said:

"Well at first we were a little concerned, but we have things under control now. I don't think we'll lose too much by it." But Hulbert, according to the *Herald Tribune*, "declined to say how much the corporation would lose because of the copyright lapse, or even to say what proportion of the books is now in the public domain."

Other publications followed with major features on the upswing of Tarzan. *Newsweek* magazine reported more than 6 million Tarzans in print. "The reason for this enormous spate of publishing is that the Burroughs heirs have refused until recently to authorize paperback reprints. But now Ballantine has been awarded rights to all Tarzan books, and Ace, after attempt-

---

*In Burroughs' ape language, "white man," "gorilla" and "black man," respectively. See Appendix F for ape English dictionary.

†Obviously no Tarzan book reader, *Time* magazine's movie critic committed the same unpardonable *gaffe* when in a review of *Tarzan and the Slave Girl* (July 25, 1949), he wrote: "Moviegoers often fret about Tarzan's morals, and write in to ask if he and Jane are married (they are not)...." Two weeks later (August 8) *Time* printed a letter from Henry Hardy Heins correcting the error. The Reverend Heins, an ardent Burroughs fan and bibliographer, is author of *A Golden Anniversary Bibliography of Edgar Rice Burroughs* (Donald M. Grant, West Kingston, R.I., 1964).

ing unsuccessfully to get similar authorization, is publishing those on which copyrights have lapsed."[4]

And *Life* magazine, in a special report on Tarzan: "...Burroughs' heirs had committed a lapse which would have sent Burroughs' hero skulking into the underbrush ... the heirs had forgotten to renew the copyrights on at least eight Tarzan books plus about 20 other Burroughs novels."[5]

Initially the Burroughs corporation assumed that the failure to renew hardcover editions of some of Burroughs' works was fatal. However, when Burroughs' attorneys subsequently looked into the matter, they declared that the works in question had all been published in magazines before they appeared in hardcover editions and that there were renewals of the magazine copyrights. They then advised their client that, in their opinion, these renewals protected the Burroughs' stories. (The Copyright Office of the Library of Congress states that if a renewal of a copyright is obtained for a story first published in a magazine it will be protected regardless of whether or not renewal is secured based on the copyright of a subsequently published book containing the same story.)

Armed with its rather late discovery of the magazine copyright renewals, Burroughs proceeded to assert its copyrights and other rights in many parts of the world. Copyright law experts have told the writer that there has never been any court decision to the effect that any Edgar Rice Burroughs work is in public domain in the United States, and Burroughs, Inc. and their attorneys are of the opinion, today, that ERB's works are protected by copyright. In fact, the Ape-man's victorious jungle cry has been heard in such distant places as the Federal Court in New York; the Supreme Court of Judicature of Jamaica, West Indies; the Supreme Court in Helsinki, Finland; and the Tribunal de Grande Instance de la Seine de Paris, France! However, whether every Burroughs work on Tarzan is protected by copyright in the United States is a question that could only be resolved by the courts.

But going back to 1962, Biblo and Tannen had moved fast in a bold leap to capture the jungle empire. They organized Canaveral Press for the purpose of publishing the Burroughs books and placed an advertisement in the April 30 issue of *Publisher's Weekly*, accepting orders (through December) for twenty-one Burroughs Books (at $2.75) including two Tarzan titles—*Tarzan and the Lost Empire* and *Tarzan at the Earth's Core*; also a juvenile, *The Tarzan Twins*.

Other publishers swung into the clearing. Ian Ballantine, president of Ballantine Books, Inc., who had a sixteen year interest in the Tarzan property (see Chapter XXI), flew to California to discuss a possible deal for a paperback series. "I found Tarzana but it took me practically half a day to locate the Burroughs office. No one seemed to know where it was." Meanwhile, Canaveral Press, Ace Books, a paperback house (which finally published a total of thirty-six Burroughs titles), and Dover Publications raced to reprint those titles which they believed to be in public domain. (Dover was first.)

Ballantine was anxious to proceed with its "authorized" paperback series, but first Burroughs had to gain rights to the two titles of which McClurg still held some control (*Tarzan of the Apes* and *The Return of Tarzan*). Proposals, counter-proposals, counter counter-proposals and accusations flew from Tarzana to Chicago and back again. Neither side was getting anywhere and the first Ace Tarzan paperback, *Tarzan and the Lost Empire* was already on the stands. Burroughs, Inc. could no longer afford to delay and a final agreement with McClurg was reached in March, whereby McClurg turned over all rights, title and interest in the two properties in return for a percentage of the gross receipts actually received by Burroughs from the book publishing rights of the two works in the United States until expiration of the copyright term.

Burroughs was now free to enter into a contract with Ballantine for fifty-cent "authorized" versions of the Tarzan stories and to make separate contracts with Canaveral Press for hardcover works. One hundred and fifty thousand paperbacks of the two first titles were published in July and Ballantine immediately went ahead with the second printing of 100,000 each for November distribution.

On November 26, 1963, *The New York Times* quoted Hulbert Burroughs as claiming an assortment locked in the safe of "close to forty or fifty pieces that have never been published." Some were said to have been written under a pen name because Burroughs wanted to see if they could sell without his name. They did not.

(On Burroughs' death in 1950, *The Times* reported that the author left "approximately fifteen incompleted Tarzan tales plus some other stories.")

However, since the Burroughs revival, the only new Tarzan novel that has appeared is *Tarzan and the Madman*, completed by Burroughs in 1940, published in hardcover by Canaveral (1964) and in paperback by Ballantine (1965) as number twenty-three of Ballantine's Tarzan series. *Tarzan and the Castaways* also had been published by both of the above houses, but this one is made up of three stories that previously had appeared in magazines.*

There is, perhaps, more than one lesson to be learned from the phenomenal† resurgence of interest in the ape-man and his friends: first, it is likely that most of us still require (and see in Tarzan) the noble (albeit lonely) figure of primitive man — our folk hero — in the electronic, rocketry age to which our civilization appears totally dedicated; secondly, never underestimate the power of a schoolteacher.

---

*"Tarzan and the Champion" in *Blue Book*, April 1940; "Tarzan and the Jungle Murders" in *Thrilling Adventures*, June 1940; and the original version of "The Quest of Tarzan" serialized in *Argosy* magazine in three parts, beginning August 23, 1941.

†*Life* magazine (November 29, 1963) "...The Tarzan [paperback] books, along with other works of their author, Edgar Rice Burroughs, are runaway bestsellers today and have been ever since they began to come out [1962]. They have sold something more than 10 million copies, almost one thirtieth the total annual sales of all paperbacks in the U.S...."

I

Formative Years 1875–1897

> *When I was young, I used to dream of living an adventurous life, and it may be that these youthful dreams more or less shape up one's later life.*
> The Living Dead,* November, 1941

1. ON, BRITANNIA

From 1912 through 1947, amidst dizzying tree-top leaps and savage and bloody hand-to-hand combat — through twenty-four† Tarzan novels of derring-do — never once did author Edgar Rice Burroughs waver from his conviction that the English were the height of aristocracy, the noblest of souls; bully gentlemen of excellent manners; mentally, physically and, of course, morally above and beyond reproach. All of these highly commendable qualities were embodied in a certain John Clayton, who rightfully could take his seat in the House of Lords as Lord Greystoke — better known to Nkima, Tantor and the tribe of Kerchak, the great apes, as Tarzan, the ape-man.

---

*Part III of a four-part serial which first appeared in *Fantastic Adventures* (Ziff-Davis Publishing Co., New York); subsequently, as the novel, *Escape on Venus*, October 15, 1946, published by ERB, Inc., Tarzana, California.
†Total of twenty-six Tarzan books by 1964.

In his first Tarzan novel, *Tarzan of the Apes*, Burroughs immediately set the character of the great *Tarmangani*. The scene is Tarzan's initial encounter with a female (other than with ape-playmate Teeka). In a gallant gesture, the ape-man gives Jane Porter the locket which belonged to his parents (he is unaware at this time that Lord and Lady Greystoke are his rightful parents and believes Kala, the great ape, to be his mother). Jane puts the locket to her lips and then:

> Tarzan took the locket in his hand, stooped gravely like some courtier of old, and pressed his lips upon it where hers had rested. It was a stately and gallant little compliment performed with the grace and dignity of utter consciousness of self. It was the hallmark of aristocratic birth, the natural outcropping of many generations of fine breeding and hereditary instinct of graciousness....

And, again:

> Clayton was the type of Englishman that one likes best to associate with the noblest monument of historic achievement upon a thousand victorious battlefields—a strong, virile man—mentally, morally and physically.
>
> In stature, he was above the average height; his eyes were grey, his features regular and strong; his carriage was that of perfect, robust health influenced by years of army training.

Examples of the author's life-long affliction with Anglophilia abound throughout both Tarzan and non–Tarzan stories. If some explanation is in order, there is this passage from *Slaves of the Fish Men*:

> On my mother's side, I can trace my ancestry back to Deacon Edmund Rice, who came to Sudbury, Massachusetts, about 1639; and from him to Cole Codoveg, who was King of Briton in the third century.*

Burroughs himself, however, could not be called English—that is, not *pure* English. His father, George Tyler, born in Warren, Massachusetts, in 1833, and his paternal grandparents, Abner Tyler and Mary Coleman Rice, also born in the Bay State, were of old English stock, but his mother, Mary Evaline Zieger, born in Iowa in 1840, was of Pennsylvania Colonial Dutch stock back to her grandparents.

The obvious comment to make upon reading the above paragraph is that something is very much amiss! How could it be that the author had his character in *Slaves of the Fish Men* declare that he could trace his ancestor back to King Cole on his "mother's" side when, in fact, it was through the side of Burroughs' father (Rice) from which he could trace his claim to English nobility?

Why did the author create this obvious discrepancy? Well, he never hid the fact that he preferred his mother to his father and that he and his father differed on practically every subject throughout Burroughs' youth and adult years: ERB's daughter, Joan Burroughs Pierce, recalled her father telling her about *his* own father:

> My father always was very stern and military in our relationship. He used to tell me with increasing frequentness—until I was thirty-six—that I always would be a failure, and until I was thirty-six he was right. He urged me time and time again to come into business with him and although I did for a short time, this did not better our relationship. Whatever warmth and sense of humor I do possess, I owe entirely to my mother's side.[1]

(In *Tarzan of the Apes*, Tublat, foster father of the young white ape, hates Tarzan

---

*The first of four connected stories, appearing under separate titles in *Fantastic Adventures* magazine (Ziff-Davis Publishing Company). "Slaves of the Fish Men" was first published in March 1941 and in novel form in 1946 as the first part of *Escape on Venus* (ERB, Inc., Tarzana.)

and Tarzan, in turn, never loses an opportunity to reveal similar feelings. But to Kala, his foster mother, he gives all of his affection.)

It is not known if Burroughs' father ever read *Tarzan of the Apes*, which first appeared complete in the October 1912 issue of *All-Story* magazine, or if he ever commented on the first published story of his youngest son, *Under the Moon of Mars*.* These would have been the only two possibilities, for George Tyler Burroughs Sr. died February 15, 1913, at age seventy-nine.

Captain George Tyler Burroughs had served four years and two months with the Union forces in the Civil War. His rank was listed as brevet major by early Chicago historians, and ERB also gave his father the rank of major, although military records and discharge papers show his highest rank as that of captain. On July 22, 1865, at Albany, New York, he was honorably discharged from service by tendering his resignation "to enable him to return to his family and to establish himself in business." With his wife of two years,† he left for Portland, Maine, to resume his position as a merchant. By July 1868, the Burroughs family had increased to four — George Tyler Jr. was born on August 29, 1866, and Henry Studley, on May 23, 1868 — and they moved to Chicago. A third son, Frank Coleman, was born on May 14, 1872, seven months after the Great Fire made a name for Mrs. O'Leary's cow (no record has been found to indicate if the Burroughs' residence was among the more than seventeen thousand buildings destroyed by the fire). A fourth son would die in his teens. On September 1, 1875, their fifth child, Edgar Rice, was born. As a sixth son died in infancy, Edgar Rice would always remain the youngest child in the family.

Of his early childhood, ERB refused to remember any events until he was twelve. All that is known of him prior to this age is that he entered the Brown School on the West Side (1758 Warren Boulevard) one month short of his seventeenth birthday, that he also was known as "Edward" and "Eddie," and that the records did not show his participation in any special or outstanding activities. When he was twelve a diphtheria epidemic broke out in the city and "much to my horror my parents took me out of public school and put me in a girls' school"[2] which was the only private educational facility available on the West Side. Next, Ed attended Harvard School. When another epidemic hit Chicago — this time, influenza — he was dispatched to his brothers' ranch in Idaho. "Unquestionably," Burroughs later remarked, "my destiny is closely woven with pestilences, which may or may not account for my having become a writer."[3]

Influenza was not the only epidemic plaguing Chicago (and much of the nation) at this period. There had been fierce labor wars racking the city over the past five years and the fallout still lingered from the Haymarket Square riot of May 1886, when a bomb, hurled by an unknown assailant during a mass labor protest, killed eight policemen and injured more than seventy other officers. Also making his presence felt in Chicago was that fiery labor leader, Eugene V. Debs (later five-

---

*First published in *All-Story* magazine in six parts, beginning February 1912. As a novel entitled *A Princess of Mars*, October 10, 1917.
†It was a war-time marriage. Stationed at a camp near White Oak Creek, Virginia, on February 8, 1863, Lieutenant Burroughs was granted a fifteen-day leave of absence. He was married to Mary Evaline Zieger on February 24 at the home of her mother in Columbus City, Iowa, and, like soldiers immemorial, overstayed his leave and did not reappear on muster roll until March 3.

time candidate for president on the Socialist ticket), who was organizing the American Railway union and pushing his ridiculous proposal for an eight-hour day.

(A milder form of lingering epidemic also hit young Burroughs at this time. When he was fourteen he began proposing to Emma Hulbert, who lived in a spacious fifteen-room brownstone only a few doors down the street from the Burroughs' residence at 650, later 646 West Washington Boulevard — now the 1800 block.)

2. Don't Fence Me In

There was talk that soon the Territory of Idaho would be admitted to the Union (as it was on July 3, 1890), but to a vigorous boy of fourteen this could not have been very important. Edgar boarded the Northern Pacific for Pocatello and there transferred to the Oregon Short Line for American Falls, where his brothers had ridden thirty miles to meet him. Recent graduates of Yale University, class of '89,* Sheffield Scientific School, George and Harry (Henry) "had entered the cattle business as the best way of utilizing their college degrees," Ed remarked some years later.[4]

The population of Idaho at the time consisted of approximately 15,000 inhabitants (including 4,274 Chinese), with ranching and mining the principal industries. The Sweetser† and Burroughs' spread, part of the extensive holdings belonging to the late Senator and cattle king "Jim" Pierce, was located along the Raft River Valley (Cassia County) in the southeastern part of the Territory. Edgar took to the absolute freedom of the West like his horse Calamity took to alfalfa. He recalled "never having been as happy or cheerful as during the short time when I did hard chores, grubbed sage brush and drove a team of broncs to a sulky plough."[5] He was starting to develop a powerful physique and his grip, even at this time, was a bone-crusher. (Burroughs later told the story of a rubber in a Turkish bath who, after looking at his hands, remarked: "We get all kinds of people in here, but this is the first time I ever massaged a blacksmith."[6])

When the mail carrier at the ranch ran off with some supplies, Ed begged for the job and he got it, but first his brothers saw to it that he knew how to use a rifle. The boy and his horse hauled the mail to the nearest railroad at American Falls and made the round-trip of sixty miles in one day, although if there was freight to bring back, it was an overnight trip with the team and wagon.

When a friend of the Burroughs' family, passing through Idaho en route to Chicago, halted at the ranch, he apparently was shocked at the boy's imaginative stories of murderers, thieves and bad men whom the boy had met. "I suppose," Burroughs later said, "they [the stories] must

---

*George and Harry, who looked like twins, described themselves in a classbook as "Two lovely berries (Burris) moulded on one stem." [Yale University class records] They were both Chi Phi and members of the crew. George was elected vice president of his junior class and also captained the junior crew. In their senior year they marched in the first rank "all over the State of Connecticut" to help elect Benjamin Harrison over Grover Cleveland as President "and see the GOP restored to power for another quarter of a century."

†Yale classmate Lewis Hobart Sweetser later became lieutenant governor of Idaho, business executive, writer and lecturer. He authored *The Alexander Talisman* and *The Inner Voice Reveals*. Sweetser for years had been interested in psychic phenomenon and revealed to Harry Burroughs in 1937 that he had been receiving written messages from his wife who had died some years before. In the 1939 Yale Class Record, Harry told of his own psychic experiences which, he said, included receiving messages from his wife, who had been killed in an automobile accident.

have constituted another epidemic,"[7] because in the following mail he received a railroad ticket from his father and orders to return to Chicago at once. In an interview twenty-eight years later, Burroughs recalled that (as a fourteen-year-old) he had ridden the ranges in the days of horse thieves, cattle rustlers and pitched battles between sheep and cattle men, "where even among men born to the leather he won a name for his mastery of bad horses, among them the locally notorious man-killer, Black Pacer."[8]

What was he doing, cavorting with rustlers and thieves? Did he not have any respect for his parents? Did he want to disgrace the Burroughs' name? (In the 1890s, several Burroughs, although unrelated, were well-known figures: naturalist John Burroughs and, more recently, William Seward Burroughs, whose new invention of the adding machine was pleasing a multitude of clients.)

"I am sending you to Phillips Academy!"

It was shortly after Edgar's return. The boy was duly informed by his father that Andover, Massachusetts, was a respectable town—that Phillips Academy was already more than one hundred years old, boasted a fine reputation for scholarship and, as well, was an excellent preparatory for Yale (the academy still boasts of these same qualifications today)—that his brother, Frank Coleman, would be joining him as a boarder at Mr. Morrill's—that Edgar not only would be receiving instruction in English and Latin grammar, but also in arithmetic, the sciences and, more especially, he would be taught the real business of living—that an ample allowance would be assured ($150.00 per month)—that among those who would be matriculating with him in the class of 1894 would be families of the Burroughs' own station in life.*

3. PHILLIPS ACADEMY

When Oliver Wendell Holmes attended Phillips Academy in 1825, he described the main school building thus: "On the side of the long room was a large clock dial bearing these words, 'Youth is the seed-time of life,'" and he expressed this comment, "I had indulged in a prejudice up to that hour that youth was the 'budding-time' of life."

Phillips Academy, as Ed soon discovered, was no "breeze." The June 1892 catalog plainly indicated that "the school is not a suitable one for boys who are idle, wayward, or averse to study, or for such as require the supervision of a teacher and the routine of a school room to enforce industry and fidelity." The 440 students (from thirty-eight states, the District of Columbia, Canada, Hawaii, Turkey and Japan) were divided into two departments: Classical and English. Ed had matriculated into the "Junior Middle" (third) class and entered the English department. The curriculum consisted of six hours of mathematics, four hours of English composition, two hours of history, four hours of Latin and two hours of chemistry. Tuition was seventy-five dollars for the three-term year, with board and lodging costing from six to nine dollars per week—fuel, lights and washing not included.

For the first semester, Phillips Academy was fun. There were fewer than two hundred students, and Andover had direct railroad connections to Boston. Young Burroughs' adventures in the "wild west" of Idaho plus the fact that he came from the great metropolis of Chicago made him

---

*Among his classmates: Irenée du Pont, later president of the du Pont Corporation (1919–26) and Hiram Bingham, later governor and then U.S. Senator from Connecticut (1925–33).

popular with the other boys and he was elected president of his class.* While there was no official distinction, there was a natural resentment between the regular students of P.A. (the "cads") and the working boys of Andover (the "townies") who were taking special courses at the academy. The result was constant friction and fighting between the two groups. Also, Burroughs, like Holmes, obviously believed that youth was the "budding-time" of life. He began to chafe at the strict Congregationalist environment. The long hours of study restricted him because as he often remarked later in life, he really never was interested in formal school, believing that practical education was the best way of learning.

At the beginning of the second semester, Edgar received notice that unless he started to shape up he would be dropped. When the warning was ignored, "Banty" (Dr. Cecil F. P. Bancroft) sent for him. Dr. Bancroft had been the principal of Phillips Academy for twenty-one years and the respected educator from New Hampshire spared no words. Author Burroughs tells a story in *Son of Tarzan* of the difficulties encountered by a Mr. Harold Moore in tutoring the young son of Lord Greystoke. As Mr. Moore explains it to the boy's parents:

> It's not that he isn't bright.... if that were true I should have hopes of succeeding, for then I might bring to bear all my energies in overcoming his obtuseness; but the trouble is that he is exceptionally intelligent, and learns so quickly that I can find no fault in the matter of the preparation of his lessons.... however, he evidently takes no interest whatever in the subjects we are studying. He merely accomplishes each task as a task to be rid of as quickly as possible and I am sure that no lesson again ever enters his mind until the hours of study and recitation once more arrive. His sole interests seem to be feats of physical prowess and the reading of everything that he can get hold of relative to savage beasts and the lives and customs of uncivilized peoples; but particularly do stories of animals appeal to him. He will sit for hours together poring over the work of some African explorer, and upon two occasions I have found him sitting up in bed at night reading Carl Hagenbeck's book on men and beasts....†

The final decade of the nineteenth century was on hand and it would prove to be one of the most interesting and exciting in which an adventurous young American could be living. However, it must be pointed out (perhaps to the chagrin of many a loyal fan) that Burroughs, turning seventeen and about to take up residence in his fourth state (Michigan), was not actively seeking adventure at this point in his life.

The 1890s saw the population of the United States surpass sixty million for the first time. If this fact escaped the notice of ERB, he must have been justifiably proud at the launching of our new battleship, *Maine*, with its twelve-inch thick side armor and its two menacing ten-inch turret guns. But it was not all good news. Certainly, there was little to cheer about in the results of the election of 1892. Grover

---

*Burroughs was class president for the first semester. President for the second semester was Truman R. Temple. In the fall of 1965 (while this book was under way), I wrote to the surviving members of the class of '94, and received the following note from Mr. Temple dated October 5: "Without moving from my wheelchair, I'll try to answer your inquiry. I remember the Burroughs name very clearly because I remember how the mathematics teacher rolled the *rrrr*'s when he called upon him to recite. I can't even remember the teacher's name in spite of this, perhaps because of the way I detested him. Yes, we had some scraps. Burroughs might have been in one or two of them but I recall nothing to discredit him ... have passed my ninety-second year. Wish I could live to see your book but doubt it. Good luck!" (Mr. Temple is the last surviving member of the class of '94.)

†First appeared in *All-Story Weekly* in six parts, beginning December 4, 1915; subsequently as a novel (Chicago: A. C. McClurg, 1917).

Cleveland defeated Benjamin Harrison (becoming the first President to win an election after losing one) and the country was entirely in Democratic hands for the first time since the Civil War (the Democrats retained control of the House and won a majority in the Senate). The results of the election must have been especially disquieting to Edgar's father, who once told him: "I would rather be found dead than found voting against the Republican party."[9] The Burroughs, father and sons, were staunch backers of the GOP for a full century — with but one exception. Joan Burroughs Pierce recalled the only time that her father was really angry at her. "It was in 1932 when I confessed to having voted for a Democrat in the presidential election, Franklin D. Roosevelt."

Things were happening in that world of the nineties in entertainment, adventure and discovery, too. Thomas Edison patented the Kinetoscope, a device for the showing of moving pictures — George Eastman's twenty-two ounce Kodak, which took a circular picture of two and one-half inches in diameter, seemed to be catching on — Nelly Bly, that daring and intrepid reporter of the *New York World*, returned to a thundering salute after circumnavigating the globe in the astounding time of seventy-two days, six hours and eleven minutes (breaking the mythical record of Phineas Fogg in Jules Verne's *Around the World in Eighty Days*) — Rudolph Diesel of Berlin showed off his new internal-combustion gasoline engine. In literature, Stephen Crane's *The Red Badge of Courage* was found to be an extraordinary novel of the late war — Mark Twain was at it again with *Pudd'nhead Wilson*, and English author H. G. Wells shocked the world with *The Time Machine*. A new game called "basketball" was invented by James Naismith, a YMCA training instructor, and at a Chinese restaurant in New York the chef concocted an American dish with a Chinese-sounding name that he hoped might prove popular — "chop suey." Clearly, those were great days in which to be going on seventeen!

Being dismissed from Phillips Academy was disgraceful! Captain Burroughs certainly told Edgar that what he required was "more discipline." Inquiries were made and Burroughs senior was impressed when he learned that Brevet Major J. Sumner Rogers had founded a reputedly first-class military academy, located at the Orchard Lake Buildings near Pontiac, Michigan (and the major *was* said to be a native of Maine). Particulars were dispatched to Chicago: Orchard Lake Michigan Military Academy had become the state's first institution of practical, civil and military engineering. It was recognized as a "diploma school," and its graduates accepted by universities without examination. General fees for instruction, room and board amounted to 450 dollars a year, with uniform and incidental expenses about 150 dollars. The interest of the Academy lay "in developing the whole man [with] moral training of the students given as much consideration as their mental training."* The captain brought two railroad tickets to Detroit. He would escort Edgar to the academy himself!

4. Orchard Lake

It was at Orchard Lake, class of 1895, that Burroughs later confessed to meeting his first (and last) idol — a person he was to admire and respect more than anyone with whom he would come into contact throughout his later years. "The Commandant was Captain Charles King, author of the best army stories ever written;

---

*"Fifty Years at Orchard Lake, 1909–1959." From the 1959 EAGLE Yearbook of the Orchard Lake Schools.

a man who has been an inspiration to me all my life because of his outstanding qualities as a soldier, a cavalryman and a friend."[10]

A graduate of West Point, class of 1866, King fought against the Apache and the Sioux, was wounded and had received the Silver Star for gallantry. While King's literary style hardly could be compared with that of such contemporaries as Robert Louis Stevenson, Mark Twain or that fine Anglo-Indian writer, Rudyard Kipling (himself no mean teller of army tales), King popularized army life in such romantic stories as *Colonel's Daughter*, *A Wartime Wooing*, *Cadet Days* and *Beyond the Lines*.

So it was here, at Orchard Lake, that Burroughs found the first of the four essential ingredients necessary for the formation of Tarzan.

1. *The Hero*—an inspirational type, with army background.

Still lacking:

2. *The Germ*—required for the African background and its wild animal life (this item is close at hand).
3. *The Reason*—for writing.
4. *The Escape*—a violent dislike and distrust of man and civilization.

Taken under the personal wing of Captain King, Ed was taught the tricks of horsemanship until he was among the academy's top riders. He was the only non-senior among the handful selected by the commandant to perform the exciting and extremely difficult Monkey Drill, consisting partly of bareback, Cossack-style riding and Greco-roman horsemanship.

Home on vacation during the summer of 1893, Ed attended the World's Columbian Exposition, commemorating the Fourth Centenary of the discovery of America. President Cleveland opened the Exposition on May first, and in the ribbon-cutting ceremonies at Festival Hall, a poem was read by Phillips Academy graduate Oliver Wendell Holmes (who died one year later at the age of eighty-five). The Fair site was Jackson Park, fronting on Lake Michigan from Fifty-sixth to Sixty-seventh streets and the crowds were coming in at a rate of more than 170,000 per day. Ed's visit to the grounds was for business as well as pleasure. His father, after twenty-five highly successful years in the distilling business as vice president of the Phoenix Distilling Company, and Abel Ames and Company, had joined the American Battery Company earlier in the year. George and Harry were still seeking their fortunes in Idaho (they had switched from cattle raising to mining), so with his brother Coleman, Ed assisted his father at the fair in demonstrating the new electric storage batteries. They were used principally for train lighting and signaling but were being promoted as the last word for the new horseless carriages.

Within the 550 acres of ground, Ed Burroughs witnessed a sight that led him closer in setting the stage for the ape-man and his friends nineteen years later. It was not "The Streets of Cairo," where Little Egypt tantalized the men and shocked the ladies with her pulsating belly dance; nor was it the sparkling magnificence of the hundreds of structures made of "staff" (a plaster of paris composition resembling marble), all in classic Renaissance style and surrounded by lagoons of deep-blue water leading to the park from the lake. But if you had happened to proceed into the fairgrounds by way of Cottage Grove Avenue to the western limit of the midway—there you would have discovered the great Hagenbeck Wild Animal Show!*

---

*In 1865, Carl Hagenbeck of Hamburg, Germany, who had inherited several animals from his father, began the business of collecting wild animals from all over the world and exhibiting his show, with great

Ed was thinking about entering Yale, from which two of his brothers were graduated, but inspired by Captain King (and perhaps his father's own military service in the Civil War) he decided to pursue a military career. (Ed's record at the academy was excellent and in his senior year he was named Captain of Cadets, Company D.) Through the influence of his oldest brother, George, on May 4, 1895, Edgar R. Burroughs was nominated for appointment as cadet to the U.S. Military Academy by the Honorable Edgar Wilson, Member of Congress at large for the District of Idaho.

Ed journeyed to West Point for the examination with 117 other candidates. "Only fourteen passed," he recalled, "I being one of the 104."[11] He was stunned. His father could not believe that Ed had failed (Orchard Lake was one of the finest schools in preparing young men for admission to West Point). Emma Hulbert, Ed's girl friend, saw her dream of a military wedding fading like the echo of a bugle call.

That summer, Ed took a job as collector for an ice company in his parents' neighborhood and in the fall of 1895, upon the urging of Captain King, he returned to the academy, having been appointed Second Lieutenant, Michigan State Troops, detailed to the academy as Assistant Commandant and Tactical Officer, Cavalry (over many more experienced members of the staff). His other assignments were as gatling gun instructor and professor of geology. "The fact that I had never studied geology and knew absolutely nothing about the subject seemed to make no difference. They needed a professor and I was it."[12]

But it was not the same. As a student, Ed had had the pick of the "brass button boys" for his friends. It had been a full round of activities. In the fall and winter months, there had been football, tobogganing and the winter "hop" held at Clinton Hall in Pontiac; in the spring baseball, tennis, golf, swimming and boating. There had been numerous lawn parties and dancing, and the academy also had a splendid marching corps, which was in demand to participate in parades throughout the stage and as far away as Washington, D.C. However, as a member of the faculty, Ed was excluded from the "beer busts" and general good times. "It was a lonesome job. I had always been impatient of restrictions and now I had less freedom than I had as a cadet."[13] Captain King had left the academy for another post and what remained to interest Ed? When ERB left Orchard Lake early in 1896, the academy had grown from a single building into a colorful and well-known institution with ten castellated buildings. It was a complete military organization, composed of a battalion of four companies under the command of an officer of the U.S. Army detailed there for duty. (However, after the death of its founder, Colonel Rogers, the school foundered and was forced to close down in 1909 because of lack of students.)

It seems likely that once back in Chicago, Ed once again proposed marriage to Emma Hulbert and that once again she had said, "No, settle down first." His father, age sixty-three, had been elected president of the American Storage Battery Company and although he urged his son to enter the business, he deferred to Ed's wishes to enter the Regular Army and win a commission through the ranks. (The fact that Ed had not entertained serious thoughts of settling in Chicago seemed to be evident in the records of the Orchard

---

success, throughout the major cities of Europe. (Hagenbeck's zoo at Stellingen, near Hamburg, has been copied by numerous U.S. and European zoos for its native-looking habitats and settings, in which the animals can be observed roaming free and in natural surroundings.)

Lake Academy. When enrolled the first year, his home address was listed as Chicago; when he entered his senior year he had it changed to the address of his brothers, Yale, Idaho.)

5. THE "BLOODY 7TH"

Ed Burroughs was four months away from his twenty-first birthday when he returned to Michigan after a brief visit home. On May 13, 1896, in Detroit (where conductors always stopped the streetcars to watch a good dog fight), he enlisted as a private in the Regular Army. On May 23, Ed arrived at Fort Grant, Territory of Arizona, whereupon he was assigned to Troop B, 7th Regiment, U.S. Cavalry, also known as the "Bloody 7th," after General Custer's Last Stand of 1876. (Misjudging the strength of the opposing Sioux forces, Custer attacked the Indians in a center and two flanking columns and his group was met by the full force of the Sioux. All 226 of the cavalrymen were slaughtered at the junction of the Bighorn and Little Horn rivers in Montana.)

What was ERB like at this time? He stood five feet eight and one-half inches tall and weighed 160 pounds. He looked wiry and tough. In a few months, the desert sun would color him as bronze as an Indian and that smart, jet black mustache he was sporting (to make up for his rapidly thinning hair) would be full-blown.

The fort was located northeast of Tucson at the foot of the Pinaleno Range. The troopers' primary job was to enforce the government's law and keep the Indians contained in their reservations—to make them behave. The men who wore the blue denim overalls (down the seams of which were sewn broad yellow stripes) were mainly old Indian fighters, who were more at home on a horse than off. But the "city boy" was able to ride with the best of them—thanks to the extra drills at the academy. (One of Burroughs' greatest pleasures in later years was pride in his ability "to ride anything that wears hair.")[14]

It has been reported that as a member of the U.S. Cavalry, ERB had chased Geronimo up and down the Territory. Actually, it was fully eight years before Burroughs' arrival at Fort Grant that Geronimo had maneuvered and outfoxed the entire U.S. Army (plus part of the Mexican army) before voluntarily "surrendering" in truce talks.* There was little excitement or adventure at the fort although "Black Jack" Tom Ketchum, the outlaw, was raiding towns in the vicinity and (while Cochise and Geronimo no longer held sway) there were persistent rumors of another Apache uprising. Meanwhile, there were minor incidents with which the troopers had to cope. Some of these were recalled by Ed in *The War Chief*, which he wrote in 1926:

> ...a rancher and his family had been murdered at Sulphur Springs ... two cowboys had a running fight with the Apaches at San Simon Valley ... two men had been killed near the Billings' ranch ... the attack upon San Carlos Agency ... the fight in Horse Show Canyon ... the flight of the hostiles along the rough crest of Stein's Peak Range, down into the San Simon Valley, and from there into the Chiricahua Mountain....†

---

*With no fewer than five thousand troops plus five hundred auxiliaries hell-bent after the old Indian chieftain, Geronimo succeeded in eluding them time and time again. His "forces" consisted of 35 men, 8 boys and 101 women!

†Published in five parts beginning April 16, 1927, in *Argosy All-Story Weekly*. Also published the same year as a novel by McClurg. Although it was written thirty years after his brief service with the 7th U.S. Cavalry, backed by Burroughs' phenomenal memory (which seldom let him down unless he *chose* to

To the men stationed at Fort Grant, there were three kinds of Apaches—the Apache of the government reservation, the Apache of the red headband (signifying that he was a scout for one of the agencies); and then there was the third kind:

> Across his swart* face, from ear to ear [was] painted a broad band of vermilion ... above and below ... a coast of blue, the base of which was a ground micaceous stone....
> Attached to his person and concealed from view was his [amulet] wrapped in a three-inch square of buckskin upon which were painted crooked lines of red and yellow, depicting the red snake and the yellow.
> Upon his legs ... long war moccasins with their rawhide soles and protecting toe armor; their tops, three feet long ... turned down just below the knee.... further protecting the lower leg from the sharp spines of the cactus ... there was a cartridge belt around his waist and a six-shooter and a butcher knife at his hips, but he also carried his beloved bow and arrows as well as the rifle....[15]

The current nemesis at the fort was the Apache Kid,† said by several Western historians to have been the wiliest Indian fighter of them all. The troops kept their eyes peeled for the Kid (after a 5,000-dollar reward for his capture was posted by the territorial legislature), and hit the trail in search of him in groups of 100 to 150.

> Whole regiments ... were in the field searching for him; but they never saw him. Strange tales grew up about him. He possessed the power of invincibility. He could change himself at will into a coyote, a rattlesnake, a lion. Every depradation, every murder was attributed to him, until the crimes upon his soul were legion.[16]

Chances are that ERB, not yet twenty-one, soon became disenchanted with regular army life. There was little enough "adventure." If members of the detachment were not patrolling, what was there to do in the desert wilds—and what could be more hellish than a sentence of blankety-blank days and nights inside the furnace of an Arizona summer, "...building roads, digging boulders out of parade grounds, erecting telegraph lines up and down over red-hot mountains and white-hot plains...."[17]

Burroughs' service with the 7th Regiment lasted less than one year. "A weak heart developed and I was twice recommended for discharge. As it seemed wholly unlikely that I should pass a physical examination for a commission, my father obtained my discharge from the army through Secretary of War Alger" [R. A. Alger of the McKinley Administration].[18]

Sixteen days after Ed's arrival at Fort Grant, the commanding general of the De-

---

ignore it), *The War Chief* accurately lists towns, forts, gaps, passes and peaks. The "Billings' ranch" likely is patterned after one that existed in the area at the time of ERB's service. It is interesting to note that the lieutenant of Troop B in the novel is named King, a West Point graduate—obviously a tribute to West Pointer Charles King, Burroughs' former commandant at the Orchard Lake Military Academy.

*A favorite adjective of Burroughs. He used a "swart face" and a "swarthy" complexion to describe many a villain—Arab, Spaniard or Russian.

†The Apache Kid was real enough. He was formerly a sergeant in the Apache Scouts of the San Carlos Agency (under famed Indian fighter Al Sieber), and when the Kid's father was murdered his duty became clear. He promptly killed the murderer, was caught and jailed. The Kid was pardoned by President Cleveland but this did not suit the local authorities, so they had him arrested for another crime and he was sentenced to a seven-year term. Fuming at the double standard of white man's justice, the Kid broke out of jail and went on a murderous rampage of robbery and killing such as the Territory had never before experienced. He never was caught, although reported seen and "trapped" hundreds of times. ERB (and others) seemed convinced the Kid had managed his escape into Mexico. He was not heard of again.

partment of Colorado forwarded to the adjutant general a Certificate of Disability for Discharge and a recommendation that Burroughs be discharged. It was indicated that he had irregular and intermittent heart action especially after exertion and that this condition existed before enlistment.

The assistant surgeon general returned the discharge on June 16 stating the young soldier should be retained for further observation as he had been under observation for one week only and the disability was not stated as definitely as desirable, since only symptoms were given. His retention in service was approved, and he remained at Fort Grant on detached service while the troop was at San Carlos. He was a stable orderly on March 11, 1897, when two Chicago businessmen wrote Secretary of War Alger in behalf of Ed's father. They indicated that ERB enlisted with the consent of his father, the intent being to obtain a commission and pursue a military career. However, due to findings of the medical inspectors, they claimed he would probably never be able to secure a commission and since it had been previously recommended that he be discharged, his parents were anxious to have him discharged as two opportunities in commercial lines were open to him.[19]

Under the provisions of Special Orders No. 60, Adjutant General's Office, dated March 15: "Private Edgar R. Burroughs, Troop B, 7th Cavalry, now at Fort Grant, Arizona Territory, will be discharged from the service of the United States on receipt of this order by the Commanding Officer of his station. This soldier is not entitled to travel-pay." He was discharged by favor as a private on March 23, 1897.

Ed returned to Chicago—via Tucson and Kansas City—courtesy of the Southern Pacific Railroad. But he had no luxurious suite nor, for that matter, even a seat. All he could manage was a precarious perch atop a cattle train! The seven cars of cattle to which he was attached were separated from the caboose by eleven other cars, belonging to another outfit. At each stop it was necessary that he prod upright the cattle that were down to prevent their being trampled to death, and then climb to the top of the cars while the train was already in motion. Another highlight of the ex-soldier's journey was the long trek back to the caboose over the swaying, bumping cattle cars in the midst of a Kansas gale. This took so much time that when he finally would arrive at the caboose, the train was slowing down for the next stop. Then it was leap to the ground, run forward, prod the cattle and back again.[20]

As Ed boarded a passenger train from Kansas City to Chicago, he must have been more than a little concerned about what lay ahead of him. Would he enter his father's business? Would Emma say yes? Were his adventures ending, or just beginning? And what of Tarzan, still incubating but lacking the final two ingredients necessary for birth:

The Reason—for writing.
The Escape—a violent dislike and distrust of man and civilization.

II

Search for Adventure 1898–1904

> *[He] was inoculated with the insidious virus of gold-fever—that mad malady which races white-hot through the veins of its victims, distorting every mental image and precluding the sane functioning of reason.*
> The Girl from Farris's, *1916*

1. REVEILLE AND TAPS

On February 15, 1898, America's fine new battleship, the *Maine*, was sunk by a mysterious explosion as she lay at anchor in Havana harbor, killing 260 officers and men. Fanned by heated editorials led off by William Randolph Hearst (*New York Journal*) and Whitelaw Reid (*New York Tribune*) and kindled through fiery speeches by such men as Theodore Roosevelt, Henry Cabot Lodge and John Hay, Assistant Secretary of the Navy, Republican Senator from Massachusetts and Ambassador to London, respectively, United States intervention on the side of the Cuban revolutionists against Spain would be a matter of only a few months.* For

---

*And indeed, on April 21, the U.S. declared war on Spain. Three months later it was over, with Spain surrendering all claim and title to Cuba and ceding Puerto Rico, Guam and the Philippines to the United States.

twenty-two-year-old Ed Burroughs, this war-fever was an opportunity to escape from the dullness and boredom of entering his father's business.

> ...he found that he had grown away from his people. Their interests and his were far removed. They had not kept pace with him, nor could they understand aught of the many strange and wonderful dreams that passed through [his] active brain.[1]

When the formation of the 1st United States Volunteer Cavalry Regiment (popularized as the Rough Riders) was announced, cowboys, ranchers, hunters and a sprinkling of Yale and Harvard graduates joined up to fight with "Teddy"—Lieutenant Colonel Theodore Roosevelt, who had resigned his position as Assistant Secretary of the Navy to command the regiment with Colonel Leonard Wood. As an ex–army cavalryman, a graduate and, subsequently, an instructor at a leading military academy, it should not have been too difficult for Ed to obtain a commission. Evidently he tried but failed.* What now? Ed turned once more toward Idaho—but he might first have again proposed to Emma:

> How tall and fine she was. Had she changed suddenly within the few hours of his absence.... she was no longer such a little girl.[2]

Harry staked Ed to a business in Pocatello, not far from where the brothers were operating a placer gold dredge. The venture was a stationery store with a large newsstand and cigar counter. Ed also established a newspaper route and delivered the papers himself, on horseback, but: "Providence never intended me for a retail merchant; the store was not a howling success and I certainly was glad when the man from whom I had purchased it returned to Pocatello and wanted it back."[3]

Mrs. Evelyn McKenzie recalled her earliest memories of her uncle, Ed:

> At the time he was making his home with us in Pocatello, while he tried out an unsuccessful business venture, financed by my father [Harry Burroughs]. Uncle Ed had just been discharged from the Army, Seventh Cavalry, and was a romantic figure to my brother and myself. My outstanding memory of him then and in the following years of my childhood in Idaho, when he visited us, [was] of his irrepressible sense of humor. He kept us in gales of laughter with his pranks and nonsense. He delighted in writing foolish verse for us and illustrating his quips with clever cartoons. I think of him as always laughing, his dark mischievous eyes crinkled at the corners.
>
> His training in the Cavalry resulted in expert horsemanship; he rode magnificently, as much one with the horse as an Indian. He was slim and dark and carried himself with military erectness.[4]

2. Proposal Accepted

Ed returned shortly thereafter to Chicago and went to work for his father, starting at the bench "to learn the business from the ground up." His salary: fifteen dollars a week.

It certainly could not have been with any great deal of pleasure that Emma looked upon her suitor's recent travels. But

---

*Prior to 1939 (to the best of this writer's knowledge), Burroughs had never mentioned applying for a commission with the Rough Riders, although he wrote his own "biography" in the *New York Sunday World* (October 27, 1929) and, with some additions, in 1934 in a bylined story that appeared in many newspapers. However, when interviewed for a *Saturday Evening Post* article (July 29, 1939), ERB revealed that "Teddy" had rejected his request for a commission. It also was reported, in the *Post* story, that ERB was refused a commission in the Chinese Army after the Sino-Japanese War of 1895–95, and that he succeeded in obtaining a commission in the Nicaraguan Army but that his father blocked it.

after Ed had stayed put for a full year and, presumably, would take over his father's storage battery company, she said yes, and Emma Centennia* Hulbert became Mrs. Edgar Rice Burroughs on January 31, 1900. ("For ten years I haunted her, when I wasn't out west, or in the Army, or at school, and for ten years I kept proposing and she kept saying 'no.' she got so tired of being proposed to that she just had to marry me to get a little rest.")[5]

Ed was the last of the four brothers to be married, although three of them all married in January 1900; George Tyler, Jr., married on a houseboat on Snake River, Idaho, January 10, to Edna McCoy; Frank Coleman, married at Minidoka, Idaho, January 24 to Grace Stuart Moss; and Ed and Emma on January 31. The fourth brother, Harry, had married in Chicago, December 30, 1891, to Ella Oldham.

A good and prosperous year for most Americans, 1899 was less than forty years after the nation had managed to survive the costliest U.S. war ever. But everyone was predicting that the twentieth century† would make the last look like the horse-and-buggy age it was.‡ Americans were spending more and enjoying it more and prices generally were low, as Ed and Emma discovered in Chicago; a sofa could be bought for less than ten dollars and a brass bed for three! William McKinley, re-elected in November 1900 with Theodore Roosevelt as his running-mate, had hit the nail right on the head with his campaign slogan of "The Full Dinner Pail."

But even in the most prosperous of times, prosperity does not come to all men and what the new year of 1900 meant to Ed Burroughs was that he had received a five-dollar raise as a wedding present and now was earning twenty dollars a week as treasurer of his father's company. They were managing — the newlyweds were just about managing — and "owing to the fact that we could eat as often as we pleased at my wife's mother's home or at my mother's we got along nicely."[6] (He especially resented going out to the Sunday afternoon dinners, calling them "Sunday Sermons.")

In September — for no special reason — and certainly never dreaming (even in the wildest Burroughs fashion) that what he was about to mail to his niece, Evelyn, would be the first of his more than ninety stories, ERB did a twelve-page illustrated poem, added a home-made hard cover and bound it all together with a shoelace. He entitled his first "published" work, *Snake River§ Cotton-Tail Tales* and (in the grand manner) on the inside cover, he printed:

AUTHOR'S AUTOGRAPH EDITION
Ed. R. Burroughs
[signature]
Limited To One Copy
Of Which This Is No. 1

The title page, dated 1900, read:

THYS BOOKE (sic)
IS DEDICATED
AND GIVEN

---

*Four months younger than her husband, Emma was born January 1 in the centennial year of 1876, and thus her middle name. She was the daughter of one of the best known and successful hotelmen, Colonel Alvin Hulbert, owner of the old Tremont House in Chicago, then also owner of the Sherman and the Great Northern hotels and, in St. Louis, the Lindley.

†While the twentieth century actually began on January 1, 1901, 76 million Americans recognized it on New Year's Day, 1900.

‡The first recorded sale of an automobile was a two-passenger Winton Phaeton, which in 1898 was sold by its inventor to a customer in Cleveland for $1,000. Ransom E. Olds founded his motor plant in 1900 and in the following year turned out several hundred "mass-produced" runabouts to sell for $650.

§After *Snake River* in Idaho, where Ed's brothers were part of a mining company.

TO
EVELYN
BY
HER UNCLE
ED

Each page contained clever and colorful drawings by the author, to illustrate these lines:

A Bull Rush in the Meadow
"As the Blue-Jay on the Wing
"Informs me," said the Rabbit
"That we'll see an early spring

"When I see the little cow-slip,"
Said the Rabbit to his chum,
"I can read the story plainly
"That another Fall has come."

"That great big ugly egg-plant, ma
"Just bit me on the leg."
"That is a hen you foolish child,"
"Well I saw her lay an egg."

"Good morning Mrs. Bunnie, could you loan
a friend some money?
"I have not tasted food for several days.
"I who used to be the real thing could eat a
cast iron cinch ring
"Who's bucked the giddy tender-foot
"Who's gi'en 'em all the snakes."

"Good morning Pinto Cayuse, you used to pass
right by us,
"Your appetite's improving of your ways.
"If you starve a little longer your manners
may grow strong.
"Since you're such a wondrous bucker
"Why don't you Buckwheat Cakes?"

"Is this what they call a cabbage, ma,
"I've been eating for an hour?"
"No, you silly little child
"It's what they cauliflower."

(Ed also authored an illustrated cook book, which he dedicated to "Mistress Evelyn," Christmas, 1901. He entitled it "Grandma Burroughs' Cook Book," and included recipes for cookies, fried chicken, chicken gravy, angel's food cake, nut candy, cream sponge cake and assorted ice creams.)

Life in the young Burroughs' household, in all likelihood, was simple and quiet. To ease her husband's twelve-hour day, Emma might have insisted that he breakfast on C. W. Post's Grape Nuts, having read the advertising claim that the product "results in a marked sturdiness and activity of the brain and nervous system, making it a pleasure for one to carry on the daily duties without fatigue or exhaustion." For reading matter, there was *McClure's*, *Munsey's*, *Frank Leslie's Popular Monthly*, *Everybody's Magazine*, *Collier's Weekly* and *Cosmopolitan*. Ed never cared too much for fiction and heartily disliked the classics—particularly Shakespeare and Dickens, as Joan Burroughs Pierce recalls him saying, "each of which bores me to extinction." His father used to read the classics aloud when Ed was a young boy—perhaps the root of his boredom. They both might have agreed, however, that Jack London's *Call of the Wild* was better than most, and Ed surely enjoyed his ex-mentor Charles King's latest novel, *A War-time Wooing*. In Chicago, Cap Anson of the White Stockings was everybody's hero—more so than Jim Jeffries, who had taken the heavyweight boxing title from lanky Bob Fitzsimmons.

In the panic of May 1901, fortunes were lost when the stock-market collapsed as the nation's leading industrialists, bankers and millionaires fought for control of the Northern Pacific Railroad. The stock climbed as high as one thousand dollars a share before the plunge, with railroads and steel heading the list. The American Battery Company was salvaged only after Ed chased around to all the fire stations to sell them storage batteries (which were beginning to be used in every installation of the electrically driven fire equipment in the city).

After three years with the American Battery Company, Ed found himself growing nervous and irritable. He still was not getting along too well with his father and might have resented being the only one of the four sons who was not out West. In the early spring of 1903, he wrote to his oldest brother, George, that he and Emma would be coming out to Idaho. Emma, a bride of only three years and a city girl to boot (and recalling how long it took her husband to settle), probably was none too happy with the idea. But she helped pack their custom-made furniture (a gift from her parents) into packing boxes, and with their collie dog they were off to a new adventure.

3. Gold Is Where You Find It

George and Harry Burroughs were still allied with their good friend and Yale classmate, and Ed became part of the Sweetser-Burroughs Mining Company. It was quite a group. Lewis Sweetser had his wife with him, as did George, Harry and Frank Coleman (Harry and his wife Ella also had two children, Evelyn and Studley).*

Coleman stayed along the Raft River Valley to operate a dredge at El Nido, near Minidoka. Ed and Emma joined George, who was operating a placer gold dredge in the Stanley Basin of north-central Idaho, described by Harry Burroughs as "at the foot of snow-capped 'Sawtooth' range — the Alps of America, with glaciers and terminal moraines that would have delighted the heart of Professor Verrill," his former geology professor at Yale.[7]

Ed and Emma pitched a tent on a hill while he built a cabin, "the construction of which was original and not too successful but timber was plentiful and I felled what I needed at no great distance from our cabin site."[8]

From *Tarzan of the Apes*:

Frightened [on] their first night ashore, he gathered her in his arms, whispering words of courage and love into her ears, for the greatest pain ... was the mental anguish of his young wife. Himself brave and fearless, yet he was able to appreciate the awful suffering which fear entails....[9]

Again, from the same story:

The task to build a cabin was an arduous one and required the better part of a month, though he built but one small room. He constructed the cabin of small logs about six inches in diameter, stopping the chinks with clay which he found at the depth of a few feet beneath the surface soil. At one end he built a fireplace of small stones from the beach.... In the window opening he set small branches about an inch in diameter both vertically and horizontally, and so woven that they formed a substantial grating that could withstand the strength of a powerful animal.... The A-shaped roof was thatched with small branches laid close together and over these long jungle grass and palm fronds, with a final coating of clay. The door he built of packing-boxes which held their belongings; nailing one piece upon another ... until he had a solid body some three inches thick.... final touches were added after they moved into the house ... piling their boxes before the door at night....[10]

While some of the men found gold flakes in the water-deposited gravels and sand near bedrock of the Salmon River, no mother lode was discovered. The next stop for the couple was a similar gold-dredging operation, managed by Harry. This one was located on the Snake River just inside the Oregon border. To get to the camp, Ed and Emma again packed their custom-made furniture and climbed aboard a freight wagon. Taking stock when they arrived, they found they had their furniture, clothes, a few utensils, the collie and forty dollars to their name.

---

*Studley later illustrated the first four books published by ERB, Inc. (1931–33).

Forty dollars did not seem much to get anywhere with, so I decided to enter a stud game at a local saloon and run my capital up to several hundred dollars during the night. When I returned at midnight to the room we had rented, we still had the collie dog.[11]

The gold-dredging operation moved slowly and, while none too successful, proved to be more worthwhile than the Stanley Basin labor — which had been a complete disaster, according to Harry.[12] Still, it was nothing at all like the big strikes of the fifties and sixties, when for a time it seemed sure that southeastern Oregon contained as much gold as the entire state of California.

After a short time, the company failed and three of the four Burroughs brothers decided they had had enough (George and Harry had been ranching and mining, unsuccessfully, for fifteen years). But one brother was not quite ready to return home — to face his father as a failure. Harry knew a friend who knew another friend so Ed and Emma packed up again and joggled and jounced aboard a freight wagon — this time heading to Salt Lake City — perhaps with dust flying in their faces from the spinning wheels of a one-cylinder Packard of nine horsepower, which would make motoring history when it arrived in New York, sixty-one days after leaving San Francisco.*

One again, Ed was in uniform — but this time in the less attractive blue serge of a railway cop at the Salt Lake City Union Pacific yards. "For the next several months, I was kept busy rushing bums out of railroad yards and off passenger trains."[13] The couple had settled in an uncomfortable shoehorn flat and made ends meet only by economizing severely. They were without funds and it is likely that Emma suggested she write home for money — at least enough to pay for the return trip to Chicago — but "pride kept us from asking for help. Neither of us knew much about anything that was practical, but we had to do everything ourselves, including the family wash."[14] Ashamed to see his wife do work of this sort, Ed insisted on doing it himself. He also halfsoled his own shoes and accomplished numerous other things "that school had not prepared me for."[15]

While the Chicagoan pounded his beat through the railroad yards, waving his big stick at those who flouted the law, a dislike and distrust of man and civilization started to envelop him. He was twenty-nine years old, married for four years and still unable to support himself, let alone a wife. He never had held any kind of a regular job (outside of working for his father) and his schooling had not prepared him for very much except a military career. He had flunked one opportunity (West Point) and his pride had kept him from remaining in the Regular Army other than in a commissioned rank. Ed had no intention of making a home in the Mormon state, he so informed his wife, but how were they to raise enough money to get out?

Emma agreed that they had nothing to their name — except for the useless custom-made furniture on which they had spent their last penny transporting from one place to the next. "A brilliant idea overtook us. We held [a furniture] auction which was a howling success. People paid real money for the junk and we went back to Chicago first class."[16] Going first class meant that Ed would have tipped the new railway cop to buy him a half-dozen Anna Held cigars and while they made themselves comfortable in the lounge car,

---

*See Appendix B for a report of the Burroughs' cross-country trip in 1916.

with Emma glancing at a magazine while sipping on a Coca-Cola—"Nothing so completely brightens your faculties"—Ed was confident he would be a success in Chicago. He would show his father. He would show Emma. He would show them all.

III

A Lord's Trial 1905–1911

You have been gone very long. You will find no friends from whence you came. You will find deceit, and hypocrisy, and greed, and avarice, and cruelty. You will find that no one will be interested in you....
Tarzan and the Golden Lion, *December, 1922*

1. "Do or Die"

The heat was stifling when Ed and Emma arrived in Chicago the summer of 1905, amidst final days of the first convention of the IWW. (The Industrial Workers of the World, organized by radical labor leaders to bring about a social revolution, worked toward abolishing the wage system and sanctioned taking over the instruments of production by the workers.)

His parents had moved into a smaller place at 493 West Jackson Boulevard, so the couple returned to where they had lived in 1900—one of the inexpensive, eight-family flats at 194 Park Avenue in the West End. For the first time since 1885, all the brothers were living and working in Chicago. Frank Coleman was sales manager of Hawtin Engraving; Harry, assistant to the manager of Automatic Electric, and George Jr. had taken over the presidency of American Battery Company upon his father's retirement. As for Ed, he was determined to "do or die."

Forced to take a job immediately, all he could find were openings for salesmen. "The next few months encompassed a series of horrible jobs. I sold electric light bulbs to janitors, candy to drug stores and Stoddard's Lectures from door to door. I hated them all and I hated myself. Most of all I hated the slant-heads I tried to sell to."[1] After deciding that he was a total failure, he spied an advertisement for an "expert accountant." Although Ed knew nothing about the work he applied for the position (The T. J. Winslow Company, manufacturer of waterproof coatings for doors, sashes and blinds) and got the job.

Throughout his life, Ed was convinced that "luck" and "the breaks," good or bad, "have fully as much to do with one's success or failure as ability. The 'break' I got in this instance lay in the fact that my employer knew even less about the duties of an 'expert accountant' than I did."*[2] He remained with the Winslow Company for a little more than one year before leaving of his own accord. Bursting to achieve "success" and ever-conscious of his late start in the business world, Burroughs saw a potential in mail order houses and "I took a job that brought me to the head of a large department"[3] — the stenographic department of Sears, Roebuck and Company. (ERB was more anxious in later years to prove that he was not a business failure and in 1941 he looked back thirty-five years to tell of his early days at Sears. See Chapter XXIII.) While the salary was only slightly higher than what he had been earning, Ed felt that it was an important step in his business career. With Sears for two years, his salary had been raised and the couple were better off than at any other time since their marriage. Ed could not yet afford to purchase that smart, one-cylinder Oldsmobile runabout, but what he promised himself one day was nothing less than a Packard.†

Two important events in the life of Ed Burroughs occurred at the beginning of 1908. Ed and Emma's first child, Joan, was born on January 12 and — seeing a promising future in the advertising agency business — Ed quit his job to start his own company. "Having a good job and every prospect for advancement, I decided to go into business for myself and rented a small office."[5] Here, the young (thirty-two) entrepreneur wrote courses in salesmanship — hiring college students to sell aluminum pots and pans and remit the proceeds back to the home office. However, the students either quit or just did not bother to remit the money.

At this time, the mail order house offered Burroughs a position if he wanted to come back. "If I had accepted it, I probably would have been fixed for life with a good living salary, yet the chances are that I would never have written a story, which proves that occasionally it is better to do

---

*One of Burroughs' rare works, *The Efficiency Expert* (1921) (familiar only to his fans), is a modern romance of a young man's struggle for success and recognition in Chicago. Our young hero (just out of college) must show his father that he can make it on his own. But he cannot land a job and is convinced that he is a failure. Then a "break" comes his way. He spies an advertisement for an "Efficiency Expert," and bluffs his way to the job although he knows nothing about it, nor what the duties entail. He comes through with flying colors, however; he is appointed general manager of the firm and wins romance. (For more about *The Efficiency Expert* and how it ties in with the author's early struggles in Chicago, see Chapter XII, *The Girl from Hollywood* and Other Romances.)

†He had a love for motoring and fine cars throughout his life. In an interview published in 1918, it was written that "next to Mr. Burroughs' devotion to his family comes his love of motoring. Rain or shine, summer or winter, you may see him every afternoon with his family upon the Chicago boulevards or far out on some delightful country road beyond the city's limits."[4] His promise to have a Packard was realized in 1916, when he bought a magnificent Twin-Six. Later, in California, Burroughs owned a series of Packards and Cords — the big, open, flashy roadsters.

the wrong thing than the right."⁶ He again was penniless — no job, no money and a second child, Hulbert, was born on August 12, 1909. "When my independent business sank without a trace, I approached as near financial nadir as one may reach. My son, Hulbert, had just been born. I had no job and no money. I had to pawn Mrs. Burroughs' jewelry and my watch in order to buy food. I loathed poverty, and I should have liked to have put my hands on the man who said that poverty is an honorable estate. It is an indication of inefficiency and no more. To be poor is quite bad enough. But to be poor and without hope — well, the only way to understand it is to be it."⁷

Burroughs later said that he got writer's cramp from answering blind ads and that he wore out his shoes from chasing after jobs. Harry was employed as office manager of the Physician's Co-Operative Association, and he landed a job for Ed placing ads in pulp fiction magazines. The ads were for a patent medicine called Alcola, described as a positive cure for alcoholism. (He later omitted mention of this job from his record of employment.) The job lasted for only a few months and then Ed took a position as an agent for a lead-pencil sharpener — secretary of Stace, Burroughs & Company at 1006 South Michigan Avenue. He and Emma were forced to give up their own home and they moved to his father's country place in suburban Oak Park for one year, while subagents were out trying, unsuccessfully, to sell the sharpener.

2. THE TARZAN SYNDROME

Was Tarzan ready to be conceived? Let us see: a gentleman of Yale caliber, *check*; English-bred and of noble stock, *check, check*; regular features and of perfect, robust health, *check, check, check*; virile, oh, by god, *yes*; the inspirational hero, *yes*, in the figure of soldier-author Charles King; the germ, *yes* in Hagenbeck (and perhaps Kipling and Jack London). How about the other essential requirements: a dislike and distrust of man and civilization, and the reason for writing?

In *The Return of Tarzan* (1913), with the unhappy experiences of his struggle to make good fresh in his mind, Burroughs said about men:

> They are all alike. Cheating, murdering, lying, fighting, and for all things that the beasts of the jungle would not deign to possess — money to purchase the effeminate pleasure of weaklings. And yet withal bound by silly customs that make them slaves to their unhappy lot while firm in the belief that they may be lords of creation enjoying the only real pleasures of existence.... It is a silly world, an idiotic world, and Tarzan of the Apes was a fool to renounce the freedom and happiness of the jungle to come into it....

Ten years later, in *Tarzan and the Golden Lion*, he had this to say about civilization:

> You will find no friends. You will find deceit, and hypocrisy, and greed, and avarice, and cruelty. I, Tarzan of the Apes, have left my jungle and gone to the cities built by men, but always I have been disgusted and been glad to return to my jungle — to the noble beasts that are honest in their loves and in their hates — to the freedom and genuineness of nature.

And ten more years later, in *Tarzan and the City of Gold*:

> With scorn the ape-man viewed the overwhelming majority of mankind.... He saw the greed, the selfishness, the cowardice, and the cruelty of man; and, in view of man's vaunted mentality, he knew that these characteristics placed man upon a lower spiritual scale than the beasts....

So much for a distrust and dislike for man and civilization. It was there! Now, the *reason* for writing. Burroughs had worked for six years without a vacation and for fully half of his working hours "I had suffered tortures from headaches [and neuritis]. Economize as we could, the expenses of our little family was beyond my income. Three cents worth of ginger snaps constituted my daily lunches for months." One might conclude, therefore, that Burroughs' *reason* for writing was not due to any urge to write "nor for any particular love of writing. It was because I had a wife and two babies, a combination which does not work well without money."[8]

George Burroughs, Jr. had had it as far as Chicago was concerned. He turned the presidency of the American Battery Company over to Charles Kaufman (an old friend of his father and secretary of the firm since 1900), and with his wife and five-year-old son departed for Burley, Idaho, where he entered the hardware business. Harry went into the insurance business, and Coleman took a job as secretary with the stationers, Champlin-Yardley Company.

Ed and Emma were now living in a cheap flat at 2008 Park Avenue, and while subagents for Stace, Burroughs & Co. were making their rounds, out of desperation more than anything else Ed began to write a story. "I had gone through thoroughly some of the all-fiction magazines and it suddenly occurred to me that people were probably paid for writing such rot."*[9] but his literary experience was zero. He never had met an author (outside of Captain King), an editor or a publisher. He admittedly knew nothing about the technique† of story writing and had no idea of how to submit a story or what he could expect in payment. "Had I known about it at all I would never have thought of submitting half a novel."‡[10]

Thomas Newell Metcalf, then editor of Munsey's *All-Story* magazine, encouraged Burroughs. "He wrote me that he liked the first half of the story and that if the second was as good as he thought he might use it. Had he not given me this encouragement, I should never have finished the story and my writing career would have been at an end, since I was not writing because of any urge to write nor for any particular love of writing."[14]

The fledgling author took two safeguards before submitting even the first half of his story:

He assumed the pen name of Normal Bean (translation: "common head"). "I was sort of ashamed of writing as an occupation for a big, strong, healthy man, so I kept it a secret.§ No one helped me. No one knew what I was doing, not even my closest friends."‖[15]

The subject of planets, especially Mars (see Chapter XV), always had held a fascination for him and he assumed it also should hold a similar fascination for others (as H. G. Wells and other authors, such

---

*Interviewed in 1918,[11] Burroughs said that he always had known that he could write, and in 1929 he even was more positive about his early success as a writer. "I knew absolutely that I could write stories just as entertaining and perhaps a whole lot more than any I chanced to read in those magazines."[12] But, in 1911 he took two safeguards (see below) before writing his manuscript.

†A favorite saying of Burroughs—in rebuttal to literary criticism of his stories—was that he never did learn the technique although, he wryly commented in 1937, "with the publication of my new novel [*Back to the Stone Age*], there are forty-seven books on my list."[13]

‡Not so unfamiliar a practice.

§A second reason: Ed did not want to be connected with another failure.

‖ This also included Emma, who was kept in the dark about her husband's latest endeavor until encouragement was received from Metcalf.

as Jules Verne, had proved). A story of strange people in a mysterious locale, yet possessed of the same desires, hopes, fear, frustrations, loves and hates as anyone else. It must have a beautiful girl—a princess, no less—and, of course, a handsome hero. (ERB's eleven Martian novels are second in popularity only to his Tarzan series and considered by some fans to be even more important. His Martian hero, John Carter, a typically Southern gentleman of the highest type, was the prototype for Tarzan.)

Metcalf liked the second half of Burroughs' story and he bought it for four hundred dollars (which included all serial rights). Entitled *Dejah Thoris, Princess of Mars*, Metcalf changed it to *Under the Moons of Mars*,* and it was published in six parts in *All-Story*, beginning February 1912. Edgar Rice Burroughs, at age thirty-six, had written and sold his first story.†

In the fall of 1911, while writing his Martian adventure, Ed found the lead pencil sharpener business at a dull point and highly unprofitable. Brother Coleman, who had worked for Champlin-Yardley, put in a good word and Ed took a job at the stationers. "With the success of my first story I decided to make writing a career but I was canny enough not to give up my job."[16]

Throughout the fall and winter and into the spring of 1912, Ed spent most of his evenings at the Chicago Public Library. His second effort was entitled *The Outlaw of Torn*, completed in December 1911. It was a historical story about a lost prince of England and a 13th century war. But Ed was not as lucky with this one. It was rejected five times and before Ed would sell it he had an idea for still another kind of setting—this one with a precedent.

Meanwhile, his job with the stationers did not pay expenses and "we had a recurrence of great poverty, sustained only by the thread of hope that I might make a living writing fiction. I cast about for a better job and [in the spring of 1912] landed as a department manager for a business magazine."[17]

---

*After having published four Tarzan books, McClurg published Burroughs' initial effort in novel form on October 10, 1917. It was dedicated "To my son Jack" (John Coleman).

†One other change was made in that first story. An over-alert proofreader changed "Normal" to "Norman," and that is how the byline came to read "by Norman Bean."

IV

Like Ulysses...

To be poor assures one an easier life than being rich, for the poor have no tax to pay....
　　　　　　　　　　　　　　　　Tarzan and the Ant Men, *1924*

Ulysses wandered ten years after the battle of Troy and made his way safely home after braving great perils and tribulations. ERB wandered twenty years after having been sacked at Phillips Academy, facing the more realistic perils and tribulations of trying to make good. By March 1912, at age 36, the log of navigator Burroughs read thusly:

1891–95	Student, Michigan Military Academy, Orchard Lake, Michigan.
1895–96	Assistant Commandant, Tactical Officer and Cavalry Instructor, Orchard Lake.
1896–97	Private, 7th U.S. Cavalry, Fort Grant, Arizona. Discharged by favor.
1898–99	Retail book and stationery business, Pocatello, Idaho.
1899–1902	Treasurer, American Battery Co., Chicago.
1900	Married, January 31, to Emma Hulbert, Chicago.
1903–04	Gold mining, Idaho and Oregon.
1904–05	Policeman, Salt Lake City, Utah.

1905–06	"Expert Accountant," T. J. Winslow Co., Chicago.	1909–11	Secretary-treasurer, Stace, Burroughs & Co., Chicago.
1906–08	Stenographic Department, Sears, Roebuck Co., Chicago.	1911	Secretary and advertising manager, Champlin-Yardley Co., Chicago.
1908	Joan Burroughs, born January 12.	1912 (March)	*Under the Moon of Mars*, written in the fall of 1911, under the pseudonym of "Norman Bean" running serially in *All-Story* magazine.
1908	Sales agency business, Chicago.		
1908–09	Magazine ad buyer for Physicians' Co-Operative Association, Chicago.		
1909	Hulbert Burroughs, born August 12.		

V

The Ape-man Cometh 1912

> ...*imagination is but another name for super-intelligence. Imagination it is which builds bridges, and cities, and empires. The beasts know it not, the blacks only a little, while to one in a hundred thousand of earth's dominant race it is given as a gift from heaven....*
>
> The New Stories of Tarzan,* 1916–17

1. THE COUNSELOR

The A. (for Archibald) W. Shaw Company, located at 5 North Wabash, 16th floor, published magazines of business like *System — The Magazine of Efficiency*. Another was called *Factory*. Ed held several jobs at *System*, one of which, ironically, was advising businessmen how to solve their problems and become more successful!

(Upon payment of fifty dollars per year, any executive could pose as many business problems as he wished, and "counselors," such as ERB, would reply with advice and suggestions.)

Ed knew he would have to revise *The Outlaw of Torn*, but first he would work on his draft of a new story and continue his research at the Chicago Public Library. What else was there to read? Stanley's *In*

---

*Subsequently published in novel form as *Jungle Tales of Tarzan*, 1919.

Darkest Africa; Kipling's *Jungle Books*; Jack London's *Call of the Wild* and *The Sea Wolf**; a most interesting article researching tales of "Wild Men and Beast Children," by E. Burnet Tylor†; and J. A. Macculoch's book, "Childhood of Fiction."‡

"While I was working there [A. W. Shaw] I wrote evenings and holidays ... in longhand on the backs of old letterheads and odd pieces of paper. I did not think it was a very good story and I doubted if it would sell. But Bob Davis§ saw its possibilities for magazine publication and I got a check ... for $700."¹ The story was entitled *Tarzan of the Apes* and it appeared complete in the October 1912 issue of *All-Story*.‖

Evelyn McKenzie recalled:

My father [Harry Burroughs] and I read the manuscript of *Tarzan of the Apes* before it was submitted to the publisher, as Uncle Ed wanted my father's opinion of it, and Dad read it aloud to me while I was making a dress for a High School dance. We thought it highly interesting, but agreed in confidence that it was much too fantastic to sell. How often we laughed over that prediction in later years!

I sometimes think [Uncle Ed] might have tried to write earlier in life if his unusual imagination had not been somewhat blighted at an early age. I remember my father tell of an incident in Ed's early childhood which may ... have had its effect on a creative mind.

Coming in from school one day [Ed] announced, wide-eyed, that he had just seen a cow in a tree. Perhaps it was a purple cow—I don't recall that part of the story. At any rate, my grandfather, who was a rather stern man, with a very positive nature, heard the statement and punished his small son for lying. [Grandfather] was an unimaginative man himself, and to him there was only black and white, truth and untruth, and he didn't want his son to lie.¹ᴬ

Burroughs admittedly liked to speculate as to the relative values of heredity, environment and training on a child reared by beasts, and in Tarzan he was playing with this idea.

Away back in the days when events were recorded only in the memories of man, and handed down by word-of-mouth from father to son, there were stories of human babes reared by beasts, and instances have been reported from time to time even to this present day. There is something in the idea which appeals very strongly to the imagination. It did to mine....

Several years ago, I had occasion to interview a young man who claimed to have been raised by a band of apes somewhere upon the coast of Africa. He attained quite a little notoriety as Dan, the Monkey Man.

Having learned quite a little about the habits and customs of the beasts of the jungle, I am inclined to think that Dan's life among the apes was as truly a contribution to fiction as my story of Tarzan, and was the result of misspent youth among the Tarzan books, for I do not believe that any human infant or child, unprotected by adults of its own species, could survive a fortnight in such an African environment as I describe in the Tarzan stories, and if he did, he would develop into a cunning, cowardly beast, as he would have to spend most of his waking hours fleeing for his life. He would be underdeveloped from lack of proper and sufficient

---

*Both London books deal with approximately the same theme. In *Call of the Wild*, it is the "civilized" dog returning to the primitive life of the wolf pack; in *The Sea Wolf*, a sophisticated man who is forced to adapt to primitive living.

†*Anthropological Review*, London, 1863, Volume 1.

‡Published by John Murray, London, 1905.

§Fiction editor of Munsey's magazines for twenty years, Robert Hobart Davis had a long, varied and prolific career as reporter, write, editor, columnist and author. He was advisor and good friend of both Irvin S. Cobb and O. Henry, and for years wrote a popular column in the *New York Sun* under the signature of "Bobdavis."

‖ Published as a novel—Chicago: A. C. McClurg & Company, 1914.

nourishment, from exposure to the inclemencies of the weather, and from lack of sufficient restful sleep.

So Tarzan is purely the product of my imagination. I always like to think of him as a real character, but the fact remains that he was merely an interesting experiment in the mental laboratory which we call imagination.[2]

2. LORD AND LADY G.

The first story of the ape-man finds an aristocratic English couple, Lord and Lady Greystoke (the Honorable Lady Alice) put ashore on the west coast of Africa by a mutinous crew. Lord G., also referred to as John Clayton, builds a cabin to protect them from the wild animals but one day a huge gorilla attacks him. Lady Alice shoots the beast but the shock of the encounter proves too much and results in unbalancing her mind. That same night a son is born to her and one year later she dies. A band of great apes breaks into the cabin, kills Lord Greystoke, and Kala, a she-ape who just lost her own little one, snatches the white babe from his cradle and treats it as her own dead child.

> As she took up the live baby of Alice Clayton ... the wail of the living had answered the call of universal motherhood within her wild breast.... High above the branches of a mighty tree she hugged the shrieking infant to her bosom, and soon the instinct that was as dominant in this fierce female as it had been in the breast of his tender and beautiful mother — the instinct of mother love — reached out to the tiny man-child's half-formed understanding, and he became quiet. Then hunger closed the gap between them, and the son of an English lord and an English lady nursed at the breast of Kala, the great ape.[3]

The story continues with Tarzan rising almost to manhood, fighting the battles of the primitive jungle after the manner of the beasts. He rises to kingship of the great apes, the Tribe of Kerchak.

> His straight and perfect figure, muscled as the best of the ancient Roman gladiators must have been muscled, and yet with the soft and sinuous curves of a Greek God, told at a glance the wondrous combination of enormous strength with suppleness and speed.... With the noble poise of his handsome head upon those broad shoulders, and the fire of life and intelligence of those fine, clear eyes, he might readily have typified some demi-god of a wild and warlike bygone people of his ancient forest.[4]

Tarzan meets Jane Porter, who also is put ashore in West Africa by a mutinous crew. Accompanying Jane are her father, a bumbling, comic professor, an assistant bumbling, comic professor, and William Cecil Clayton, who, coincidentally, happens to be related to Tarzan. Clayton will be heir to the Greystoke title unless Tarzan proves his rightful claim to the Greystoke name. When Jane is carried away by Terkoz, son of Tublat, foster-brother of Tarzan, the ape-man swings to the rescue. He catches up with the pair.

> Jane Porter — her lithe, young form flattened against the trunk of a great tree, her hands tight pressed against her rising and falling bosom, and her eyes wide with mingled horror, fascination, fear and admiration — watched the primordial ape battle with the primeval man for possession of a woman — for her.... It was a primeval woman who sprang forward with outstretched arms toward the primeval man who had fought for her and won her.
>
> And Tarzan?
>
> He did what no red-blooded man needs lessons in doing. He took his woman in his arms and smothered her upturned panting lips with kisses.[5]

3. SELF-EDUCATION

Tarzan's first spoken language was not English, but French taught to him by Paul D'Arnot, French naval officer with whom Tarzan became great friends. In return for saving D'Arnot's life, the ape-man writes a note: "Teach me to speak the language of men." (*Tarzan of the Apes.*) But — how is it that Tarzan can write and read and yet not speak?

> The development of Tarzan from infancy to manhood, and the manner in which he learned to read English, although he knew no spoken language outside of the meager vocabulary of the apes, while apparently preposterous, was so interesting to me that I thought it worth while to make it seem plausible.[6]

Not so preposterous at all, as it turned out, for Burroughs brought about the self-education of Tarzan through development of the "recognition" method of reading — based on associating pictures with accompanying letter groups.

Finding the cabin in which he was born, the ten-year-old boy opens a primer to a picture of a little "ape," similar to himself, albeit covered with clothes. Beneath the picture are three little "bugs" which spell out B-O-Y. He finds these same "bugs" always stuck to every picture of the little "ape," and also finds many other combinations of B-O-Y (like in the pictures of other little "apes" and four-legged creatures). Beneath one of these pictures, the "bugs" spelled out A B-O-Y AND A D-O-G.

By the time he was fifteen, Tarzan knew the various combinations of letters which stood for every pictured figure in the primer. His search through the various books inside the cabin convinced him that he had discovered all the different kinds of "bugs" most often repeated in combination, and these he arranged in proper order from the alphabet picture book. When Tarzan discovered the arrangement of words in alphabetical order, he looked for the combinations with which he was familiar. Thus he learned that he was a M-A-N and not an A-P-E, that Sabor was a L-I-O-N-E-S-S,* Histah a S-N-A-K-E and Tantor an E-L-E-P-H-A-N-T. Tarzan also found several lead pencils in the cabin and discovered they leave black lines. His attempts to reproduce some of the "bugs" leads to *writing*, and by copying the "bugs" (and noticing how many there are), to *arithmetic*.

So before Tarzan is eighteen, he knows reading, writing and arithmetic but he is unable to speak! It was at this point in his young life that he meets up with D'Arnot. At first, the French officer thinks Tarzan is a deaf mute, not realizing that the ape-man never had spoken to a fellow human being. D'Arnot pointed out familiar objects and repeated their names in French. Of course, it made no difference to Tarzan whether it was French or English — he had no way of telling one language from another. Tarzan soon mastered a few basic sentences until he and D'Arnot were able to converse. The ape-man also studied English but French was his first spoken language and thus was realized the self-education of Tarzan. Preposterous?

Although Tarzan knew the meaning of many words, one word puzzled him above all others. This was the word *God*.

> It attracted him because it was short, and because of the number of "he-bugs" which figured in its definition. (Tarzan called the capital letters "he-bugs" and the lower case, "she-bugs.") The definitions of *god* were in "he-bugs"— Supreme Deity, Creator or Upholder of the Universe.... *God*— he thought — must be a great chieftain, king of all the Mangani — but that might mean that *God*

---

*In the magazine story of *Tarzan of the Apes*, which was published two years prior to book publication, Sabor was a T-I-G-E-R. Letters poured into the magazine by those who knew something of the wild life in Africa and pointed out that Africa contained no tigers! So in the novel, Burroughs changed Sabor into a L-I-O-N-E-S-S.

was mightier than Tarzan and this he would not believe. But although he tried, he never found a picture of God and Tarzan determined to look for him.*

A wise old ape told him that the power which made the lightning and rain and thunder came from Goro, the moon.... Tarzan climbed to the highest branch of the tallest tree, and was surprised that Goro was still as far away as when he was on the ground. Tarzan yelled at Goro and challenged him to come down and fight it out with Tarzan, but Goro did not move; when a cloud hid Goro's face, Tarzan was convinced that Goro was hiding from him.[7]

Tarzan was then told that the witch doctor in the village of Mbonga was God. But the ape-man discovered that under his masquerade he was a mere native.

An orchid, dangling close beside his head, opened slowly. A thousand times had Tarzan of the Apes witnessed the beauteous miracle; but now.... What made the flower open? What made it grow from a tiny bud to a full-blown bloom. Why was it at all? Why was he? Who planted the first tree? How did Goro get way up into the darkness of the sky to cast his welcome light upon the fearsome nocturnal jungle? And the sun! Where and how, anyway, did they all come from — the trees, the flowers, the insects, the countless creatures of the jungle?

An idea popped into the ape-man's head: in following out the many dictionary definitions of God, he had come upon the word *create*—"to cause to come into existence; to form out of nothing."

Ah, now it was all explained — the flowers, the trees, the moon, the sun, himself, every living creature in the jungle — they were all made by God out of nothing.

And what was God? What did God look like? Of that, he had no conception; but he was sure that everything that was good came from God. Yes, Tarzan had found God and he spent the whole day in attributing to Him all of the good and beautiful things of nature; but there was one thing which troubled him. He could not quite reconcile it to his conception of his new-found God.

Who made Histah, the snake?†[8]

Joan Burroughs recalled years later:

Dad never discussed religion at home. He said he wanted us to choose our own church when we were grown up and possessed of sufficient intelligence to make our own decision. He did not go to church and we didn't either. He lived by his own conscience, of which honesty and humility were important.[9]

The author revealed his philosophy of religion in many of his stories, such as:

The Lord of the Jungle subscribed to no creed. Tarzan of the Apes was not a church man yet like the majority of those who have always lived close to nature he was, in a sense, intensely religious. His intimate knowledge of the stupendous forces of nature, of her wonders and her miracles had impressed him with the fact that their ultimate origin lay far beyond the conception of the finite mind of man, and thus incalculably remote from the farthest bounds of science. When he thought of God he liked to think of Him primitively, as a personal God. And while he realized that he knew nothing of such matters, he liked to believe that after death he would live again.[10]

---

*For another native of Africa who was determined to find God, read *The Adventures of the Black Girl in Her Search for God*, by George Bernard Shaw (New York: Dodd, Mead & Company, 1933).

†The little black girl who strode off into the African jungle in search of God met a poisonous mamba snake, and said to the mamba: "I wonder who made you, and why he gave you the will to kill me and the venom to do it with." (From Bernard Shaw's *The Adventures of the Black Girl in Her Search for God*.)

VI

Breakthrough 1913

Tarzan [lived] as the lion lives — a true jungle creature dependent solely on his own prowess and his wits, playing a lone hand against creation....
Tarzan the Terrible, *1921*

1. An Author's "Rights"

The "make" or "break" year for ERB was 1913. His third child, John Coleman, was born on February 28, thirteen days after the death of Ed's father, and the author made the decision to devote himself full time to writing: "We were a long way from home. My income depended solely upon the sale of magazine rights.... Had I failed to sell a single story during these months we would have been broke again."[1] But he sold them all. That Burroughs worked hard to make a success of his newly found career was evidenced by a graph that he used to keep on his desk, showing word output. In 1913, he wrote 413,000 words (equivalent to four 300-page books). This amazing output resulted in: *The Cave Girl, The Monster Men, The Warlord of Mars, The Eternal Lover, The Mad King, At the Earth's Core, The Mucker* and *The Return of Tarzan*, the latter written in December 1912 and January 1913. Another story, *The Gods of Mars*, was written in the fall of 1912.

Also, in August of his "breakthrough" year, Ed finally sold *The Outlaw of Torn*, after having revised it. The story was purchased by Street & Smith's monthly *New*

Story Magazine and published as a five-part serial beginning January 1914. This one had an extended publishing history, not appearing in novel form until February 1927, when it was published by A. C. McClurg & Company, Chicago.

The author was now starting to shop for his rights, particularly after Metcalf (who had encouraged him to complete his first story) turned down *The Return of Tarzan*, which ERB then sold to *New Story Magazine* for a thousand dollars. Bob Davis, Munsey's chief editor, was greatly upset that the Tarzan sequel was turned down and he saw to it that it would not happen again.*

Burroughs received no payment from the wide newspaper serialization of *Tarzan of the Apes* (the original copyright was taken out in the name of Frank A. Munsey Company, 1912), but he preciously guarded his rights forever after. He expressed his feelings on the subject to the *Author's League*:

> I am very *recent* in the writing game, and so, like most *recent* people in any field, feel fully qualified to spill advice promiscuously among my betters.
>
> But the very fact of my newness is the strongest argument I have in favor of my propaganda—that writers never part with any of their rights except for value received. Though my literary fontanelle is scarce closed, and my name a household word only in my own home, I am making more real money out of the second serial rights to my stories than some famous authors whose work is of infinitely greater value than mine.
>
> They relinquish their second serial rights either to magazine or book publisher. I retain mine in all events. I sell mine for cash or not at all.... I sold three stories to magazines before I discovered that second serial rights had a value. From then on I have retained these rights and the fourth story [*The Return of Tarzan*] has already brought in $729.00 in cash and is still selling. I have received as high as $300.00 for the newspaper rights to a story for a single city.²

Burroughs called for a syndication plan, where all writers would pool the information on how much they were getting per story from magazines and newspapers so they could reach a price basis that was fair to both writers and newspapers. He suggested that the league undertake the syndication of all its members—and thus cut out the agent. Although many favorable comments were received from other writers, nothing ever was done. Burroughs wrote to another writer: "Way in the backs of our heads we could harbor the hope that some day the syndication bureau could develop into that ideal [for the writer] organization—an author's publishing house, by means of which we could not only get our royalties, but also a share of the profits from our books."

Notwithstanding that early loss in "second rights," the income of ERB—resulting from his prodigious efforts in 1913—probably amounted to between $10,000 and $15,000, rather than the "more than $20,000" that has been reported in several sketches of Burroughs. Also, he was not getting ten cents a word for his copy (as stated). If this were true, his earned income from the 1913 output would have totaled more than $40,000. Burroughs himself later acknowledged that he did not receive ten cents a word for magazine stories until several years *after* publication of *Tarzan of the Apes* in book form, and not from Bob Davis, the author said, but from Ray Long of *The Red Book*.†

---

*Forty-seven of ERB's stories appeared in the Munsey publications and its successors from 1912 through 1941.

†A Burroughs story appeared only once in *The Red Book Magazine* (forerunner of today's *Redbook*). This was in 1919 when *The Red Book* pre-printed the first half of *Tarzan the Untamed* in six parts, from

2. Tarzan—The Novel

Ed Burroughs enjoyed telling the story of his attempts to have *Tarzan of the Apes* published in book form: "Every well-known publisher in the United States turned it down, including A. C. McClurg & Company who finally issued it. The popularity of *Tarzan of the Apes* and its final appearance as a book was due to the vision of J. H. Tennant, managing editor of the *New York Evening World*."[3]

The author might have allowed a small amount of vision to the Munsey Company — holder of the original copyright — which serialized the magazine story to the *World*. It appeared in forty-six daily (except Sundays) installments beginning January 6, 1913 — three months after publication in *All-Story*. A striking center-page illustration of Tarzan battling a lion plus two smaller illustrations appeared under a head that read: "Not Like Any Other Story That You Have Ever Read." To further tantalize its readers, the *World* further explained the story as "A romance of the African Jungle, With a Hero Who Grew to Wild Manhood Among the Beasts Before Seeing a Human Face." A second top-of-the-page "teaser" read: "A 'Forest God' Youth and Yankee Heroine Who Met in a Primitive World. Man's Battle Against Brutes in the Dark Continent."

Other newspapers also serialized the story to make it widely known, "resulting in a demand from readers for the story in book form which was so insistent that A. C. McClurg finally came to me after they rejected it and asked to be allowed to publish it."[4]

Burroughs later acknowledged that the book idea also had been pushed by Herbert A. Gould, director of McClurg's retail book store on Wabash Avenue, that Gould discussed the possibility with Joseph Bray, head of the firm's publication department (later to become president of the firm and a good friend of the author's), and that Bray "was equally enthusiastic." But at no time (to the best of this writer's knowledge) did Burroughs ever give credit to an individual by name of William G. Chapman, and twelve years later it was Chapman *vs.* Burroughs in the Circuit Court of Cook County, Illinois.

The plaintiff, Chapman, claimed he had entered into an oral or verbal contract (shortly before May 1, 1914) to negotiate for the defendant, Edgar Rice Burroughs, a contract for the publication in book form of *Tarzan of the Apes* ... by which Burroughs agreed to pay him ten per cent of any and all royalties which the defendant might thereafter receive from publication of said book. It was further stated that Chapman did negotiate a contract with A. C. McClurg & Company but that Chapman had never received any commission on royalties paid to Burroughs upon sale in foreign countries, and had received no commission on royalties based on U.S. sales since the end of December 1920.

The case was settled out of court when on June 1, 1926, Burroughs paid Chapman one thousand dollars and the latter thereupon released Burroughs (and McClurg) from future claims and action concerning royalty payment.

In the original contract for book publication of *Tarzan of the Apes*, dated April 20, 1914, the signature of William G. Chapman appears as witness to Burroughs' signature, and it is also written into this contract that "all royalty payments together with the semi-annual statements of sale shall be made by McClurg to ERB

March through August. Burroughs received a total of $2,800. (However, *The Red Book* editor was not Ray Long but Karl Edwin Harriman.)

through his agent, W. G. Chapman of 1325 First National Bank Building, Chicago, Illinois."

On June 1, 1914, McClurg published an announcement to the book trade:

EXTRA!
We take pleasure in announcing that there
Will be issued on June 17 one of the most
ORIGINAL and *remarkable* stories ever written
TARZAN OF THE APES*
By Edgar Rice Burroughs

One part of the blurb read:

Reminiscent perhaps in spirit of the "Jungle Books" and in human interest of the "Call of the Wild," but there the likeness ceases. TARZAN is *unique*—one of those books that appear only once in a while, *fascinating, absorbing*, and—DIFFERENT.

3. The Critics

Book reviewers in 1914 agreed that *Tarzan of the Apes* was "interesting" and "imaginative."

New York Tribune

The author sometimes strains our belief a little but he has worked out his extraordinary invention with so much ingenuity that one reads on, genuinely interested in what will happen next in the career of Tarzan of the Apes.

Chicago Post

It is highly improbable fiction ... very odd and very interesting. But it is hard to leave it half-read. This book is well-written and the author displays an astonishing amount of knowledge about ape-life. At least it must pass as knowledge among those who know apes only at a zoo.

Omaha World Herald

As a whole the book is impossible, but each individual incident is so well handled by the author as to make it altogether probable and altogether interesting.

Milwaukee Journal

This wildly impossible book is nevertheless an uncommonly good book, interesting to the very last page. For sheer imagination and a certain ingenious appeal to the reader's credulity, this yarn stands nigh well unsurpassed.

Boston Advertiser

Fact and fiction gracefully mingled is the best prescription for a story that is to succeed. "Tarzan of the Apes" belongs in this class of fiction; there is enough of fact, or what claims to be fact to delight the reader of adventure stories.

San Francisco Argonaut

This story succeeds in being wildly ridiculously impossible, and at the same time interesting.... The reader will laugh consumedly, but he will probably persevere to the last page.

St. Paul Pioneer

"Tarzan of the Apes" is not literature, yet if you do not scorn the movies, you will probably read through.

Galveston News

Rather long drawn-out—yet a wonderfully imaginative story! A real genius in the writer might have become manifest had he not set out to make the foster-child of an ape entirely too human and turned quite the most striking figure of a jungle lad into a conventionalized Englishman at heart.

---

*Dedication was to the author's wife—"To Emma Hulbert Burroughs."

Toronto Globe

If the author of "Tarzan of the Apes" had gone to Darwin for the improbable basis of his tale, he has at least given it all the air of reality which one expects to find in a novel that treats the ape as a distant ancestor of man.

*The New York Times**

As the result of a mutiny aboardship, an English nobleman and his wife are marooned in a jungle inhabited by anthropoid apes. Here a child is born; a year later the mother dies. A great ape kills the father, but the baby boy is adopted by a female ape whose own child had just been killed by a fall. The subsequent adventures of Tarzan, as the boy is named by the tribe, make a story of many marvels.... With adventures and perils the book is replete, nor is a strange love story wanting. It closes with great renunciation, but with the promise of another Tarzan book, which leads the reader to hope that the renunciation was not final. Crowded with impossibilities as the tale is, Mr. Burroughs has told it so well, and has so succeeded in carrying his readers with him, that there are few who will not look forward eagerly to the promised sequel.

4. SALES

Burroughs' book-publishing history has been one of phenomenal success and, as well, one of equally phenomenal exaggeration — particularly in the early years. For instance, it has been reported innumerable times (and accepted as valid) that more than 1,000,000 copies of *Tarzan of the Apes* were sold before the first year was out. Other reports claimed 3,000,000 and one even 5,000,000! McClurg's initial printing, however — in cloth, at $1.30 — has been reported to be only 5,000 copies. True, the Chicago firm† did reprint two additional times before the end of 1914, but the combined total likely was no more than 15,000.‡

---

*Review of July 5, 1914. *The New York Times* also gave the book a pre-publication date review (June 14) which was no more than a brief synopsis of the story. (McClurg preprinted a number of paperbound review copies.)

†McClurg & Co. never was a major publishing house, per se. Its principal business was that of wholesaler and distributor and it also carried on a successful retail bookstore operation. But McClurg became a name in the publishing field mainly through sharing the ape-man's jungle. It seldom printed more than short-run first editions, preferring to contract with other houses for reprinting purposes and then sharing a percentage with the author. The A.L. Burt & Company began reprinting *Tarzan of the Apes* in 1915 (in a fifty-cent edition) and continued reprinting this work and the next four Tarzan titles innumerable times through 1929. Grosset & Dunlap had a much longer run, beginning with *A Princess of Mars* in 1918 and continuing with other titles until 1962. (For more on G & D's run, see Chapter XXI.)

‡In 1934, a list of best-sellers since 1875 was compiled for the Institute of Arts and Sciences of Columbia University by Edward Weeks of *The Atlantic Monthly*. Sixty-five titles were included and *Tarzan of the Apes* ranked twenty-seventh, with sales of 750,000, a few thousand below Winston Churchill's *Richard Carvel*. (American literary taste ran heavily toward works of religious or sentimental nature; sixty of the sixty-five titles were works of fiction, and the number one best-seller — approximately eight million copies — was *In His Steps*, by Charles Monroe Sheldon, a work depicting what the world might be like if everyone followed Christ's teachings literally.)

Frank Luther Mott's *Golden Multitudes* (New York: The Macmillan Company, 1947) lists overall best-sellers in the United States by decades, with the criterion being that to attain best-seller status, sale of the particular book had to be equal to one per cent of the population of the U.S.A. for the decade for which it was published. In the decade from 1910–19 (with one per cent representing sales of 900,000 or more) *Tarzan of the Apes* is listed (along with Zane Grey's *Riders of the Purple Sage*; Eleanor Porter's *Pollyanna*; Booth Tarkington's *Penrod*; Kathleen Norris' *Mother*; Harold Bell Wright's *The Winning of Barbara Worth* and *When a Man's a Man*; and Gene Stratton Porter's trio, *The Harvester*, *Laddie* and *Michael O'Halloran*).

In what might be called a footnote to a footnote: Frank Luther Mott, director of the School of Journalism, University of Iowa, first requested the information relative to the sale of *Tarzan of the Apes* in a letter to McClurg on March 27, 1942. McClurg wrote to Mott the following day, saying that a copy of his letter had been forwarded to Burroughs with a covering letter urging compliance with his request.

Mott wrote to McClurg again on May 7, not having heard regarding his inquiry. McClurg immediately followed up with a second letter to Burroughs and, subsequently, a reply to Mott in which the publisher suggested that since "we have so far been unable to obtain any response, we can suggest only that you write Burroughs directly...." Since no further correspondence was found between Mott and McClurg, the sales figure used by Mott in his *Golden Multitudes* (1947) was likely that furnished him directly by Burroughs, Inc.

VII

Tarzan and Friend

As he stood there in the red light of the oil lamp, strong, tall and beautiful, his long black hair sweeping over his shoulders, the knife swinging at his neck, and his head crowned with a wreath of white jasmine, he might easily have been mistaken for some wild god of a Jungle legend.
The Jungle Book, 1894
Rudyard Kipling

The young Lord Greystoke was indeed a strange and warlike figure, his mass of black hair falling to his shoulders ... with the noble poise of his handsome head upon those broad shoulders, and the fire of life and intelligence in those fine, clear eyes, he might readily have typified some demigod of a wild and warlike bygone people of his ancient forest.
Tarzan of the Apes, 1912
Edgar Rice Burroughs

1. MOWGLI

At seventeen years old he had the strength and growth far beyond his age:

He could swing by one hand from a top branch for half an hour at a time.... He could stop a young buck in mid-gallop and throw him sideways by the head. He could even jerk over the big, blue wild boars that lived in the Marshes of the North. The Jungle-People who used to fear him for his wits feared him now for his strength, and when he moved quietly on his own affairs the mere whisper of his coming cleared the wood-paths. And yet the look in his eyes was always gentle.*

Tarzan at seventeen! But — is this Tarzan? It looks like him. It even sounds like him — especially when he calls his faithful jungle companion "with a long, low howl that rose and fell." But responding to the call is Bagheera, the black panther, and not Tantor, the elephant, and the seventeen-year-old is not Burroughs' Tarzan the ape-man, but Rudyard Kipling's Mowgli, the man-cub.

The striking similarities between Mowgli and Tarzan are many, as are certain undeniable similarities between their respective authors (noted elsewhere in this chapter), and in 1938 fate stepped in to unite Kipling and Burroughs in fictional marriage. There were a number of witnesses, and the Los Angeles Times dutifully reported the occasion with this headline:

REAL TARZAN FOUND IN INDIA

Expedition Forms to Go
in Search of Jungle King

SIMLA (India) Nov. 19. (Exclusive) — A real-life Tarzan who is believed to have some strange control over wild animals is to be sought by an expedition which will set off soon into the heart of India's biggest jungle....

Tarzan was first seen a few weeks ago by the members of a hunting party.... Losing their way, the huntsmen were resting in their tents when they suddenly heard a weird, piercing cry. They at first thought it was the wail of some animal, but when it continued they realized that it was a human voice.

Climbing some tall trees, they saw in the distance a giant ape-like man, naked, bearded and over six feet tall. His body was covered with long hair. The weird cry came from him.

Suddenly as they watched a huge tiger came out of the undergrowth and bounded up to "Tarzan," who put his arms around its shoulders. One of the huntsmen fired at the tiger and both man and beast looked up in amazement. Then they vanished into the jungle, but for many minutes the party heard the piercing cry mingled with the tiger's roar.

The huntsmen searched the forest for two full days but no other trace of the Tarzan was found.[1]

Simla! Kipling stamping grounds as a seventeen-year-old journalist. How incredible that a "real live" Tarzan should be found in Rudyard's own backyard! Burroughs and Kipling ... Tarzan and Mowgli ... one happy family. Certainly it is no secret that writers do borrow from one another — a scrap here, a bone there — before completing their own soups. But there is one proviso. The borrower must come up with the twin ingredients of talent and imagination or all he will find in his bowl is a poor and tasteless imitation.

(Burroughs always said that Tarzan was based mainly on the legend of Romulus and Remus.† Kipling readily admitted to his close friend and fellow-author H. Rider Haggard,‡ that the impulse for

---

*This passage as well as all others in this chapter describing or referring to Mowgli and his jungle habitat and friends are from Kipling's *The Jungle Book* (London: The Macmillan Co., 1894). Doubleday and Company published it in the United States.

†In Roman mythology, the founders of Rome. Left to die on the banks of the river Tiber when they were babies, the twin brothers were reared and suckled by a she-wolf. Later Romulus killed Remus and became the first king of Rome.

‡Author of such popular adventure "classics" as *She, Cleopatra* and *King Solomon's Mines*. In ERB's *The Return of Tarzan*, the ape-man stumbles onto the lost civilization of Opar, where a lost race of white men are ruled by the beautiful La, high priestess of the Temple of the Sun — she herself a descendant of people who came to that locale ten thousand years before in search of gold. A "lost civilization" and a beautiful (and ageless) princess made up Rider Haggard's *She* (and there were others who wrote of this same theme long before Haggard). A little-known story of Burroughs', which first appeared in 1918, is

Mowgli of the *Jungle Books*,* was derived from the latter's Zulu romance, *Nada the Lily*, where a character was presented as running with a pack of wolves.)

Publicly, ERB never acknowledged any indebtedness for his creation of Tarzan, but in private correspondence with Professor Rudolph Altrocchi, former professor of Italian at the University of California at Berkeley, he admitted having been influenced by Kipling.†

Mowgli is a member of the Seeonee wolf pack, reared and suckled by a mother wolf. Tarzan, member of the Tribe of Kerchak, reared and suckled by a mother ape. Kipling divided the jungle's inhabitants into "Jungle-People" and "Monkey-People," the latter he named the Bander-log. "The flight of the Monkey-People through tree-land is one of the things nobody can describe. They have their regular roads and cross-roads, up hills and down hills, all laid out from fifty to seventy or a hundred feet above ground."

While everybody knows that Tarzan can climb trees and swing from branch to branch faster and higher than any of the great apes, Mowgli also has talent in this direction. "From early infancy he had used his hands to swing from branch to branch ... speeding through the tree-tops with his brothers and sisters. He could spring twenty feet across space at the dizzy heights of the forest top ... [flinging] himself through the branches almost as boldly as the grey ape."

When the man-cub was being taken to the Monkey City (known as "Cold Lairs"), "Mowgli could not help enjoying the wild rush through the tree-tops though the glimpses of earth far down below frightened him ... his escort would rush him up a tree till he felt the thinnest topmost branches crackle and bend under them, and then with a cough and a whoop would fling themselves into the air outward and downward...."

Like Tarzan, Mowgli hates mankind, though not nearly as vehemently. But it is there, nevertheless:

Mowgli
He loathed them, their talk, their cruelty and their cowardice.

Tarzan
...he saw the greed, the selfishness, the cowardice and the cruelty of man....[3]

Mowgli
They are idle, senseless and cruel; they play with their mouths and they do not kill the weaker for food, but for sport. When they are full-fed they would throw their own breed into the "Red Flower."‡ It is not well that they should live here any more. I hate them!

---

entitled *H.R.H. the Rider*. While the title specifically refers to "His Royal Highness the Rider," could this not have been ERB's tribute to H. Rider Haggard?

*Kipling wrote his *Jungle Books* between 1892–95 while he and his American wife were staying in Brattleboro, Vermont. Born in 1865, ten years before Burroughs, the English author was already a literary success prior to his jungle stories, and *Captains Courageous*, *The White Man's Burden*, *Kim* and many other stories, ballads and honors—including the Nobel Prize for Literature (1907)—were still ahead of him.

†"What, then, were the sources of Mr. Burroughs? For his [Tarzan] story did not spring full-grown from his imagination, no matter how fertile this may be. Indeed he frankly admitted his sources in two letters to me.

"First of all, as he says, he was always interested in mythology.... Secondly, he admits having been influenced by Kipling who, in his two *Jungle Books* (1894–95), developed most entertainingly the life of a boy, Mowgli, lost in the jungle, who fantastically hobnobbed with wild animals.... Mr. Burroughs also admitted that he browsed in the Chicago Public Library for books which would give him exotic flora and fauna...."[2]

‡Kipling's "Red Flower" meant fire. In *Tarzan at the Earth's Core*, a fiery maiden is Jana, the Red Flower of Zoram.

Tarzan
The cruelty of the blacks toward a captive always induced in Tarzan a feeling of angry contempt.... It was the cruelty of wanton torture of the helpless....[4]

Mowgli, like Tarzan, is a beautiful man:

Kipling
Have any told thee that thou art beautiful beyond all men. Thou art very beautiful. Never have I looked upon such a man.

Burroughs
[Tarzan's face] was one of extraordinary beauty ... a perfect type of the strongly masculine, unmarred by dissipation, or brutal or degrading passions.[5]

As man is drawn and must go to man, so must Tarzan and Mowgli leave their jungle friends to find their fellows.

Kipling
Take thine own trail; make thy lair with thine own blood and pack and people but where there is need ... remember, Master of the Jungle, the Jungle is thine at call. And Mowgli cried, in answer: "I would not go, but I am drawn by both feet."

Burroughs
Tarzan is not an ape. He is not like his people. His ways are not their ways, and so Tarzan is going back to the lair of his own kind by the waters of the great lake.... You must choose another to rule you, for Tarzan will not return. (And thus young Greystoke took the first step toward the goal which he had set — the finding of other white men like himself.)[6]

Kipling
The dawn was beginning to break when Mowgli went down the hillside alone, to meet those mysterious things that are called men.

When it came to tempting fate, Burroughs toyed tirelessly with the grand dame and Kipling rather appreciated a like contest.

Burroughs
Tarzan had lived as the lion lives— a true jungle creature dependent solely on his own prowess and his wits, playing a lone hand against creation....[7]

Kipling
There was nothing Mowgli liked better than — as he said himself — "to pull the whiskers of death," and make the jungle know that he was the overlord.

Writing about their respective deserted cities and ancient civilizations, the phraseology of the two authors is remarkably similar:

Kipling
The Cold Lairs was an old deserted city, lost and buried in the jungle.... Some king had built it long ago on a little hill. You could still trace the stone causeways that led up to the ruined gates where the last splinters of wood hung to the worn, rusted hinges. Trees had grown into and out of the walls; the battlements were tumbled down and decayed, and wild creepers hung out the windows of the towers on the walls in bushy hanging clumps.

Burroughs
On the far side of the valley lay what appeared to be a mighty city, its great walls, its lofty spires, its turrets, minarets and domes showing red and yellow in the sunlight.... Crumbling edifices of hewn granite loomed ... upon the crumbling debris along the face of the buildings trees had grown, and vines wound in and out of the hollow, staring windows.[8]

Kipling
A great roofless palace crowned the hill, and the marble of the courtyard and the fountains was split, and stained with red and green, and the very cobblestones in the courtyard where the king's elephants used to live had been thrust up and apart by grasses and young trees.

Burroughs
...but the building directly opposite them seemed less overgrown than the others.... It

was a massive pile, surmounted by an enormous dome. At either side of its great entrance stood rows of tall pillars [each] capped by a huge, grotesque bird carved from the solid rock of the monoliths.⁹

Kipling

From the palace you could see the rows and rows of roofless houses that made up the city looking like empty honeycombs filled with blackness; the shapeless block of stone that had been an idol, in the square where the four roads met ... the shattered domes of temples with wild figs sprouting on their sides.

Kipling never pretended to invent — he recorded. Burroughs never pretended to record — he invented. To illustrate: Kipling's ancient city of Cold Lairs was the ruins of an ancient city which the then-young journalist had seen for himself. Burroughs, on the other hand, never having visited Africa or seen a "lost city," used his inventive powers to produce a similar scene. It is interesting to speculate on the following: did ERB plant a tiger in Africa (in the magazine story of *Tarzan of the Apes*) because he recalled that Kipling had placed the dreaded tiger, Shere Khan in India? (Tigers are native to India but not to Africa.)

Both ERB and Kipling were conservative in politics and colonial in their thinking. Like Burroughs, Kipling also had his own personal kind of religion. Neither accepted a formal, organized type of religion and each preferred to work out his own beliefs according to his own personal philosophy and desires.

Communication is as important in the jungle as out of it, but while Mowgli and Tarzan each speak the language of their respective habitats there apparently is little similarity between the animal mother-tongues of India and Africa. The closest match is Kipling's *KAA* (snake) and Burroughs' *Ska* (vulture). It would take a true arboreous etymologist to track down the whys and wherefores of the author's jungle *patois*. (And wouldn't this be a meaty thesis for a language major?) Below is a literal translation of some proper nouns from English-to Ape-to Wolf*:

English	Ape	Wolf
Baby†	Balu	____
Brown Bear†	____	Baloo
Buffalo	Gorgo	Mysa
Elephant	Tantor	Hathi
Jackal‡	Ungo	Tabaqui
Panther	Sheeta	Bagheera
Snake	Hista (h)	KAA
Tiger§	Sabor	Shere Khan

The Kipling-Burroughs confrontation boasts of several other coincidences. In *The Return of Tarzan*, the ape-man meets up with those fierce warriors, the Waziri, of which he forever after becomes their chieftain and they his "children." But what business does the Waziri tribe have in Africa when Waziristan — as can be found in any good atlas of India — belongs in Kipling's country!

A more personal matter. When Kipling returned to England in 1899, after nearly seven years in India, he wrote two ballads for *Macmillan's Magazine* (and perhaps because he was starting to write in a

---

*While the ape language is spoken and understood only by apes and some sub-humans in Tarzan's jungle, the wolf language is spoken and understood by other animals than wolves in Mowgli's jungle.

†There is no translation for "baby" in the wolf language and none for "brown bear" in the ape language, but "balu" (baby) and "baloo" (brown bear) are pronounced exactly alike so I assume that the two are interchangeable.

‡Ungo, the jackal, often turns into Dango, the hyena.

§Sabor is a lioness as well as a tiger.

new country, he took the pen name of Yossuf).*

Burroughs, too, tried his hand at poetry and adopted the use of his pen name. Perhaps the author of Martian tales and Tarzan adventures envisioned himself — at least during the beginning of his writing career — as an American Kipling?

The Climate and the View.[10]

When one first comes to southern Cal
And gloms the cloudless blue,
   One swallows nearly everything
   While listening to the natives sing
The Climate and the View.

And when one's robbed and bilked and bled
And flimflammed through and through,
   The native tries to ease the pain
   By bleating loudly and amain
Of Climate and the View.

The lean and hungry realty man
Adheres to one like glue.
   He has not eaten for a year,
   Yet still one hears him bravely cheer
The Climate and the View.

And when one comes to leave for home,
And bids the south adieu,
   One must admit, would one be fair,
   That Sunny Southern Cal is there
With Climate and with View.*

San Diego, Normal Bean
And nothing else.†

"THE CONTRIBS OF YESTERYEAR"[11]

From out the yellow, musty past
   Of faded files and drear
I wriggle from oblivion
   To answer, "Master, here!"
My old blood starts and almost flows—
   Ah, memory sublime!—
Of long gone day when first I made —
   (Aw, shucks! That doesn't rime.)

Yet once again before I go
   To reap reward condign,
I'm glad that I have heard the call—
   The old call of the Line;
The call that's old, yet ever young,
   Nor time, nor age can stint;
The ancient call for which I fall —
   To see my name in print.
            NORMAL BEAN

The two authors were jungles apart in one area. Burroughs had an obvious relish for publicity—(though not the personal kind; he was not often mentioned in the gossip columns and, according to his daughter Joan, "he appreciated that Hedda‡ never said anything bad about him"[12]). Kipling had an obvious distaste for publicity of any kind and for all attempts to lionize him. He twice refused knighthood (and wouldn't Burroughs have loved this!) and, as well, reportedly turned down the honor of being appointed England's Poet Laureate.

ERB prided himself on the fact that he never had hired a personal publicist or press agent, but he had his own little tricks of obtaining maximum mileage in this regard. Through letters to the editors of various papers he expressed his viewpoint on the popular issues of the day (life on Mars, Darwin and evolution, women in politics, Hawaiian Territorial dispute, etc.). He enjoyed giving newspaper interviews (when they did not concern his private life). Burroughs also employed a rare trick in the books published by his own corporation (as well as in the last few McClurg editions). On the top of every right-page appears the name: *Edgar Rice Burroughs*.

---

*The second ballad, written at age twenty-four, immediately made a name for Kipling. This was "The Ballad of East and West" and contained the memorable line, "Oh, East is East, and West is West, and never the twain shall meet."

†Written after a vacation to San Diego, California (in the winter and spring of 1913–14). ERB signed the poem with his pen name of Normal Bean, only used once before — in the publication of his first story, *Under the Moons of Mars*.

‡The late Hedda Hopper, syndicated columnist and one-time Tarzan film actress (*Tarzan's Revenge*, 1937).

Rudyard Kipling did all he could to discourage a society in England that was formed in 1927 to honor him.* "Even more than the flatterings of the Kipling Society, he disliked the activities of bibliophiles who trafficked in his private letters, draft manuscripts, rejected trifles, and unauthorized editions. All this was what he called the 'Higher Cannibalism.'"[13]

Burroughs, however, heartily enjoyed the activities of his fans such as *The Burroughs Bibliophiles*,† a loosely knit band of his admirers, tightly bound together by a fiercely charged devotion to the Master. ERB encouraged their newsletters and bulletins and found time to write a few words in their "fanzines."‡

---

*Originally formed with 100 members, in 1965 the Kipling Society listed 1,200 members all over the world, according to Carl T. Naumburg of New York, vice president and secretary (U.S. branch).

†Numbering more than 1,200 members as of December, 1965. (The author is card-carrying member No. 1142.)

‡ERB's son, Hulbert, vice president of Burroughs, Inc., is even more actively involved. He keeps members abreast of the latest Burroughsania — in and out of the jungle — and is constantly being quoted in the "fanzines." In *The Gridley Wave* (December 1965), Hulbert: (1) supplied the editors with a list of publishers who produce Gold Keys (comic book) Tarzan in foreign-language editions; (2) revealed the dates of the *Chicago Tribune* issues which carried ERB's early poems (two of which are reproduced in this chapter); (3) was announced as guest of honor of the Burroughs Bibliophiles' Dum-Dum '66 (James and Joan Burroughs Pierce, Tarzan and Jane of the early Tarzan radio series were the honored guests at the 1965 Dum-Dum held in Chicago over Labor Day weekend); (4) took a back page in the publication to advertise: "FOR SALE — WHILE THEY LAST" eleven Tarzan books and two non–Tarzan novels (originally published by ERB, Inc.). The prices, including postage, from six to fifteen dollars. The same announcement also apprised fans that books for sale showing smoke discoloration would have this label affixed to the inside front cover:

"*THIS BOOK* is one of the few survivors of a near-disastrous fire that occurred in our storeroom on Saturday, May 3, 1958. The fire started as a result of the spontaneous combustion of old Tarzan motion pictures printed on nitrate film.

"Although this book shows some fire damage, we are told it has considerable value among collectors. We sincerely hope it will add to the worth of your own personal collection."

VIII

Those Crazy Moving Pictures 1913–1918

...It's Hollywood — we all try to be something we're not, and most of us succeed only in being something we ought not to be.
  Tarzan and the Lion Man, *1933*

1. "California, Here I Come"

In the winter of 1913, Edgar Rice Burroughs — the successful magazine writer — was able to take his first vacation since his "do or die" period, which started in Chicago eight years before. This would make up for the bad news earlier in the year: the income tax, declared unconstitutional by the Supreme Court in 1894, had been ratified by two-thirds of the states and was now a law of the land — much to the displeasure of Ed and of 90 million other Americans. And if this was not enough, Teddy Roosevelt and Taft split the GOP right down the middle and allowed Woodrow Wilson to become president, the first Democrat to hold that office since Grover Cleveland.

This was Ed and Emma's first trip to California and the climate of San Diego was just the right medicine to soothe his neuritis. He was hard at work on his third

Tarzan story (*The Beasts of Tarzan*), but had not yet had his first book published.

It was while at San Diego that Tarzan for the movies was first suggested to ERB in form of an inquiry from a New York music publisher and play broker:

Joseph W. Stern & Co.
(Edna Williams) to ERB
March 23, 1914

Your address* has been handed to me by Mr. Albert [Payson] Terhune of the *New York World*, and I write to ascertain whether you have placed the producing or moving picture rights of *Tarzan of the Apes*.

I read your story† with very much interest and it occurred to me that it would be an excellent vehicle for moving pictures, and as I am in very close touch with the prominent manufacturers, I believe I could place same to your advantage.

My firm, the above, are not only music publishers, but play brokers as well, and if you have done nothing with Tarzan, we would be pleased to hear from you, also in regard to any other works which you think might have a dramatic value.

Evidently nothing resulted from this proposal and the Burroughs' returned to Chicago and moved to the suburbs of Oak Park, 6415 Augusta Street. On April 30, Ed signed the contract with McClurg for book publication of *Tarzan of the Apes*. He had mailed his completed manuscript of *The Beasts of Tarzan* from San Diego and this appeared in five parts in Munsey's *All Story–Cavalier Weekly*, the first of which was published on May 16.

Meanwhile, Ed had selected the Authors Photo-Play Agency in New York to promote the motion picture sale of *Tarzan of the Apes* and received the following letter in answer to his inquiry.

Cora C. Wilkening to ERB
September 22, 1914

Your letter of September 19th, in regard to "TARZAN OF THE APES," received, and in reply I wish to tell you that I am making every effort to dispose of the photo-play rights of your book on the following basis: $500 cash advance on 5% royalty. At the present time the work is being favorably considered by three Companies, and if necessary, I will try to hasten their decisions within the next few days.

Your story has aroused a great deal of interest among the Film Companies, and one scenario-editor, to whom I sell a great deal of material, is urging his Company to purchase the work.

On December 4, Ed signed his second book contract with McClurg (*Return of Tarzan*‡), and it clearly showed his recognition of the new movie industry as a possible source of additional revenue. There were several important changes in this contract as opposed to his first signed eight months earlier. For one, he received an advance of 500 dollars against the original 250 dollars. He had replaced William Chapman as his agent with Elsie Schroeder of New York, and all monies were to come to him directly (after which he would pay the agent his commission). In the event of publication of a cheap edition of his book (commonly known as a "popular reprint"), Burroughs was to receive five cents per copy. Most important was this clause — typed into the contract: "It is ex-

---

*4036 Third Street, San Diego.
†It was not yet published in novel form; she could have read the story either in *All-Story* magazine or in the *New York Evening World*, where it was serialized in 46 daily installments beginning January 6, 1913. Despite this interest, however, when ERB signed the contract for book publication only one month later (April 30), no mention was made of the author retaining "moving picture" rights.
‡Published by A. C. McClurg March 10, 1915. The original magazine story, which appeared in seven parts in Street & Smith's *New Story*, was illustrated by the famous American artist and illustrator, Newell Convers Wyeth.

pressly understood and agreed that all dramatic and moving picture rights are owned by said author."

Impatient to make his first moving picture sale — and having received no favorable report from Cora Wilkening — Ed mailed a copy of *Tarzan of the Apes* together with an unpublished manuscript to Colonel William N. Selig,* president of the Selig Polyscope Company of Chicago (with studios in Chicago, Los Angeles and Prescott, Arizona), "Producers and Manufacturers of High Class Motion Pictures."

The unpublished work was entitled *The Lad and the Lion*,† and it related the story of what happens to a prince of a lad when he is forced into exile — with a lion as companion. What happens, of course, is that the lad and the lion end up on the coast of Africa (where else?) and there is a beautiful Arabian princess and ... but read it for yourself, as Colonel Selig was planning to do, as he said:

W. N. Selig to ERB

Dec. 4, 1914

Want to thank you kindly for the copy of "Tarzan of the Apes." I shall read this book and will let you know what I think of its moving picture possibilities. Also "The Lad and the Lion." Shall read the latter first so that I can return to you your manuscript, as it is the only copy you have.

It would perhaps be just as convenient for you to see me Tuesday evening, when we could have lunch together at the Athletic Club, as I have an engagement with my dentist generally around the noon hours, so that it would be rather hard to make such an engagement unless we made it at a later time. Kindly phone me regarding this matter.

In mid–January Selig made a firm offer for *The Lad the the Lion*. Unsure if it was a good deal or not, Ed dispatched a night letter to his agent and on the following day received this telegram in reply.

C. C. Wilkening to ERB

Jan 29, 1915

CONSIDER PROSPECT OF FUTURE WORK FOR SELIG SUFFICIENTLY IMPORTANT TO ACCEPT ONE HUNDRED DOLLARS A REEL FOR THE LAD AND THE LION IF THIS IS HIS OFFER.

Ed accepted Selig's figure and received an advance payment of five hundred dollars, covering five reels. The contract called for him to receive an additional hundred dollars per reel for all over five. ERB enclosed a fifty-dollar check to his agent — her commission was the usual 10 per cent — and advised her that Selig would not decide about Tarzan until he could see the jungle pictures to be made by a man whom the Colonel was sending to Africa.

Burroughs tried selling another story to Selig — *The Cave Girl*.‡

W. N. Selig to ERB

April 20, 1915

I have read your story "The Cave Girl" with a great deal of interest. However, it does not appeal to me as exceptionally well adapted for photoplay purposes — it does not contain sufficient dramatic action. I am returning the story under separate cover.

As 1915 began, business in the United States was never better, with goods and

---

*Selig, along with Thomas Edison, was one of the true pioneers of the motion picture industry. In 1910, his film, *Roosevelt in Africa*, created a furor when it was discovered that the "leading man" was not the popular ex–President at all, but an actor who bore a resemblance to Teddy. Roosevelt's African hunting expedition was shot in the Chicago studio of producer Selig.

†First published in *All-Story Weekly* in three parts, beginning June 30, 1917. (The original magazine version was written in 1914. For the book version in 1938, ERB added European "intrigue" to the original story through the insertion of alternate chapters.)

‡First published in *The All-Story* magazine in three parts, the first of which appeared July 1913.

weapons of all kinds being rushed to the European belligerents, chiefly for the allied nations.* Business also was bullish for Ed Burroughs who, equally, was hell-bent for fortune. In 1914 and 1915, eleven† of his stories were published in magazines and newspapers as serials or novelettes (subsequently as novels). But the author's eyes were focused on those moving pictures (which had come into their own as an art form with the sensational success of D. W. Griffith's *The Birth of a Nation* in March of 1915).

ERB next submitted a wild-animal comedy, *The Lion Hunter*,‡ to Selig. But when he was offered only sixty dollars, the author went to Hollywood with the submission (plus a second manuscript) instead of signing the enclosed contract. The reply from the Pacific Studio of Universal Films was months in coming; meanwhile, Ed and his family had moved into the former country home of his parents, 414 Augusta Street, Oak Park.

Universal Films to ERB

October 15, 1915

We are returning you herewith the two stories submitted by you some time ago entitled The Lion Hunter and The Mad King.§

We have submitted these to several of our directors but they are not suitable to any of their requirements.

Regretting that we cannot use these and hoping to receive more of your material....

Ed turned back to Selig after *The Lion Hunter* was rejected by Universal, saying that sixty dollars was not enough money, that his name was known to a great number of readers by this time. But Selig repeated that he could go no higher and the script was returned to Burroughs at the author's request. Concerning a possible film version of *Tarzan of the Apes*, Selig either said no or else delayed so long in making a decision that Ed turned elsewhere with this property: to the American Film Company, with headquarters in Chicago.

The American Film Company never became a major film studio, and if there is anyone still around with some of its worthless securities hidden far down in an attic trunk — read the following and weep.

American Film Company to ERB

April 22nd, 1916

We acknowledge receipt of yours of the 12th, enclosing review on "TARZAN OF THE APES" and in reply, state that we are obliged to conclude that we are not interested in this production for moving pictures. It no doubt has many gripping incidents for fiction, but *these will not be practicable for picture purposes.*‖

On June 6, Burroughs signed a contract with a Chicago life insurance man, William Parsons, granting him the movie rights to the first book, *Tarzan of the Apes*. Parsons had never produced a movie or seen one made, but Burroughs was satisfied with the deal. One week later, ERB and company set off for a camping trip to Maine. Ninety-nine days and 3,527 miles later, what was left of the rolling stock (and the rolling passengers) arrived in — of all places — Los Angeles!

---

*We were still exporting to Germany and Austria-Hungary through 1916, although it was a trickle compared to what it had been prior to the war.

†*The Outlaw of Torn, The Eternal Lover, The Mad King, At the Earth's Core, The Beasts of Tarzan, The Mucker, Sweetheart Primeval, Pellucidar, Barney Custer of Beatrice, The Man-Eater* and *The Son of Tarzan*. (*The Man-Eater* never appeared in magazine form, but was published in the *New York Evening World*, November 15–20, 1915).

‡No story with this title ever appeared under ERB's name in magazine, newspaper or book form. Ed's submission to Selig was a 1,500-word story outline.

§*The Mad King* appeared in *All-Story Weekly* complete, March 21, 1914.

‖ Italics added.

The Burroughs-Parsons deal[1] for the latter to make a movie of *Tarzan of the Apes* probably was the most unbelievably confused episode of its kind — in that day or in any day. It went something like this: Parsons asked for 60 but was given 120 days to raise $5,000 for payment to Burroughs as an advance against royalties. Burroughs also was to receive $50,000 (for his help and good will) in capital stock of the new film corporation and become one of its directors. He also was to receive 5 per cent of the gross receipts over the cost of production. Parsons was to complete the film within 16 months and market same within 28 months.

Ed and his family, in the formidable Twin-Six, ended their cross-country trip in Los Angeles on September 23. They checked in at the Hollenbeck Hotel, but although the stipulated 120 days almost was up there was no word from Parsons. Ed dispatched a reminder to Parsons that he would consider the contract cancelled if $5,000 was not forthcoming by October 6. He also chided Parsons for not having sold the stock (in the film corporation) after Burroughs had voluntarily doubled the option period from 60 to 120 days.

On the 30th, Ed sent a wire to Parsons saying that if the latter wanted to extend his option for 30 or 60 days, such an offer would be entertained, but — *only* after a substantial amount of cash were paid to him. Ed then asked an old friend, Robert D. Lay, a Chicago insurance man, to represent his interests with Parsons.

Parsons, unable to sell stock in New York or Chicago, hied himself off to Wyoming and Montana, hoping that he would have an easier time of it with cattlemen and ranchers. He did have better luck and was able to send ERB two checks for $500 each, but with each check he asked for an extension in time — first, 60 days and then 30 days.

On October 18, Ed again reminded the self-styled producer that the latter had not kept his part of the agreement — that $50,000 in capital stock of the company should have been made out to him and had not, that the money that was rightfully due him, under terms of the contract (Ed had now received a total of $2,000), had been used by Parsons to purchase an extension. Ed also said he was not interested in becoming president of the company, the title having been tendered to him.

(Ed mentioned to Parsons that he and Emma had seen D. W. Griffith's *Intolerance* at Clune's Auditorium and while he thought it was a magnificent spectacle, neither he nor his wife had found it as full of thrills and heart throbs as *The Birth of a Nation*. They also announced their move from the Hollenbeck to 355 South Hoover Street.)

Through Lay's intervention, Ed received an additional $1,000 around the 20th of October, and he wrote his Chicago friend a lengthy letter ... the trip out West had cost him about three times more than he had estimated ... Los Angeles was doing nothing to ease the pain of his neuritis ... he thought the world of his Twin-Six; it was far superior to Fords, Pierce-Arrows, Saxons and Locomobiles ... if Lay thought it was to his advantage to accept the presidency of the company he would take it (but with reservations — he did not want to be associated with another failure) ... it was not cheap to rent a typewriter these days — five dollars for three months....

On October 28, Ed received 10,000 shares of stock in the company and, subsequently, the balance of the $5,000 due him. He also assumed the title of director general.

Away from his home state, Ed was unable to cast his vote in the November election but if he had, his vote certainly would have gone to the GOP candidate, Supreme Court Justice Charles Evans Hughes (who went to bed on the night of

November 7th, certain that he would awaken as the twenty-ninth President of the United States).*

On New Year's Eve, 1917, Ed might have counted his efforts of the past year, which were not inconsiderable: nine magazine serials and novelettes and one novel *published*,† four additional stories‡ completed for publication in the first few months of 1917, and the news from Colonel Selig that *The Lad and the Lion* would be ready for release shortly.

What of *adventure*? It was available to those who were after it. General Pershing had led an American expedition into Mexico earlier in the year in an attempt to capture the revolutionary bandit, Pancho Villa, after the latter had crossed the border to raid towns in New Mexico. And while we were busy defending our interests south of the border, there was that other conflict, "over there," which few Americans felt was our concern. As for Ed Burroughs, he was on his way to becoming a "success," and whatever quest he once might have had for adventure he now relegated to the ape-man and his friends.

Burroughs' fans have been prone to make much of their hero's lust for adventure—confusing the creator with his creation. ERB's "adventures" during the fifteen-year period (1897–1912) might more rightfully be termed "misadventures," the result of one failure after another. When his application in 1898 for a commission with Teddy's Rough Riders was turned down, could Ed have joined the forces as an enlisted man — or, perhaps, a non-commissioned officer? And what about service during the First World War? Joan Burroughs recalled:

> Dad always regretted not having been active in the First World War. He was forty-one and responsible for a family of four but he still wanted to go. Mother told him he had to take care of us and she won out.[2]

Under the Selective Service Act, which became effective May 18, 1917, initial registration was for men between the ages of 21 and 40. On the 28th, Ed received an appointment as Captain of the 1st Battalion, 2nd Infantry, Illinois Reserve Militia. The official order was not mailed to ERB until January 1, 1918, and he took the oath of allegiance on May 3. The militia was not a federally recognized unit. It had no active Federal service and was organized primarily for local protection against any pro–German elements.

ERB cut short his vacation in Los Angeles after it became apparent in February that, with Germany's declaration of "unrestricted submarine warfare," followed by the hasty withdrawal of Pershing's (unsuccessful) expedition into Mexico, the United States soon would be involved in the World War. The family returned to Oak Park, 700 Linden Avenue. On April 2, Congress was asked by President Wilson to declare that a state of war existed between the United States and Germany. In his message to Congress April 2, 1917, Wilson declared, "It is a fearful thing to lead this great, peaceful people into war, into the most terrible and disastrous of all wars, civilization itself seeming to be in the balance. But the right is more precious than

---

*The election was so close that the result was not known until one week after the polls had been closed. Then it was determined that California had gone to incumbent President Woodrow Wilson by 3,773 votes (electoral vote was Wilson, 277; Hughes, 254).

†*Beyond Thirty, Thuvia, Maid of Mars, The Return of the Mucker, The New Stories of Tarzan, The Girl from Farris's, The Capture of Tarzan, The Fight for the Balu, Tarzan and the Jewels of Opar, The God of Tarzan*. The novel was *The Beasts of Tarzan*.

‡*Tarzan and the Black Boy, The Witch-Doctor Seeks Vengeance, The End of Bukawai, The Lion*.

peace, and we shall fight for the things which we have always carried nearest our hearts...."

The following day, after twelve unsuccessful attempts to interest British publishers in what was near to the hearts of Ed and his publishers, A. C. McClurg, a contract was signed with Methuen and Company Ltd. of 36 Essex Street, Strand, London, to reprint three works: *Tarzan of the Apes, The Return of Tarzan* and *The Beasts of Tarzan*.*

On April 12, Burroughs signed a contract with McClurg for something even nearer and dearer to his heart — book publication of his very first story, *Under the Moons of Mars*.† Terms called for him to receive an advance payment of one thousand dollars against royalties of 12½ per cent of the first five thousand copies sold, and 15 per cent thereafter. (Selling price was $1.35.)

The Selig production of *The Lad and the Lion*, in five reels and starring Vivian Reed (neither the Lad nor the Lion) was released on May 14.

> Director Al. Green has succeeded in visualizing Edgar Rice Burroughs' adventure story with fine realism. The story calls for marine views that include shipwreck, fire aboard another vessel at sea, its abandonment by the crew and the escape of the sole survivor and a captive lion from the wreck; an Arab village and the desert surrounding it; wild picturesque scenes along the shore nearby, and desert brigands dashing across the sands on their Ishmaelite adventures. All these invest the pictured story with an atmosphere that succeeds in carrying the spectator away beyond his or her accustomed ken, forming perfect surroundings for the action of the photoplay....
>
> Vivian Reed looks charming in the dress of Nakhla (beautiful daughter of an Arab sheik), and bears the role with becoming grace and pride. Will Machin's "Lad" is always equal to the occasion. In his association with the big lion he will cause many to wonder; for this animal is really a fierce brute that resents intimacy from all but his trainer. Charles Le Moyne's Ben Saada is arrogant and cruel, as he should be, and Al. W. Filson's Sheik, Ali-Es Hadji, is dignified and decorous.[8]

2. THE INDUSTRY

With *The Lad and the Lion* behind him and a production date set for *Tarzan of the Apes*, one might expect that Ed Burroughs would be delighted to find himself in the midst of an exciting new motion picture industry. But, no. The fight with Parsons over monies rightfully due the author now enlarged into story say-so, production know-how and a struggle over control of the film. Burroughs already had complained that *The Lad and the Lion* was *not* his story by time it reached the screen. And now — in the early scripting and blocking out of scenes for *Tarzan of the Apes*— Ed, who had been promised a voice in the production by Parsons, got nowhere when he asked that the scenario be submitted to him.

Ed also sincerely believed (or, at least had convinced himself) that his background included a successful record as a business executive and this was more than Parsons could claim. But the author's principal concern for wanting a voice in the production was not difficult to understand: a poor film could have an adverse effect on the sale of his books. And was this really the time for a Tarzan feature? The

---

*The first of the three titles was published in England on September 13, 1917. (In the same year Methuen, which had printed much of Kipling throughout the early 1900s, published his poems, *The Five Nations*.)

†Published as *A Princess of Mars*, October 10, 1917.

first war films were being released and both the public and press were heatedly lining up into pacifist or preparedness camps, while our government made it known to moviemakers that "selling the war" was the patriotic thing to do.

Ed was in no position to halt Parsons from proceeding in any way the self-styled producer wanted to go, although he could console himself by promising he would have no more dealings with producers. (But he *would* sell motion picture rights to any of his stories in return for a substantial cash payment and a proper contract.)

ERB never appreciated the literary agent, per se, and after 1916 had no one representing him. While *Tarzan of the Apes* was in production, E. V. Durling,* Pacific Coast representative of *The Morning Telegraph* (Los Angeles), proposed that he act as the author's agent in the sale of his stories to film. Ed's requirements and conditions, however, precluded any possible arrangement. Ed Burroughs would not crawl. Ed Burroughs would not humble himself. Not any more. He had already gone that route. Four *long* years ago. Job-to-job, door-to-door; *selling*. What could be lower? No, he would not ask anyone to purchase one of his stories; he would not voluntarily submit a story to a producer; he would not even furnish a copy of one of his stories. And if all this were not enough to discourage a prospective agent, Ed insisted he would never pay anyone a commission for selling motion picture rights to one of his stories.

3. A Jungle Production

To stir up interest in the forthcoming Tarzan film, a number of form letters went out under Burroughs' name to a special mailing list.

ERB to "Friends"

Feb. 21, 1917

Tarzan of the Apes is about to be produced on a large scale for the screen by The National Film Corporation of America, and a question has arisen relative to this production which can best be answered by the readers of the Tarzan stories.

As you have expressed an interest in my work I am taking the liberty of asking your advice in the matter, since the producers are as anxious as am I to release a film which will meet with the entire approval of the majority of Tarzan's friends.

The screen has, of course, certain limitations which the novel has not, and so a few slight changes and contractions are absolutely imperative; but the important questions are these: Shall we adhere to the rather unpopular ending of the first Tarzan story in which Tarzan renounces his birthright and the woman he loves, or shall we take something from the second story and have a happy ending?

And shall we confine the entire production to the jungle, which is the natural setting for Tarzan's life and romance?

Or, shall we follow the story verbatim?

The National Film Corporation of America contemplates a jungle production such as has never before been attempted and which I sincerely believe will stand for years to come as *the* wild animal classic of motion photography. Mr. Parsons tells me that he had arranged for the largest and finest specimens of apes to be found; that he will show, not two or three lions; but a herd of twenty or thirty; that lions will be actually roped and killed by Tarzan; that two or three thousand cannibals will take part in the battle and village scenes under Mbonga the chief; that hyenas, wild boar, leopards, antelope and all the other numerous fauna of Central Africa will appear in various scenes, and that nothing will be omitted which may in any way add to the truth and realism of the picture.

Under the circumstances you can understand why it is that we all wish to profit by

---

*Subsequently, a popular syndicated columnist with the Hearst newspapers.

the advice of every friend of Tarzan, and I sincerely hope that you will write and give me the benefit of your interest in and knowledge of Tarzan of the Apes.

The locale for filming of *Tarzan of the Apes* was Louisiana. Stock shots and background were filmed in Brazil. Tarzan as a boy was to be played by ten-year-old Gordon Griffith; Tarzan as a man, by an actor from New York, Winslow Wilson. But even before the actual filming got under way, Parsons ran out of money and had to scamper back to his "stock field" in Montana and Wyoming for additional capital.

Griffith later recalled:

> Winslow went with us to Louisiana, but a few days later he enlisted in the army and left us stranded. The director sent out a call for help, and we got Elmo Lincoln,* the strong man, to play the part. He was so hairy that they had to shave him twice a day so that the audience could tell him from the apes. In those days we didn't use animals. Instead, we hired a bunch of husky young fellows from the New Orleans Athletic Club who put on ape skins and swung through the trees. I was supposed to be nursed and cared for by an ape named Kala. The director was afraid to risk me with a real chimp, and we got a fellow to put on an ape suit and play my foster mother.[4]

Fred Miller, who later became a prominent theatre owner in Los Angeles, was called in to adapt the book. Miller recalled:

> I was called in to adapt the book and worked with Edgar Rice Burroughs as well as Parsons. By this time Parsons was surrounded by self-appointed advisers. The adaptation was changed, for I had departed to another studio. More advisers and more changes. A director was engaged. More changes in the story.
>
> The shooting began. More changes in the scenario. Until they shot without it, devising "things" as they went along.
>
> When the picture was finished it was poor in every way.† To make matters worse, it was cut in the worse way. The titles were worst of all, if that were possible.
>
> That was the "Tarzan" picture that made Bill Parsons wealthy.[5]

Parsons scheduled the film for January release, and hired the well-known press agent, Harry Reichenbach, as publicity manager. Shortly before opening day, Reichenbach dressed up an ape in a tuxedo and top hat and attempted to register the "guest" at the fashionable Knickerbocker Hotel in New York. He chose a Saturday night for the stunt, when the lobby was crowded with society folk and legitimate guests. The ape landed in police court, but it made the front pages.

Reichenbach to ERB

January 16, 1918

> "TARZAN OF THE APES" in picture form, based on your story, opens at the Broadway Theatre Sunday Evening, January 27.
>
> I would be gratified to have you present for the opening and will hold a box pending advice from you whether you will honor us with your presence that evening.
>
> Rex Beach, Irving Cobb, Woodhaven and all of the other boys in the Dutch Treat Club will be there and I will look forward to your being there.
>
> I have not seen the picture yet but am handling the exploitation of it and I am quite sure your presence will add to the dignity of the occasion.
>
> I have been talking to Mr. Parsons and everybody seems to report very enthusiasti-

---

*Contrary to much that has been written about Elmo Lincoln (real name: Otto Linkenhelt) he was no novice, and the role of Tarzan was not his first part. He had appeared the year before in D. W. Griffith's magnificent flop, *Intolerance*, playing The Mighty Man of Valor in the Babylonian story. He had also played The Blacksmith in *The Kaiser*.

†Not according to the critics.

cally on the picture and the fact that Mr. Parsons has given me "cart blank" in the matter of publicity, can make you rest assured that the story will suffer none at the hands of this Company.

Kindly let me hear from you and also advise me if there is anybody in New York you would like me to forward invitations to, to the opening.

An ad in *The New York Times* of Sunday, the 27th, announced:

THE MOST STUPENDOUS, AMAZING, STARTLING FILM PRODUCTION IN THE WORLD'S HISTORY ... PRODUCED IN THE WILDEST JUNGLES OF BRAZIL AT A COST OF $300,000 ... STAGED WITH WILD LIONS, TIGERS, ELEPHANTS, BABOONS, APES, CANNIBALS ... FROM THE ORIGINAL STORY BY EGAR [sic] RICE BURROUGHS....

The competition in New York was Mabel Normand in Goldwyn's *Dodging a Million*, at the Strand; Charles Ray in *The Hired Man*, at the Rivoli; Dorothy Dalton in *Flare-Up Sal*, at the Rialto. At the Plaza, three top films were showing for that week: Billy Burke in *Arms and the Girl*, Mary Garden in *Thaïs*, and Mae Marsh in *The Cinderella Man*. Also playing was Rita Jolivet, a survivor of the *Lusitania*, in *Lest We Forget*, immortalizing the sinking of the Cunard liner on May 7, 1915. There were other events in town: at Carnegie Hall, Burton Holmes was lecturing on "Japan, 1917"; at Aeolian Hall, John Masefield was making his first public appearance in New York, in a lecture on his war experience; and at the end of the week Jascha Heifetz was scheduled to play at the Waldorf-Astoria in a morning concert.

The film was fairly true to the first book. Lord and Lady Greystoke are marooned on the African coast by a mutinous crew. She dies shortly after giving birth to a child and a tribe of apes kill Lord Greystoke, with Kala, the she-ape, rescuing the baby and bringing him up as her own. Tarzan grows up in the jungle, educating himself through the books left by his father. Then it differs. Instead of Tarzan learning French as his first language (from Lieutenant Paul d'Arnot), he learns English from a sailor who had befriended his parents. The sailor, captured by slave traders, escapes and finds his way back to where the English couple had been put ashore. He realizes the young boy is the Greystoke heir and sailor Binns makes his way to England to inform Greystoke's lawyers of Tarzan's existence. An expedition is formed to go to Africa. Included are the Greystoke nephew (heir to the family fortune) and his fiancée, Jane Porter. Tarzan meets Jane, falls in love with her and she with him. Tarzan fights with lions and natives and then he and Jane return to England.

TARZAN OF THE APES
Released through First National Exhibitors' Circuit

The players:

Tarzan, the boy . . . . Gordon Griffith
His Father . . . . True Boardman
His Mother . . . . Kathleen Kirkham
Jane Porter . . . . Enid Markey
Professor Porter . . . . . . Thomas Jefferson
The barmaid . . . . Bessie Toner
Binns . . . . George French
Captain of Fuwalda . . . Jack Wilson
Greystoke's nephew . . . Colin Kenny
Tarzan, the man . . . . . . Elmo Lincoln
Directed by: Scott Sidney in 8 reels

The New York Times

"Tarzan of the Apes," which excited considerable interest among the readers of popular-priced fiction several years ago, was shown at the Broadway Theatre last night in film form. Being the story of a primeval man — or, rather, of a man brought up among apes and endowed with many of their abilities — it presents now a few difficulties to the movie maker. All of these have been overcome in the film at the Broadway, and apes swing realistically from bough to bough in the jungle the while lions and leopards seek their prey on the ground below. Intertwined with the jungle story is a domestic narrative which grows tedious at times, and the expedient of the cut-back is resorted to a trifle too freely. All of this is more than compensated for, however, by the stirring scenes of the jungle. A majority of these were photographed in Brazil, and several hundred natives appear before the camera. The picture as a whole, in addition to being interesting, also has a touch of educational value. An actor named Elmo Lincoln meets the difficult requirements of the hero satisfactorily.[6]

Chicago Journal

There have been all kinds of moving pictures, from "Nellie the Beautiful Knitter" to the most educational of travelogues. We've become so blasé that to see someone jump from a flying express to the top of a telegraph pole finds most of the audience wearily searching their programmes to learn what the "show" will be tomorrow. It's that everlasting desire for something new.

Well, folks, there's a brand new picture in town. And it's different from anything that's gone before. It's "Tarzan of the Apes," and is shown at the Colonial (May 14). Do you remember how you sat up most of the night to finish your first real adventure story? Well, it's better than that! And do you remember your first lover story? Well's it's better than that! And all the wondering that's been done as to how they get animals to act in the movies—wait until you see the apes and lions and elephants "acting" in Tarzan....

Darwin's theory isn't particularly complimentary. Let's hope there was not one "missing link" but quite a chain of 'em. But anyway be sure to see "Tarzan."[7]

Columnist Kitty Kelly

That good novelty was worth while Edgar Rice Burroughs demonstrated with financial convincingness in his Tarzan books, and has redemonstrated in this initial picture made from the first one. In itself, the speculation on the development of a well-born child left to animals for training is a mental fascination, and clothed so richly in jungle settings, as here, consideration is much enhanced.... It is beautifully staged in a jungle tangle of vegetation ... tinted to restful softness. Wild beasts lurk and prowl realistically, and savages peer through the twisted growths and creep about fearsomely.... It's an open-air, primitive affair, which won't appeal to tea party people, but for those who like queer things and "Tarzan of the Apes," it's a picture to be sought.[8]

Motion Picture Magazine

A thrilling, spectacular drama that contains a little of everything, including wild animals, African jungles, English lords and ladies, ships, yachts, dance-halls, fights, villains, heroes, high-brows and low-brows.

A very pretty story connects them all nicely, and we are conducted from one period to another and from England to South Africa as if years were but minutes and leagues were but inches. The photography is superb, and the acting, for the most part, fine. The story is so absorbing and so well handled that one wants to sit right thru to the end of the seventh reel and see the young ape-man win Enid Markey, the heroine, and have them return to England to wrest their landed estates from the usurpers. But it doesn't take us that far. With a murmured "I love you, Tarzan," and the usual embrace, "Finis" is flashed and we are to imagine the rest, which is perhaps just as well.[9]

The film was a decided success and triumph and, as Fred Miller said, "it made Bill Parsons a wealthy man." *Tarzan of the Apes* grossed more than a million dollars—one of the first half-dozen films to pass this magic mark. But all was not yet milk and honey between Parsons and Burroughs, and if Ed had guessed what the insurance man turned producer was up to, he would have strongly rephrased what he had written to E. V. Durling, five months before: "of all [the business people] the motion picture producer is the only man I care to have no further dealings with."

4. BACK AT THE RANCH

Meanwhile, back in Oak Park, the typewriter never stopped pounding and ERB completed his twelve-chapter magazine serial for *Blue Book Magazine*, which ran under the title of *The New Stories of Tarzan*. The stories ran every month from

September 1916 through August 1917. They were subsequently published in book form (1919) under the title of *Jungle Tales of Tarzan*.

"Were I literary," Burroughs said, in a 1918 interview, "and afflicted with temperament I should have a devil of a time writing stories, for now comes Joan with Helen in one hand and Helen's severed arm in another, strewing a thin line of sawdust across my study floor. I may be in the midst of a thrilling passage — Tarzan may be pulling a tiger out of Africa by the tail*— but when Joan comes even Tarzan pauses, and he stays paused until I have tied Helen's arm to her torso once again for the hundredth time.

"Then may come Hulbert with an orange to be 'turned inside out,' or with a steam calliope announcement that he has discovered a 'father long legs,' and about the time he has been shunted outdoors with his velocipede Jack tumbles out of his go-cart with a vocal accompaniment that would drive the possessor of a temperament to the mad house."[10]

The younger son, Jack, fairly lived the part of Tarzan, it was reported in an interview with ERB.

> None are more delighted readers of their father's books than are the children of the author.... It was with difficulty that [Jack's] father and mother could persuade him to eat cooked meat. He wanted to eat it raw, for did not Tarzan prefer it so? One day the astonished father saw his son following him across the yard on all fours with his nose to the ground. "What in the world are you doing, Jack?" Mr. Burroughs questioned. "Why, father," replied the boy, "I am following your scent spoor...."[11]

Joan Burroughs recalled:

> Even when Dad was busy writing we used to bounce on and off his knee, at times, and he was always in good humor. Later, we used to vie with each other to see who would be first downstairs in the morning to read his writings of the day or night before. He told us bedtime tales every night, without fail. They were continued in serial form, and he always started off exactly where he had left off the night before. Two of our favorites were "Arabella, the Coyote" and "Grandpa Gazink and His Flying Machine."[12]

Burroughs had a devotion to motoring and a love for automobiles, and this was as evident in 1918 as it was throughout his later years.

> Rain or shine, summer or winter, you may see him every afternoon with his family upon the Chicago boulevards or far out on some delightful country road beyond the city's limits. He loves the country, too, and the great outdoors, and every sport and game that needs the open for its playing. Yet in few such sports does he excel. In football and horsemanship he climbed close to the top, and if he should confide in you I think that you would soon discover that his greatest pride lies in his ability to ride anything that wears hair.
>
> All in all there is nothing very remarkable about Edgar Rice Burroughs except his imagination. He is a sane, healthy American gentleman, very much in love with his wife and children and inordinately proud of them. Of himself or his work he is never very serious....[13]

But if there was one thing about which Ed Burroughs was damned serious, it was m-o-n-e-y. Particularly if he were caught on the short end of the stick. It was not a fair battle as Ed faced the heavy artillery of Parsons; Ed was inexperienced and not yet committed to combat. When the earth ceased trembling from the barrage, Ed did not know what struck him.

---

*Obviously said with tongue in cheek, after criticism of his first Tarzan story had led the author to change Sabor, the tiger, into Sabor, the lioness.

The ink was still drying on the reviews of the first Tarzan film when the author discovered that Parsons was making a *second* motion picture. Parsons claimed his new film was really the second half of the book, *Tarzan of the Apes*, and it was in the contract, Parsons said, that the National Film Company of America had purchased the rights to produce *Tarzan of the Apes*. So if, as producer, he saw fit to double the book into two parts...

Ed immediately began legal action, also charging that as late as November 1918 he still had not received one cent in royalties from the first film although the picture supposedly was doing very well. But there was nothing he could do to prevent Parsons from making the second film. *Romance of Tarzan* was released just prior to the end of 1918.

"Based on the concluding chapters of *Tarzan of the Apes* by Edgar Rice Burroughs" (read the notices), the story began where the first film had ended. Just before they all sailed for England, the party is set upon by natives and Tarzan is believed to have been killed. (This according to the Greystoke nephew, who was after the inheritance even more than he was after Jane.) Tarzan is very much alive, however, and he manages to get to San Francisco (in the book, Jane is from Baltimore). Tarzan meets up with another girl, Jane suspects he is in love with her, Tarzan can't get used to the ways of civilization and he returns to his jungle. Jane, realizing the error of her ways, sets out after him. *Finis.*

Motion Picture Magazine

The sequel to "Tarzan of the Apes" has also Elmo Lincoln and Enid Markey as the girl. Lincoln's chief action, when he reaches civilization from the jungle, seems to be to tear off first one coat and then another. As a matter of fact, he looks so uncomfortable in them we are glad when he goes back to the jungle and can remain coatless. This is not especially well done, but there is an adventurous spirit about it which is at least entertaining.[14]

Romance of Tarzan was directed by Wilfred Lucas, with scenario by Bess Meredyth. The "other woman" was played by Cleo Madison.

One month after the Armistice was signed, President Wilson made a move for peace by journeying to Paris to meet with delegates from other nations. Ed, too, made a move (for gain) and it was "California, here we come!"

Nineteen-eighteen hadn't been a bad year for the author. In magazines, he had published *The Oakdale Affair*, *The Land That Time Forgot*, *The People That Time Forgot*, *Out of Time's Abyss*, and *H.R.H. The Rider*. In book form, *Tarzan and the Jewels of Opar* and *The Gods of Mars*. (His royalty was a straight 15 per cent on the Tarzan book.) On October 26, McClurg and Methuen entered into a contract for a British edition of *A Princess of Mars*. And—there were those moving pictures. Ed Burroughs would not be taken for a chump the second time around! Before leaving Chicago (Oak Park), Ed turned in to *Red Book* magazine the first parts of a six-chapter serial, with the background of World War I. Six years later, this story in book form succeeded in doing the impossible—killing off the ape-man's popularity in Germany ever afterwards.

IX

On to the City of Gold 1918

> ...It is good to be alive. It is good to live in the cool shadows. It is good to look upon the green trees and the bright colors of the flowers — upon everything which God has put here for us. He is very good to us.... He provides for each the food that each likes best. All that HE asks is that we be strong enough or cunning enough to go forth and take it. Yes, Tantor,* it is good to live. I should hate to die.
>
> Jungle Tales of Tarzan, 1916

1. THE LORD

Captain Edgar Rice Burroughs† of the Illinois Reserve Militia (writing "from an intimate knowledge of conditions affecting the Reserve Militia and the Volunteer Training Corps gained by actual experience") proposed a national reserve army to the editor of the *Army and Navy Journal*.‡[1] Then, on the evening of Janu-

---

*Elephant.
†Promoted to major on September 14, 1918.
‡See Appendix D for Burroughs' proposal of a national reserve army.

ary 28, 1919, Ed stopped packing long enough to attend a dinner in his honor at the Hotel LaSalle in Chicago.

It was given by the authors and artists who composed the White Paper Club, where word got out that "Ed Burroughs had discovered a new branch of gold mine on the Pacific Coast, from which one may get rich without doing any digging."*² But Joseph Bray, publishing head of McClurg & Co., thought that "besides gold mining and a few sidelines, including a small ostrich farm, Ed would continue his novel writing."

The population of Los Angeles was approaching the million mark when the Burroughs' arrived in February. They occupied a house at 1729 North Wilton Place while looking for a place to buy — perhaps something suitable for a lord ... even for a Lord Greystoke!

While keeping an eye open for real estate, Ed, who was still attempting to collect royalty money from Parsons (he had not received a cent other than the advance), found out he was not the only one looking for his dues. Scott Sidney, who directed *Tarzan of the Apes*, was in the process of suing Parsons for the bonus which he claimed he had been promised for bringing the picture in on schedule, and both Ed and Elmo Lincoln testified in Superior Court.

On March first, Ed found a place that was indeed suitable for a lord — in fact, it belonged to one of the most powerful and successful "press lords" of the early part of the century, General Harrison Gray Otis, founder and publisher of the *Los Angeles Times*. What did Ed get for $125,000? Mil Flores, the 540-acre estate, lay along the south side of Ventura Boulevard in the San Fernando Valley, a short distance northwest of Los Angeles and at the foot of the 47,000-acre ranch acquired by the Los Angeles Suburban Homes Community, of which General Otis and his son-in-law, Harry Chandler, were directors.†

The ranch itself (a large Spanish-type home on a hilltop) was a marvel of quaint architecture, priceless carved furnishings, huge fireplaces bricked to the ceiling, inglenooks, and a sunny library and schoolroom where the children were properly tutored. Outside, through a vista of flowers and vines was a swimming pool and the gym; down an odd Indian-rugged stairway, the ballroom and theatre. The patio was filled with foliage and flowers, about which the ranch house encircled itself with a high iron gate which rose early in the morning and closed early in the evening — lending itself to a touch of Mexican splendor and exclusiveness. The stables held finely bred horses and trappings and just past the stables was "Coonskin Cabin," a rough structure of logs in the shadow of the hills.³

They planted trees and more trees until the hillsides looked like a forest dell. Then they added pools, five of them, one underneath the other, and connected them by waterfalls.⁴

Eight years earlier, in 1911, only an Ed Burroughs could have had such a dream, and only an Ed Burroughs—"poor and without hope"—could have made it come true. Joan Burroughs recalled:

Friday nights at the Rancho were something special. The ballroom and theatre were below the servants' quarters and each Friday, my father issued a standing invitation to those living in and around the Rancho to

---

*According to club president Emerson Hough.

†Burroughs' acreage was known as Runnymede until 1928 when the community's 1,133 inhabitants decided to adopt another name. A meeting was called by the Chamber of Commerce (of which Ralph Rothmund of ERB, Inc. was secretary) and four names were proposed. "Tarzana" received 95 per cent of the votes and the name officially was adopted on August 8. The author coined a slogan for the new community, "Tarzana, Gateway to the Sea" (which yet remains to be fulfilled).

come up for a free movie. There was no theatre for miles around and perhaps one hundred and fifty or two hundred people used to come by every week. Both a drama and a comedy usually were shown.

My father loved his life at the Rancho. He used to get up at five A.M.—never later than six o'clock—and go riding. Most of the time, one or more of us would accompany him. There were two bridle paths, a long and a short one, and the first one down to the stables would leave his name and the time he left on the blackboard. We all loved to ride and later I appeared in many horse shows. Once, shortly after we had moved to the Rancho, Dad and I were out riding together. We paused at a high point from where we could look out on most of the Valley below, stretching across the Santa Susanna mountains across the far end. Neither one of us spoke and then my father waved his arms to indicate the vista before us and he said, half-seriously and half-joking, "This is mine, all mine."[5]

Mary Evaline Zieger Burroughs, the author's mother, died at the Rancho on April 5, 1920. She was seventy-nine. In 1914, she presented the members of her family with a book which she wrote and had privately printed—*Memoirs of a War Bride*, based on her experiences in the Civil War when (along with other army wives) she followed her husband from camp to camp.

2. THE OAKDALE AFFAIR*

Ed's second non–Tarzan movie, if it were released today, might be considered by some as a profound study in neo-realism and, by others, the "newest" of *la nouvelle vague*. The following was a suggested "catch line" for the exhibitors' use in promoting the film: "Girls, did you ever think of putting on your brothers' clothes and starting out on an adventure? It is great fun if you can get away with it. See how Evelyn Greeley does it in 'The Oakdale Affair.'"[6]

Produced by the World Film Company, directed by Oscar Apfel and starring Evelyn Greeley,† the five-reeler was released October 6, 1919.

Moving Picture Herald
...The theme is a familiar one ... the overworked idea of a girl who bursts the bonds of her environment in order to find romance in her own way disguised as a young man. And just as familiar is the development wherein the would-be-husband, traveling incognito as a tramp, wins the girl.

It is astonishing how the heroine comes through unscathed when one considers her association with underworld thugs, gypsies and types far removed from her select circles. The plot hinges upon the anxiety she causes her father and the chief interest is derived in watching Evelyn Greeley's efforts to appear at ease in masculine disguise.... The picture has its interesting points which are realized in its spontaneous action, its adventurous spirit and its colorful photography....[7]

A press notice read: "...Mr. Burroughs is never conventional in his writings and in the present story he has evolved a tale which fairly teems with originality and action."[8]

---

*The story appeared complete in *Blue Book Magazine*, March 1918.
†The love interest was actor Charles Mackay. Also appearing in the film, Reginald Denny.

X

Tarzan bei den Affen 1919–1932

Tarzan blamed his weakness, as he considered it, upon his association with the effeminating influences of civilization ... for in the bottom of his savage heart he held in contempt both civilization and its representatives....

Tarzan the Untamed, *1920*

1. IT WAS HATE!

Until 1925 ERB could count more than two million German readers of his works. Tarzan stories outsold those of any other foreign author ever translated into German. *Tarzan the Untamed*, his seventh Tarzan novel, was the only Tarzan book up to that time not reprinted in the German language, but despite the deliberate omission it marked the end of Tarzan's popularity in Germany.

Tarzan the Untamed has an interesting publishing history. Written in Oak Park (1918) and Los Angeles (1919), Part I was published in *Red Book* in six episodes, beginning March 1919: *An Eye for an Eye, When the Lion Fed, The Golden Locket, When Blood Told, The Debt, The Black Flyer.* Ed received $2,750 for the complete serial, $450 for each of the first five parts and $500 for the sixth and final episode.* These six parts would become chapters 1–13 in the novel. Part II, *Tarzan and the Valley of Luna*, was published in *All-Story Weekly* in five parts, beginning March 20, 1920, and would make up book chapters 14–24.

All Story Weekly played up the serial in a big way. Besides a front-cover illustration and a prologue (the prologue described the action which had graced the pages of *Red Book*), the editor ran a two-column box which stated simply:

> It is surely a work of supererogation like gilding refined gold, painting the lily or "throwing perfume on the violet" to write an introduction of any great length to a story by Edgar Rice Burroughs, and this is especially true when the story deals with the famous ape-man, *Tarzan*. Both the character and his creator are too well known and too universally popular to need any introduction, so we will only say that in this story which marks the return of *Tarzan of the Apes* to the pages of the ALL-STORY WEEKLY where he began his career, Mr. Burroughs has lived up to his reputation of making every story he writes a little better than the last.

On June 2, Burroughs signed a contract with McClurg for publication of the serial as *Tarzan the Untamed*. It was a good contract for the author. His royalty payment had gone up — it was now 15 per cent of the first 25,000 sold and 20 per cent thereafter, with the selling price of $1.90. He still reserved all motion picture and serial rights, and in the event of a popular reprint was to receive royalties of not less than 5½ cents. But the contract was to be a dear one. Let us see why. Shortly after the story opens, Tarzan returns to his plantation from Nairobi. From the book:

> Silent and deserted was the vine-covered cottage. Smoldering embers marked the site of his great barns.... [He] stood beside the little couch and the inanimate form which lay face downward upon it.... For a long time he stood there, just looking down upon the dead body, charred beyond recognition.... As he turned the body over and saw how horribly death had been meted he plumbed, in that instant, the uttermost depths of grief and horror and hatred.... When his eyes discovered and recognized the rings upon her fingers the last faint ray of hope forsook him.

In the same scene, when it first appeared in *Red Book*, the body was *positively* identified as "that had once been Jane Clayton, Lady Greystoke," and nothing was mentioned about her being "charred beyond recognition" or about the "rings upon her fingers."

Burroughs obviously had changed his mind about the demise of Jane between the time he wrote the story for *Red Book* and when it later appeared in *All-Story Weekly* and as a book. In the *Red Book* version, when Tarzan discovered the body it obviously was that of Jane and she was quite dead. In the book the body merely was "charred beyond recognition." Joan Burroughs recalled:

> Jane was supposed to stay dead, but when Mother read the story she talked Dad out of it, and so Tarzan's mate was brought back to life in the revised version.[1]

But bringing Jane back to life was not what disturbed the German public.

It was Hate — and it brought to [Tarzan] a measure of solace and of comfort — it cen-

---

*Some comparative prices in *Red Book*: Samuel Hopkins Adams received $600 for *A Stand-Off*; Sinclair Lewis, $800 for *Speed*. The latter received another $800 for *The Shrimp-Colored Blouse*, which appeared in the August issue. (It was illustrated by J. Allen St. John, who illustrated Burroughs' stories for twenty-eight years, 1915–43.)

tered about the slayer of his mate, of course; but it included everything German, animate or inanimate....

Never one to dilly-dally, Tarzan follows a lead to locate an officer named Schneider, whom he knows to have been the commandant in charge of the slaying of his mate (and, as well, many of his faithful Waziri warriors). He captures his man and leads the cringing Schneider to a terrible fate — clutching a branch of a tree as a starving lion, pacing underneath, awaits a certain meal.

Tarzan subsequently makes a pet of the lion and the two of them join the 2nd Rhodesian Regiment and just raise all kinds of mischief behind the German lines:

> Inch by inch at first Numa advanced. He was growling now and presently he began to roar. Suddenly he leaped forward and Tarzan knew he had caught the scent of meat ahead.... A dozen men were jammed, and leaping upon them and rendering with talons and fangs was Numa, a terrific incarnation of ferocity and ravenous hunger.... [As for Tarzan] it was a wild beast whose teeth fastened upon the shoulder of the Hun — it was a wild beast whose talons sought that fat neck.... The eyes of the Hun bulged with terror as he vainly struck with his futile hands.... Tarzan suddenly spun the man about and placing a knee in the middle of his back and an arm about his neck ... something snapped and Tarzan cast him aside, a limp and lifeless thing.

Is this the end of Tarzan's revenge? No, for the ape-man discovers that he had fed the wrong Schneider to Numa. He really wanted the brother, and soon he was to have him dead to rights.

> Tarzan brought the sharp point [of his knife] to the lower part of the German's abdomen. "Thus you slew my mate," he hissed in a terrible voice. "Thus shall you die!"

There is a beautiful girl in this story — she plays the role of a double spy — and now she staggers forward and cries:

> "Oh, God, no! Not that. You are too brave — you cannot be such a beast as that!"
> Tarzan turned to her. "No," he said, "you are right, I cannot do it — I am no German," and he raised the point of his blade and sunk it deep into the putrid heart of Hauptmann Fritz Schneider.

The *Red Book* story ends as our beautiful spy flies off to safety with British pilot Lieutenant Harold Percy Smith-Oldwick.* "Before I go," she says to Tarzan, who is seeing them off, "won't you tell me that you don't hate me anymore?" But the stoic ape-man does not budge and his only comment, as the plane soars off into the wild blue yonder, is: "It is too bad that she is a German spy for she is very hard to hate."

However, the novel ends like the ending in *All-Story Weekly*. Tarzan allows Fräulein Bertha Kircher to make her way to British headquarters in the company of the British pilot, although "he knows his country was at war with Germany and that not only his duty to the land of his fathers, but also his personal grievance against the enemy people and his hatred of them, demanded that he expose the girl's perfidy...."

Is it possible that for once the unerring instinct of the ape-man has let him down? Is it possible that the Fräulein has bewitched the inscrutable Lord of the Jungle? Never — as the British colonel explains about the girl whom Tarzan only knows as Bertha Kircher:

> She is the Honorable Patricia Canby, one of the most valuable members of British Intelligence Service attached to the East African forces.

---

*Burroughs enjoyed employing the hyphenated English name and made frequent use of it (a kind of *noblesse oblige* from one aristocrat to another).

Then, to round things out (in the *All-Story* version, as in the novel), Tarzan is shown the diary of Hauptmann Fritz Schneider, and reads:

> Played a little joke on the English pig. When he comes home he will find the burned body of his wife in her boudoir — but he will only *think* it is his wife. Had von Goss substitude the body of a dead Negress and char it after putting Lady Greystoke's rings on it — Lady G will be of more value to the High Command alive than dead.

2. CAME: THE REVOLUTION

Burroughs' German publisher, Charles Dieck & Company,* Stuttgart, had reprinted *Tarzan of the Apes*, July 1923; *Return of Tarzan*, February 1924; *Beasts of Tarzan* in May; *The Son of Tarzan* in June; *Tarzan and the Jewels of Opar* and *Jungle Tales of Tarzan* in October. Meanwhile, *Tarzan the Untamed* had been reprinted in Arabic, Italian, Icelandic, Rumanian, Polish, Spanish, Danish-Norwegian and Urdu — all prior to 1925.

Although hard-pressed to get enough Tarzan books into print, Dieck was not anxious to publish *Tarzan the Untamed*. The atmosphere in Germany hardly was conducive to a favorable reception of this work. The mark was plunging — already it was four thousand to the dollar (and soon would go to four and five *billion* marks); the fledgling German Federal Government, which both left and right extremists sought to topple, made no move to curb the galloping inflation, bankrupting everyone but the industrialists; the occupation of the Ruhr by the French was cause for sabotage and strong resistance; riots and disorder were prevalent throughout the nation, especially in Bavaria.

On the evening of November 8, 1923, in Munich's *Buergerbraukeller*, a political agitator took over a party rally by leaping atop a table, firing a shot into the air and screaming: "The national revolution has begun!"

Adolf Hitler escaped in the ensuing gunfight with the police but was later caught and jailed. His trial on February 26, 1924, was responsible for giving this spellbinding orator the national sounding board he so desperately wanted, and although a five-year sentence was imposed on April 1, he was freed on December 2 and relaunched the Nazi party at a rally in Munich the following February.

Such was the scene facing Charles Dieck, who thought it prudent to pass up *Tarzan the Untamed* and await another Tarzan book, which the German public would be more likely to appreciate. However, as it turned out in March 1925 — six months before publication of *Mein Kampf*— the German public took note of another work first.

Stefan Sorel, a journalist, had received a copy of *Tarzan the Untamed* in English — which he could read quite well. He also could write quite well and proceeded to pen a summary of the book. He entitled it *Tarzan the German-Devourer*. It was published by Carl Stephenson, Berlin, and the newspapers took it from there:

> *Frankfurter Zeitung* (Frankfurt)
> One of the best known potboilers is Edgar Rice Burroughs ... and what the inventors of atrocities in England and France could not accomplish, the writers of trash here [New York] did, and Burroughs stands at the head of the list.... The potboiler is so full of lies about the German nation that there is no excuse to be found for it....[2]

---

*Contracts for German publishing rights were drawn directly between Dieck and Burroughs; McClurg also held certain foreign rights, but whose rights were whose remained a question throughout the McClurg-Burroughs relationship.

Lokal Anzeiger (Berlin)

We Germans ought to feel ashamed and our faces should get red when we learn that Mr. Edgar Rice Burroughs ... is one of the basest German-devourers existing in Anglo-Saxon countries. Stefan Sorel deserves credit for this little issue he makes accessible to the German people in his summary of "Tarzan the Untamed," which, wisely, was never translated into the German language.... The greatest piece of stupidity ever thrown on the book market.... The accumulation of rudeness, slander and every conceivable vileness, as piled up in this "Tarzan the Untamed," can even terrify us, who through ten years of horror propaganda became thoroughly hardened....[3]

Berliner Tageblatt (Berlin)

...This book, from which no German translation should ever appear, is a common insult and a miserable lying slander and misrepresentation of the German people.... We have learned much from the war but ... we were not prepared, however, to learn to like the silly admiration for outlandish bungling literary compositions which are of inferior worth....[4]

Neue Freie Presse (Vienna)

To Rudyard Kipling, Burroughs compares like a shoemaker's bench to a throne ... but Tarzan books were sold in enormous quantities ... through the skill of the publishers, Dieck & Co. of Stuttgart. Five thick volumes. Only the one volume which appeared during the war, the book wherein Tarzan hunts for Germans in Africa and kills every German he can get into his clutches like vermin, this one volume the German public did not see.... Why should they? [After all] business is business. When this Tarzan-fever will finally be over, it will be impossible for people to read just a few pages without becoming thoroughly disgusted.... That little poison which reached the public from these books was hardly enough to cause any serious damage. For even as a poison-mixer, Burroughs has not enough talent.... Never had an author described the wonderful rich vegetation of the tropics anymore poorly than did Edgar Rice Burroughs. If he actually has been in Africa,* his senses have no real conception of the wonderful nature and the great outdoors....[5]

Burroughs tried to salvage what he could from the German market, which he saw slipping away. He gave his version to the German press:

I fully understand the very natural resentment that this story has aroused in Germany.... As a matter of fairness, however, to myself and Mr. Charles Dieck, my German publisher ... "Tarzan the Untamed" was written during the heat of an extremely bitter war and not six years later as claimed, nor was it written for German readers.... But perhaps my publisher's success has been his undoing in the jealousy that it has aroused.... If I have been stupid in not realizing the harm that "Tarzan the Untamed" might do, I have at least tried to remedy the wrong by instructing my publishers and agents to withdraw the book from circulation as rapidly as possible throughout the world and never offer it again† ... the war has been over a long time. None but the most mercenary or shortsighted would lend themselves in any way to the rekindling of national animosity.... This is a matter of deepest regret to me, for I really am not half the terrible creature that the German press seems to think of me....[6]

Part I of the Burroughs-Germany affair concluded with a newspaper article in the *Frankfurter Zeitung* as follows:

MR. BURROUGHS OPENLY CONFESSES
[in a letter to this newspaper] his regret that his book may have hurt German readers, but that it originated during the war and that excuses a great deal. Mr. Burroughs wrote his books for one purpose: TO ENTERTAIN. He did not want to offend and the book is really not written for Germans. The ingenuousness of this confession is disarm-

---

*Author Burroughs never set foot on African soil.
†It was often reprinted again, in English and other languages.

ing for there certainly is more pleasing material for entertainment than the cruelties of German officers in Africa.... We are glad that he acknowledges it. Unfortunately though this realization comes a little belated....[7]

3. Germany vs. Burroughs, Part II

On May 10, 1933, four months after Hitler had taken over as Chancellor, thousands of fired-up students were parading along the Unter den Linden — torches held high to light up the new Third Reich across the midnight sky. Before the University of Berlin, stacks of books — twenty, perhaps thirty thousand — were piled, and these, too, lit up the night sky. Einstein, Thomas Mann, Freud, Zola, Upton Sinclair, H. G. Wells, Jack London and, yes, Edgar Rice Burroughs. The *Berliner Tageblatt* and the *Frankfurter Zeitung* — so perturbed in 1925 about that terrible "German-devourer" — had more pressing affairs at the moment. The directors and staffs of these two most important and respected newspapers were purged — cleaned out of all "undesirable elements" and, like the rest of the nation's press, henceforth were told what to write, when to write it and how to write all the news that Herr Goebbels thought was fit to print.

The film industry also was tightly controlled, but the most popular motion pictures were the two or three Hollywood B-movies still being shown. Then, a new blow to moviegoers: In March 1934 the Berlin Film Control Board prohibited any further showings of *Tarzan of the Apes*!

The contention was that "the film was dangerous to Nazi principles of race-consciousness and offensive to Nazi ideals of matrimony and womanly dignity." According to the film board,

> A picture which places mere instincts in the foreground and which has a tendency to argue that a jungle man, even a monkey, is capable of the noblest sentiments and is worthy to be a partner in matrimony, is in contradiction to the repopulation policy and the tendencies of National Socialism.
> In its effects, the picture works against the official propaganda and enlightenment in this sphere, even if the naive spectator should not realize it immediately.... The picture is liable to hurt the sense of race and to work against the government's efforts on behalf of enlightenment. It is of vital importance for the state to uphold a vital sense of race.[8]

The official decision scored the cruelties in the fights of humans and animals in *Tarzan* and those of the animals themselves, as "liable to excite sadistic sentiments in the spectators."[9]

XI

King of the Serials 1919–1925

The beasts of the jungle acknowledge no master, least of all the cruel tyrant that drives civilized man throughout his headlong race from the cradle to the grave—Time, the master of countless millions of slaves. Time, the measurable aspect of duration, was measureless to Tarzan....
—Tarzan the Invincible, *1930*

1. THE CLIFF HANGER

The outpouring of Burroughs' "Early Rancho" crop of stories emerged in a steady flow from the sanctity of the author's 540-acre estate, couched between the low-humped Santa Monica mountains and the dusty yellow floor of the San Fernando Valley. *Auslanders* were not yet making the valley their home in the early twenties, and in this tranquil setting, while the Lord of the Manor balked at society's growing demands on the gentry, he never stopped writing the adventures of Tarzan.

Like any magazine serial writer would, Burroughs—a master of the "cliffhanger" ending—followed *Tarzan the Untamed* (where Tarzan thought Jane had been killed by the Germans only to discover that she had been taken prisoner) with *Tarzan the Terrible** (where in the search for his mate, the ape-man enters a vast waterless steppe called the land of Pal-ul-don, populated with prehistoric monsters and a race of white men with the tail, thumbs and great toes of a monkey), on to *Tarzan and the Golden Lion*† (where, with Jane and their son Korak, Tarzan leads the way back to their burned-out estate), ending with *Tarzan and the Ant Men*‡ (and what happens when the women take over).

How did ERB bridge the gap between one serial and the following? He would commence the new work from where the last one had ended, sometimes following a closing paragraph in one book with an immediate continuation in the opening sentence of the succeeding work. Other times, the author would interject a new lead before picking up from the previous story. For instance, *Tarzan the Terrible* ends:

> And then they turned once more toward the north and with light hearts and brave hearts took up the long journey toward the land that is best of all—home.

Tarzan and the Golden Lion opens with Tarzan, Jane and Korak en route home from Pal-ul-don. But first they discover a magnificent lion cub and decide to take it along.

> The long journey from Pal-ul-don was almost completed—inside the week they should be again at the site of their former home. Whether anything now remained of the ruins the Germans had left§ was problematical.

Where *Tarzan and the Golden Lion* ends:

> ...upon the banks of the Ugogo, in the village of Obebe, the cannibal, Esteban Miranda lay in the filth of the hut that had been assigned to him ... as he entered upon a life of captivity....

Tarzan and the Ant Men opens:

> In the filth of a dark hut, in the village of Obebe the cannibal, upon the banks of the Ugogo, Esteban Miranda squatted upon his haunches and gnawed upon the remnants of a half-cooked fish ... for a year Esteban had been chained thus....

2. More Than Adventure

ERB had other matters on his mind. Parties (at least at this point) seemed to be a bore, although "prohibition" liquor apparently packed a wallop like Dempsey.

In *Tarzan the Terrible*, the ape-man is first introduced to the influence and effects of partying and drinking.

> ...a single draught of this potent liquor would bring happiness and a surcease from worry, while several would cause even a king to do things that he would never think of doing or enjoying while not under the magical influence of the potion.... [To Tarzan] the banquet was a dismal and tiresome affair, since so great was the interest of the guests in gorging themselves with food and drink that they had no time for conversation, the only vocal sounds being confined to a continuous grunting....

Tarzan the Terrible also reveals the author's determined negativism (lasting throughout his writing career) on the subject of organized religion, its leaders and practices.

---

*First appeared in *Argosy All-Story Weekly* in seven parts, beginning February 12, 1921.
†First appeared in *Argosy All-Story Weekly* in seven parts, beginning December 9, 1922.
‡First appeared in *Argosy All-Story Weekly* in seven parts, beginning February 2, 1924.
§When the German troops of *Tarzan the Untamed* destroyed Tarzan's estate.

"[The high priest] fully realizes ... the falsity of the faith he preaches ... the falsity of [the priests'] teaching has been demonstrated to you today in the utter defeat of priesthood. Take then the temples from the men and give them instead to the women that they may be administered in kindness and charity and love." A murmur of approval ran through the throng. Long had they been weary of the avarice and cruelty of the priests.

But even as bits of philosophy are thrown to the readers now and then, ERB seldom forgets that he is first and foremost a storyteller — and one with imagination. From the same story:

> "This thing that you call a *gryf* is a triceratops and it has been extinct for hundreds of thousands of years...." Instantly the great bony hood over the neck was erected and a mad bellow rolled upward from the gigantic body. Full twenty feet at the shoulder the thing stood, a dirty slate-blue in color except for its yellow face with the blue bands encircling the eyes, the red hood with the yellow lining and the yellow belly. The three parallel lines of bony protuberances down the back gave a further touch of color to the body, those following the lines of the spine being red, while those on either side are yellow. The five and three-toed hoofs of the ancient horned dinosaurs had become talons in the *gryf*, but the three horns, two large ones above the eyes and a median horn on the nose, had persisted through all the ages.

Burroughs had an excellent sense of humor and while there was little amusing about his long struggle for recognition, now that he had "arrived" more humor cropped up in his stories. An example is when the author gives us a lesson in Pal-uldon grammar; the word, *kors*:

> I have used the Paul-ul-don word for *gorge* with the English plural, which is not the correct native plural form. The latter, it seems to me, is awkward for us and so I have generally ignored it throughout my manuscript, permitting, for example, *Kor-ul-ja* to answer for both singular and plural.
>
> However, for the benefit of those who may be interested in such things I may say that the plurals are formed simply for all words in the Pal-ul-don language by doubling the initial letter of the word, as *K'kor gorges*, pronounced as though written *kakor*, the *a* having the sound of *a* in *sofa*. Lions, then, would be *j'ja*; men, *d'don*.

Again, the author's fertile imagination, as he describes the strange group of gorilla-men in *Tarzan and the Golden Lion*:

> Of almost gigantic stature, the creature was walking erect with the stride of a man.... His face and head were almost those of a gorilla, and yet there was a difference.... It was Bolgani [gorilla, in ape language] with the soul and brain of a man.... It wore ornaments — and such ornaments! Gold and diamonds sparkled against its shaggy coat, above its elbows were numerous armlets and there were anklets upon its legs, while from a girdle about its middle there depended before and behind a long narrow strip that almost touched the ground and which seemed to be entirely constructed of golden spangles set with small diamonds.

3. WOMEN, WAR AND TAXES

The third product of ERB's "Early Rancho" period, *Tarzan and the Ant Men*, is the most significant — spelling out in lengthy passages the author's sentiments about war, peace, prosperity, woman suffrage and, certainly not the least on his mind, taxes. Also, for the first time the subject of age and immortality (to loom very important in subsequent works) came to the fore. When Tarzan's daughter-in-law* says she is afraid for him, that he takes

---

*Meriem became his daughter-in-law in *Son of Tarzan*, marrying Jack. Of course, she is a princess in her own right besides being the daughter of French general Armand Jacot.

too many risks, "one would think you considered yourself immortal," he replies:

> If you and my wife had your way my nerves and muscles would have atrophied long since. They were given to me to use and I intend using them — with discretion. Doubtless I shall be old and useless soon enough, and long enough as it is.

Ed had fun at the expense of woman suffrage (albeit later he became very bitter toward women), and how he must have put his head back and roared loud and long as these words emerged from his typewriter.

> ...manlike by its physical attributes, yet vaguely inhuman; a great brute [that] carried a club in one horny, calloused hand. Its long hair fell, unkempt, about its shoulders, and there was hair upon its chest.... Its face was massive, with a broad nose, and a wide, full-lipped mouth; the eyes, of normal size being set beneath heavy, beetling brows, topped by a low, wide forehead....

If you have not guessed it, the author was describing one of the Alalus, a race of females! But he doesn't stop here —

> As it walked it flapped its large flat ears and occasionally moved rapidly portions of its skin on various parts of its head and body to dislodge flies, as you have seen a horse do with the muscles along its sides and flanks.

Burroughs continued with his theory behind the creeping dominating influence of females in our society.

> The hideous life of the Alalus was the natural result of the unnatural reversal of sex dominance. It is the province of the male to initiate love and by his masterfulness to inspire first respect, then admiration in the breast of the female he seeks to attract. Love itself developed after these other emotions. The gradually increasing ascendancy of the female Alalus over the male eventually prevented the emotions of respect and admiration for the male from being aroused, with the result that love never followed.
>
> Having no love for her mate and having become a more powerful brute, the savage Alalus woman soon came to treat the members of the opposite sex with contempt and brutality with the result that the power, or at least the desire, to initiate love ceased to exist in the heart of the male — he could not love a creature he feared and hated, he could not respect or admire the unsexed creatures that the Alali women had become, and so he fled into the forests and the jungles and there the dominant females hunted him lest their race perish from the earth.

But the author cannot end the story with the female race winning out, so he had Tarzan teaching the son of the First Woman everything that the ape-man knows. He makes the son proud again to be a *man*. The son then trained other men, who saw in him something special. With their newly found courage — and instructed in the art of the bow and arrow and spear — the men stand firm in their first major combat with women and even dared to chase after them.

> Then the son of the First Woman overhauled a comely young female, disarmed her and said he was going to keep her to cook for him. The [other men] watched the experiment. She refused. He insisted and this time, struck her down with the heavy shaft of his spear. Then he kicked her on the side, to show her he meant business.
>
> Slowly she crawled to her knees and embracing his legs gazed up into his face with an expression of doglike adulation and devotion. "You will cook for me!" he demanded again. "Forever!" she replied.

The editors of the *Los Angeles Examiner* must have read *Tarzan and the Ant Men*, for they asked ERB to interview Mrs. Nellie Taylor Ross, ex–Governor of Wyoming, upon her arrival in Los Angeles. (The bylined story was syndicated to other newspapers.)

> By reason of heredity and sex I am congenitally antagonistic to the idea of lady sheriffs, lady governors and lady everything

else except lady ladies.... I am, like other men, afraid that if women get the reins they may show us up....

But most of all, I am afraid of what political power and political associations may do to the ladies themselves.

Ex-Governor Nellie Taylor Ross of Wyoming does not agree with me upon the point at all. She told me today that women's participation in the politics of Wyoming ever since has tended to elevate and dignify the profession of politics there. So much participation by the women of the entire country would have a similarly beneficial effect on the politics of the nation.

Perhaps active participation of women in Wyoming's politics is a good thing for Wyoming and her women. But I shudder to think of the possibilities inherent in an automobile full of Chicago flappers campaigning with machine guns.

To be fair though, Governor Ross does not advocate wholesale participation in politics by women. She realizes that all women are not physically, or temperamentally, or intellectually fitted for leadership. This judgment she doubtlessly deduced from an examination of the male record of leadership during the past four or five thousand years, concerning which the less said the better.

She believes that a woman's first business and prime duty lie in homemaking and the raising of children — the making of good citizens. Modern conditions of life give women more leisure. This she believes they should devote ... to a study of the political conditions of the day and in the acquiring of such other knowledge as will fit them to exercise their suffrage intelligently....

Mrs. Ross was not at all as I had mentally pictured her. I may say that her type ... suggests for greater sincerity than the run of "statesman" that I have met. But can they hold that ideal untarnished by the game of politics, greed and personal ambition any better than man has been able to?[1]

In Burroughs' stories, most tribes were divided into good guys and bad guys and *Tarzan and the Ant Men* proved no exception, except the names were funnier than most. The good guys of pygmyland were known as the Trohanadalmakusians, and naturally they were from Trohanadalmakus; the bad little guys were the Veltopisimakusians, from the cross-town suburb of Veltopisimakus.

But aside from adventure, jungle lore, magic (the royal physician was able to turn normal-sized people into pygmies), the gentle chiding of the suffrage movement — all this aside, the importance of *Tarzan and the Ant Men* lies in Burroughs' comments on the prevailing diseases plaguing our society at this period — sin, scandal and corruption — from the murder and gangsterism bred by prohibition, to the vice and scandal rampant in Hollywood (more on this in the next chapter), and the wide corruption in government which reached inside the door of the White House.*

Ed Burroughs used as his version of Harding's "insiders" the six cabinet members who composed the Royal Council of Veltopisimakus:

> They had become corrupt and self-interest guided their every act and thought.... they could be bought even while professing their virtue.

What had brought the nation to such a pass? One of the "insiders" offers this explanation:

---

*While scandals came to light in many departments of the government, under the Harding Administration the major scandal concerned the secret leasing of naval oil reserves to private individuals. Secretary of the Interior Albert B. Fall had leased the Teapot Dome fields in Wyoming and the Elk Hills fields in California to Harry F. Sinclair and Edward L. Doheny, respectively. A Senate investigating committee found that Doheny had loaned $100,000 to Fall, and that Fall also had received a "loan" of $25,000 from Sinclair. Fall resigned, was indicted and convicted for bribery. Sinclair and Doheny were acquitted of bribery charges but Sinclair was sentenced to nine months in prison and fined $1,000 for contempt of court. The Little Green House at 1625 K Street was the rendezvous for Harding's "inner circle," where many deals were said to have been fixed.

The trouble is too much peace.... The material prosperity that has followed peace has given us the means to satisfy our every whim ... we have been forced to invent new whims to be gratified ... more and more extravagant and exaggerated ... until even our wondrous prosperity has been taxed to meet the demands of our appetites....

[To solve our problems and restore our happiness] we must have war. As we have found there is no enduring happiness in peace or virtue, let us have a little war and a little sin.... War and work, the two most distasteful things in the world, are, nevertheless, the most essential to the happiness and the existence of a people.... Peace turns us into fat worms. War makes men of us....

[But don't misunderstand.] War and wine alone will accomplish nothing but our ruin. I have no quarrel with peace or virtue or temperance. My quarrel is with the misguided theorists who think that peace alone, or virtue alone, or temperance alone will make a strong, a virile, a contented nation. They must be mixed with war and wine and sin and a great measure of hard work — especially hard work — and with nothing but peace and prosperity there is little necessity for hard work, and only the exceptional man works hard when he does not have to.

Philosopher, successful author, property owner (and taxpayer) Burroughs also had a few things to say about wealth and taxes:

To be poor assures one an easier life than being rich, for the poor have no tax to pay, while those who work hard and accumulate property have only their labor for their effort, since the government takes all from them in taxes.

And this oft-told apocryphal tale:

Once there was a man who was very rich.... For several years after the new tax law was enforced, he struggled to earn enough to insure that his income would be at least equal to his taxes and the cost of his living; but he found that it was impossible. He had one enemy, a man who had wronged him grievously. This man was very poor, and to him he gave all of what remained of his great fortune and property. It was a terrible revenge. From being a contented man, this victim of another's spleen is now a haggard wreck, laboring increasingly eighteen hours each day in a futile attempt to insure himself an income that will defray his taxes.

4. The "Monkey Trial"

It was only natural that ERB would have some comments to make about the Scopes "Monkey Trial," after one of the students who testified at the trial said that in order to arouse their flagging interest, the biology teacher had pointed out *Tarzan of the Apes*.

It really does not make much difference what Mr. Scopes thinks about evolution, or what Mr. Bryan thinks about it. They cannot change it by thinking, or by talking or by doing anything else.... If we are not religious, then we must accept evolution as an obvious fact. If we are religious, then we must either accept the theory of evolution or admit that there is a power greater than that of God. And why? Because if we are intelligent we must realize that we are constantly surrounded and influenced by manifestations of the universal law of Nature. We witness the evolution of the infant into the adult, of the seed into the plant, of the bud into the flower.... If Nature, or God, had seen fit to produce the adult, or the plant, or the flower without requiring them to pass through any preliminary stages of development it would probably have been a more remarkable feat for Omnipotence than the marvelous miracle of evolution that has been slowly and laboriously unfolding since ... the thing called Time.... I do not believe that the most ardent anti-evolutionist will question the Cro-Magnon race or hesitate to admit the possibility of our descent from him; nor will he deny that man's mental attainments ... have broadened and improved in 25,000 years when the people of this extinct race lived.... Going back through the Neanderthal man, the Rhodesian man, the Heidelberg man and the Piltdown man ... we go even lower in the scale showing that evolution has been going on within the human race [until] it is difficult for science to determine whether some of the lower forms discovered in fossil remains are those of ape-like men, or man-like apes.... It is immediately obvious, even if we get no farther back than the Cro-Magnon, that Nature did not produce the finished product originally.... If that is not a heretical admission than there is nothing heretical in the whole theory of evolution, which simply goes back a little farther — to the beginning — and tries to follow up the workings of one of Nature's laws ... one of God's laws, which men who had not progressed as far as we have tried to interpret some 2,000 years ago. It is not strange that they made mistakes. They were ignorant and superstitious.[2]

XII

The Girl from Hollywood *and Other Romances 1916–1922*

For a city-bred man whose boyhood had been surrounded with every luxury and whose spending allowance had been practically unlimited, he was remarkably clear. His high ideals were still unsullied, and though a man's man mentally and physically, morally he was almost a prude.
                                           The Girl from Farris's, *1916*

1. THE SHAME

McClurg published every Burroughs book (Tarzan and non–Tarzan) between 1914 and 1929 with one major exception*— *The Girl from Hollywood*, written between November 1921 and January 1922, after Ed had observed the Hollywood scene for three years. The author's other attempts at the "big-city" or "modern" romance are two novelettes, unknown to all but members of the ERB cult: *The Girl from Far-*

---

*A second exception: *The Tarzan Twins* (P. F. Volland Co., Joliet, Ill., 1927).

ris's,* published in 1916, and *The Efficiency Expert*,† 1921.

If one were to rank the ten worst "modern romances" ever written, these two hardly could be excluded. As to *The Girl from Hollywood*—few critics were kind to it.

The "girl" from Farris's is Maggie Lynch, whose real name is June Lathrop. As our story opens, it is two A.M. and a plain-clothesman sees Maggie climbing down the fire escape of Farris's—a notorious place in the Red Light district of Chicago. The officer threatens to frame her for the murder of a mysterious man (who had died of a heart attack in the hallway of Farris's) unless Maggie consents to testify against Farris as keeping a disorderly resort. The following "synopsis" introduced part four of the serial:

> Rev. Theodore Pursen tries to make capital of her as a savior of souls, but she sees through his hypocrisy. Young Ogden Secor, foreman of the grand jury for which Farris is held, becomes interested in Maggie in a thoroughly honest way, and after the jury has of necessity found a "no bill" against Farris, Secor speaks to the girl.... Isn't there something he can do to help her....

Ogden cannot believe that Maggie is as bad as the prosecution makes her out to be. He could not believe she practiced *that* profession. Why does he want to help her? Maggie suspects the worst, but...

> There must have been a sudden, subconscious appeal to the protective instinct [in him] that is supposed to have been very strong in primitive man.

Maggie assumes her rightful name of June Lathrop and studies typing and stenography. She lands a job with John Secor & Co., not realizing that the firm's president, Ogden, is the same person who befriended her. She is horrified. Will her benefactor recognize her? He does not. Meanwhile, Sophia Welles, Ogden's fiancée, is working for the Reverend Pursen (a "heavy" in the story), assisting the minister in his project, The Society for the Uplift of Erring Women.

When the same plainclothesman recognizes Maggie, he reports this bit of news to the firm's manager, who makes a play for her. He is properly told off. The firm is robbed and Ogden suffers from loss of memory and illness after being slugged. Suspicion falls on Maggie and she is warned to leave town. Ogden's business fails and his fiancée jilts him. He starts to drink.

> A little drink would do him no harm—then he would stop. He would never touch it again; but just now his nerves required the stimulant. Then, too, was it not a well-known fact that in too sudden a cessation of the habit lay grave danger?
>
> Ah, criminal fallacy! To you how many countless thousand graves owe their poor, miserable inmates!

The situation is next to hopeless when Ogden suddenly remembers that he owns a small ranch in Idaho.‡ Out West he goes with his last two hundred dollars, which a stranger fleeces from him. A mere shell of the man he used to be, Ogden returns to the town of Goliath where June, who is now a waitress, hardly recognizes him. But she is determined to make Ogden stop drinking and pull himself together.

The Reverend Pursen and Sophia Welles arrive in Goliath on their honey-

---

*Appeared as a four-part serial in *All-Story Weekly* beginning September 23.
†Appeared as a four-part serial in *Argosy All-Story Weekly* beginning October 8.
‡ERB, who had been to Idaho several times, ranching and then operating gold placer dredges for his brothers' company, made good use of this background in the last part of the serial.

moon and the sight of the couple restores Ogden's memory. He realizes what a cad Pursen has been all along. Then — a stroke of luck. The old farm that Ogden has been trying to rework is found to be located right smack in the center of a new government reclamation project. All seems to point to a happy ending when our old friend, the plainclothesman, suddenly shows up in Idaho and arrests Maggie (or June) for the murder of John Secor.

The trial brings its surprises. Stickler, manager of the firm, is convicted of the robbery, and then the state brings forth a witness to testify. She turns out to be June's mother, who explains why her daughter was living at Farris's. It seems that a Mr. Smith, who had stopped his auto at the Lathrop place in the country, courted and later married June. The couple moved to Farris's and June, of course, had no idea what kind of place it was. Not at first. Smith turns out to be John Secor, who is already married! When Smith (or Secor) drops dead in the hallway one night, Farris tries to blackmail June to stay on. She refuses and it is with this scene — as she flees down the fire escape — that our story opens.

After it is all over, Ogden insists that June marry him. She says she cannot, but then sighs,

> I guess there is no other way; but it seems that the world must be all awry when hope of happiness appears so close within my grasp.

2. TRY AND TRUST

The Efficiency Expert* has as its protagonist Jimmy Torrance, outstanding athlete and "most likely to succeed" type — a recent university graduate. His father is a midwestern manufacturer and Jimmy is reminded of the unlimited money he has gone through; now it is expected that he will become serious and take his place in the family business.

Jimmy decides to show his father that he can make the grade and become a success on his own. Arriving in Chicago, he places an advertisement in the newspaper, offering his services as a general manager, and awaits the flock of replies. There is not one offer. Soon Jimmy is out of money, he cannot find a job and becomes convinced that he's a failure. But he will try one final time before returning home.

First, Jimmy meets a friendly pickpocket named Lizard and a friendly B-girl, Little Eva — both with hearts of gold. Jimmy also runs into a pair of well-to-do young ladies everyplace he turns. The first time, he finally has landed a job as a clerk in the hosiery department of a store and he serves them. The second time, as a waiter in a low-class restaurant where the girls are slumming (Jimmy punches a loudmouth who tries to flirt with one of the girls). Again, their eyes meet in a boxing gym, where our young man has been engaged as a sparring partner to make the other man look good (but when Jimmy sees the girls he flushes and then delivers a K.O. punch). Finally, as a messenger when he delivers a package to them.

Jimmy and Little Eva are bemoaning the fact that he cannot find a suitable job when he spies an ad in the paper for an "Efficiency expert — capable of thoroughly reorganizing large business along modern lines, stopping leaks and systematizing every activity."† But before he can apply

---

*Story stems from ERB's trying to find a job when he was down and out in Chicago, and then finally landing one as an "expert accountant."
†In 1912, ERB worked for *System — The Magazine of Efficiency*.

for this job, Jimmy requires letters of recommendation, and although he hates to do it he accepts credentials forged by Little Eva (she has had secretarial training in the old days).

The ad was placed by the father of one of the girls. Business is good but profits are down and Mason Compton wants to know why. Enter Harold Bince, assistant general manager of the plant and fiancé of Elizabeth.

Jimmy is highly suspicious of the assistant general manager after Bince refuses to show him the payroll. One night, Mr. Compton invites Jimmy to his home. There he is confronted by Elizabeth and she demands to know what he is doing posing as an efficiency expert. Jimmy pleads with her not to give him away — at least, not until he can straighten out the trouble at the plant. When she is determined to speak out, he says (regretfully) that he will have to tell her father about the type of places that she has been frequenting. This threat silences her.

Jimmy calls in a CPA to go over the payroll. (Meanwhile, he also gets a job for Little Eva as Mr. Compton's stenographer.) Compton is found murdered before he has a chance to see the report. Jimmy is charged with the crime and Little Eva is booked as his accomplice. She is soon cleared and disappears to search for the Lizard so they both can help their friend.

A lawyer appears to defend Jimmy (but he won't say who is paying his fee). The Lizard finds certain papers which incriminate Bince and friends. Jimmy goes to thank Little Eva and finds her on her deathbed, suffering from pneumonia. She tells him that it was not Elizabeth Compton who paid for the lawyer (and who believed in him all the time). It was the "other" girl — Harriet Holden! Sinking fast, Little Eva says of Miss Holden: "She is a — good girl. Go to her — Jimmy — when I am gone — She loves you. Good-by — Jimmy."

Jimmy does go to Harriet and both agree "what a good little girl" Eva had been. Elizabeth Compton now asks Jimmy to remain and run the plant, and apologizes for the condescending manner in which she had treated him. Jimmy returns to Harriet:

"And now after all you have done for me I came to ask still more of you."
"What do you want?" she asked. She was standing very close to him, looking up in his face.
"You, Harriet," he said.
She smiled tremulously. "I have been yours for a long time, Jimmy, but you didn't know it."

3. THE SIN

Burroughs' theme of sin, debauchery and dope in *The Girl from Hollywood* was far afield from the tranquil mayhem of the civilized jungle — in which he was more at home — but the wrath of the Lord of the Rancho had not been aroused for naught. Three successive bombshells exploded on the movie set, allowing ERB and the general public to preview the Bacchanalia of Hollywood's leading lights, and the features played to "standing room only" throughout the nation.

On September 10, 1920, the girl who had everything — Vogue model, Ziegfeld showgirl, popular actress — the stunning brunette Olive Thomas, age 20, was found dead in her Paris hotel suite — a suicide, from an overdose of deadly pills. Why? Everyone asked why. She was young, she was beautiful, she recently had married handsome leading man Jack Pickford — brother of America's Sweetheart, Mary Pickford — and he was about to join her in a belated honeymoon. Then it was discovered that the beautiful Olive was a habitual "user."

This news was a terrible shock to the moviegoing public, which had fallen in love with the stars. Olive Thomas was America's ideal girl; Olive and Jack were America's ideal couple! How could it be? But — perhaps this was an isolated case (it happens in the best of families).

Roscoe "Fatty" Arbuckle, that overweight, sly rogue of a Keystone Cop, was a high-living Mack Sennett star whose parties were the talk of the town, and until 1921 his managers, agents and studio somehow had managed to keep his extracurricular activities off the front page. But not this time. Fatty was hosting a real swinging affair in San Francisco. There were several carloads of guests, several cases of booze and a 23-year-old beauteous brunette starlet, Virginia Rappe.

Sometime during the festivities, Fatty and Virginia retired to an adjoining room. When the rest of the gang joined them, Virginia lay nude on the bed moaning that she was dying (which indeed she later did), but Fatty only roared and committed a perverted act before his gallery of clowns. Fatty was arraigned by San Francisco police on a murder charge. It was changed to manslaughter, after an autopsy revealed that Virginia had died of peritonitis caused by a ruptured bladder. There were two trials and two hung juries. In the third trial, Arbuckle was acquitted, but his pictures already had been withdrawn and the $5,000-per-week roly-poly comedian was not laughing any more. He was all washed up.

It was time, editorialized the scandal sheets — while reporting every lurid detail of the happenings — "to clean up the sin and scandal of Hollywood." It was time, said the Women's Christian Temperance Union — which claimed credit for the Prohibition Law (but not for what followed in those thirteen dry years) — "to clean up the sin and scandal of Hollywood." It was time, chorused the public — as they raced for their copy of the scandal sheets — "to clean up the sin and scandal of Hollywood."

It *was* time. While Fatty's second trial was upcoming in San Francisco, the third bombshell rocked the film capital. On February 2, 1922, William Desmond Taylor, a leading director at Paramount and president of the Screen Director's Guild, was shot and killed by a bullet fired through the window of his Los Angeles dwelling. Again, the "yellow press" and the sensation-seeking tabloids carried every aspect of this bizarre mystery to the public. The Desmond affair had everything that a lurid story should have — and much more. It was brought out that the handsome director had been having affairs, simultaneously, with two important Hollywood figures: Paramount's blonde and beautiful Mary Miles Minter, and the Sennett comedy star, dark-haired Mabel Normand. With each passing day, there was another story. Taylor's butler had disappeared the night of the murder and never was heard from again. Further investigation revealed that both Mabel Normand and Mary Miles Minter had visited Taylor the night of the murder — at different hours. A witness claimed to have seen someone leaving Taylor's place on the run — someone dressed like a man, but *running like a woman.*

Stacks of saucy photographs were found in one of the rooms, plus letters of erotic content (which had been overlooked by studio officials who had "tidied up" before calling the police). A collection of ladies' lingerie was found in a locked closet, with each article initialed and dated — many with the initials "M.M.M." At Taylor's funeral, both Mary Miles Minter and Mabel Normand collapsed. An aftermath of the sensational unsolved murder: Mabel Normand was discovered to be a confirmed drug addict! Her career was finis, as was that of Mary Miles Minter.

This was too much for the new industry. A "family image" was needed and Will Hays, Postmaster General in the corrupt-ridden Harding Administration, became the Mother Hubbard of filmland. But even as Hays took over there was still another scandal and it concerned one of the most popular leading men of the day — handsome, athletic, "All-American" Wallace Reid. Supposedly at a rest home suffering from "exhaustion," it was revealed that Wally was undergoing a cure for drug addiction!* This was insane! Like telling the American public that Tarzan swore!

4. The Drama

Subtitled "A Modern Drama of City and Country Life in Southern California," *The Girl from Hollywood* first appeared in *Munsey's Magazine*† in six parts (and thirty-seven chapters) beginning June 1922. It was published in book form on August 10, 1923, by Macaulay, New York, at $1.90. The book had three additional printings, the last in 1925 at seventy-five cents. Methuen published it in England in 1924. No record could be found of total sales.

Joan Burroughs later recalled:

> My father did considerable research on the story and our ranch was used as the basis for the background. Dad even installed some of my speeches and mannerisms into the character of one of the girls. He believed very much in this story and always felt that it was killed quickly by certain Hollywood elements.[1]

Burroughs' morality was evident in *Girl from Hollywood* as it was in his earlier "big-city romances," *The Efficiency Expert* and *the Girl from Farris's*. Here, too, the young man of good breeding could take the hard knocks dealt out by life and come back off the canvas to win the fight. And if the fight was going badly, no matter, chin up and remember who you are. Also, this moral: In the worst of men, there is something decent and, sooner or later, it will show.

A synopsis:

In the foothills of the Southern California mountains is the Rancho del Ganado, owned by Colonel Pennington, a Virginian of wealth and good family, and a smaller ranch on which Mrs. Evans, a widow, lives with her daughter Grace and her son Guy. Grace and Guy Evans are engaged to Custer and Eva Pennington, respectively. Grace feels that she has dramatic talent and she decides to go to Hollywood and make a bid for fame as an actress before she settles down to married life in the country.

Custer Pennington, in his eagerness for money to enable him to marry Grace Evans, becomes involved in the schemes of Slick Allen, a discharged employee of the Ganado Ranch, who is selling whiskey stolen from a government warehouse.

Another neighbor of the Penningtons is Mrs. Burke, whose daughter Shannon, known professionally as Gaza de Lure, is in Hollywood bit parts. A beautiful girl, Shannon attracts the attention of Wilson Crumb, a prominent actor-director, who tricks Shannon into the morphine habit. Crumb is also a partner of Slick Allen, to whom he owes several thousand dollars for drugs. To avoid paying the debt, he informs on Allen, who is arrested and imprisoned as a drug peddler.

Mrs. Burke is taken seriously ill, and Shannon is summoned to her mother's bedside. She takes with her a week's supply of morphine. Her mother is dead when she

---

*While locked up in a padded cell, Wally Reid, age 30, died under mysterious circumstances on January 8, 1923.

†One of the most popular magazines of the period, it was part of the vast publishing empire of Frank A. Munsey, which included *All-Story* and *Argosy*.

arrives, and the hospitable Penningtons take Shannon into their home. Here, impressed by the beauty of the life led by her hosts, she battles desperately—but with little hope—to "kick" the habit.

The ending is another of the author's whirlwind attempts to tie everything together with a neat bow of hope, cheer—and morality. Young Custer Pennington is about to be executed for the murder of actor-director Crumb. His father pays a final visit to the cell.

> You'd better go, Dad. Go back to Mother and Eva. Don't take it too hard. It isn't so bad, after all. I have led a bully life and I have never forgotten once that I am a Pennington. I shall not forget it tomorrow.

However, Shannon rushes over to the ranch with real good news. It seems that Guy Evans (who had been in a mental blackout) has recovered in the nick of time to confess to the murder of Crumb. Why? Because Crumb was responsible for the dope addiction and (subsequently) the death of Guy's sister Grace. Then why was young Custer about to be executed? Because Slick Allen—who never liked the Penningtons—heard the shot that Evans fired, but planted false evidence to point the finger of suspicion at Custer.

But there is one important question that remains unanswered. Why did Slick Allen clear the entire matter with his "confession"? Shannon explains:

> It's a hard thing for me to tell you. Allen is a bad man—a very bad man; yet in the worst of men there is a spark of good. Allen told me this morning in the district attorney's office what it was that had kindled to life the spark of good in him. He is my father.

(Shannon resolves the final problem when she tells Eva not to worry—that her boyfriend, Guy, surely would be let off on a plea of "temporary insanity.")

Some reviews[2]:

The New York Times

...we are so genuinely sorry to learn all these terrible things about Hollywood. It makes us tremble for the future of the motion picture industry. If the directors and stars spend all their time sinning, who is going to make the pictures that have become almost a necessity in our drab and dreary lives?

Indianapolis News

In this book, Burroughs has taken a sensational theme and served it up as so much sensational hash.... The jacket on the book pictures a woman dropping a robe to expose her naked shoulders.... Within the jacket is the appealing line, "Women are cheaper in Hollywood than in any town this side of Port Said." No doubt here is a situation for a novelist. But he must be a Zola. He must be more than an Edgar Rice Burroughs, writing feebly for a multitude that sees in a nation's shame nothing more than a cheap diversion.

Portland Oregonian

If a standard musical concoction were once established, such novels might be punched on rolls and reproduced on piano players....

Sacramento (California) Bee

"The Girl from Hollywood" may be described as a piece of purely machine-made gurry. It has neither moral nor artistic value. Its only significance is a perfect example of what happens when the methods of modern industrialism are applied to literary output.

But not all reviews were unfavorable:

New York Herald

Mr. Burroughs is taking himself a great deal more seriously here ... evidently writing from a genuine indignation, and unexpectedly, with much more restraint than the reader looks for.

New York Post

There is an undercurrent of righteous indignation on the part of the author which gives dignity to the book.... The accounts of debauchery and crime are not much overdone, and sometimes the book even succeeds in being impressive in spite of its crudities.

Passaic (New Jersey) Herald

...Written about Hollywood, the home of movies and movie scandal stories, one is prepared to believe it is almost a human document, or, perhaps, a piecing together of the stories of many who have fallen by the side of the primrose path.

Top: Edgar Rice Burroughs at the age of ten, 1885. *Bottom:* Edgar Rice Burroughs (front row, left end) on football team at Michigan Military Academy, Orchard Lake, Michigan, 1893.

ERB as a cowboy on his brothers' ranch in Idaho, 1891.

ERB in his senior year at Michigan Military Academy, 1895. He returned the following year as Assistant Commandant and instructor in Geology and Gatling Gun.

Burroughs at the brink. The author relaxes with newspaper account of his third story, "Tarzan of the Apes," 1912. The public response was so great that it was serialized in newspapers in 1913 and published in book form in 1914, after which the author's future was secured. It became a movie in 1918.

Top: Ed and Emma Burroughs with their three children, Joan, Hully and Jack, at their Oak Park, Illinois, home in 1915 (one year after publication of *Tarzan of the Apes* in book form).

Left: Success at last! ERB at Pacific Ocean, 1916, after publication of his first three Tarzan books. (Photograph copyright Edgar Rice Burroughs, Inc., 1975.)

Top left: Signed photograph of Burroughs at the age of 43 (1918). *Top right:* Edgar Rice Burroughs as a major in the Illinois State Militia, 1918–1919. *Bottom:* Tarzana ranch house, 1919, the hub of ERB's new 540-acre spread in the San Fernando Valley. The ranch was purchased from Gen. Harrison Gray Otis, publisher of the *Los Angeles Times*.

Edgar Rice Burroughs takes a bow as animal trainer on his Tarzana Ranch, 1923.

Jim Pierce (Tarzan No. 4, 1927) married the author's daughter Joan on August 8, 1929. Together they played Tarzan and Jane on radio when the series began in 1932.

At age 58, ERB decided to take up flying. Here he is with his private plane at the Santa Monica Airport, 1933. He designed the circled "doodle" on the tail of the plane as the official logo for his book publishing business.

Top: Edgar Rice Burroughs on the set of ***Tarzan and His Mate*** with the stars of the film, Johnny Weissmuller and Maureen O'Sullivan, 1934. (Notice the fake ears on the Indian elephant to make him appear African.) *Bottom:* Edgar Rice Burroughs and his favorite "Cord" automobile, 1934. He had driven his father's first electric car at the Chicago Columbian Exposition in 1893 and was fascinated with cars for the rest of his life.

Top: Florence Gilbert was ERB's second wife. She had come to Hollywood as a teenager at the urging of "America's Sweetheart," Mary Pickford, whom she closely resembled. Her marriage to ERB lasted only seven years (1935–1942) but they parted as friends. *Bottom:* ERB and Florence on their honeymoon in Hawaii, April 1935.

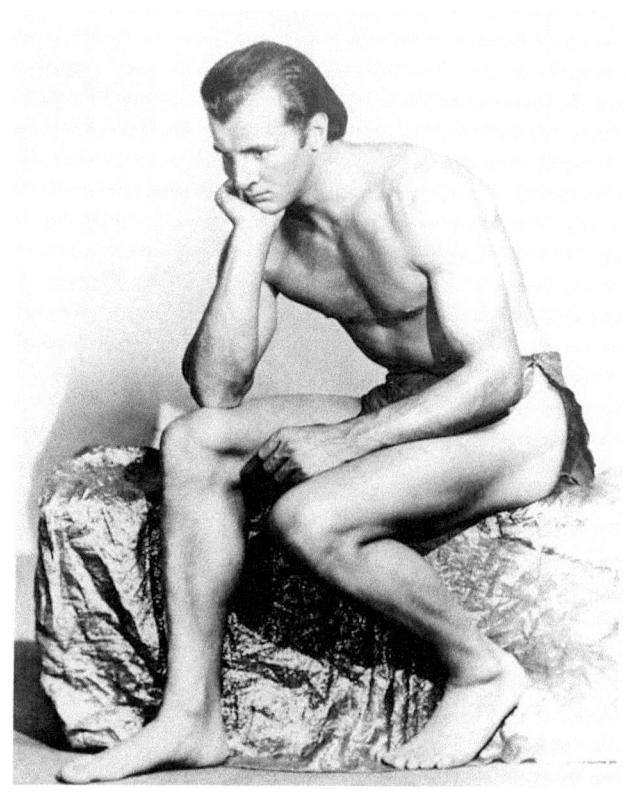

Top: A pensive Herman Brix (Tarzan No. 8) poses for the camera before leaving for Guatemala to film *The New Adventures of Tarzan*, 1935.

Left: ERB and Tarzan actor Glenn Morris on the set of *Tarzan's Revenge*, 1938.

Top: ERB dictates his latest novel at his office on Ventura Boulevard in 1935. His secretary, Mildred Jensen, transcribed the stories from the dictaphone, and ERB went over the final version for errors or non-sequiturs in the plot before publishing it. *Bottom:* Edgar Rice Burroughs and his son, John Coleman Burroughs, began their collaboration as author and artist in 1937 with the publication of *The Oakdale Affair and the Rider.*

Top: ERB in full uniform as war correspondent in 1942. He had personally witnessed the Japanese attack on Pearl Harbor and offered his services to the government. He was the oldest reporter in World War II. *Bottom:* War correspondent Burroughs interviews an old friend, Brig. Gen. Truman ("Ted") H. Landon, 7th Bomber Command, at Tarawa in the Gilbert Islands in 1944. The author flew in several missions in Landon's B-24, *Pacific Tramp.*

Top: ERB (left) with his favorite movie producer, Sol Lesser (center) and scriptwriter Richard Siodmak at Palm Springs, California, 1947. *Bottom:* Last known photograph of ERB before his death. Standing on the set of *Tarzan and the Slave Girl* are (left to right): Vernell Coriell, founding editor of the *Burroughs Bulletin*; ERB's grandson Michael Pierce; and Tarzan actor Lex Barker. Burroughs died on March 19, 1950, one week after the release of the new movie.

Top: Robert Fenton, author of this biography, in Tarzan regalia, ca. 1966. *Bottom:* Robert Fenton and friend admiring Fenton's newly published Burroughs biography, *The Big Swinger*, in 1968.

XIII

Tarzan Swings 1920–1929

> *Everyone was staring at Balza with open admiration, Orman, with the eye of a director discovering a type, Pat O'Grady with the eye of an assistant director— which is something else again.*
> Tarzan and the Lion Man, *1933*

1. THE GREAT RACE

Motion pictures (no longer called "moving" pictures) were getting bigger and more complex and so was the business and producing end of film making. Everyone wanted "in" on the Tarzan property, and with *Tarzan of the Apes* and *The Romance of Tarzan* still playing to full houses, a race was on to see who would produce the third of the ape-man series. Principal contenders were the Great Western Producing Company (for Weiss Brothers' Numa Productions) and Pioneer (for First National).

The Return of Tarzan, billed in some theatres as *The Revenge of Tarzan*, a full-length feature, and two fifteen-chapter serials, *Adventures of Tarzan* and *The Son of Tarzan*, all were released in 1920–21 and often ran at the same time in the same cities.

The Return kicked off first, for summer release in 1920. This was a Numa-Goldwyn Production, for release by Goldwyn Pictures. Numa was the production name for the Weiss Brothers; Max, Adolph and Louis were well-known in the picture field for having sponsored such popular productions as *The Open Door*, *The Unfair Sex* and other feature-length specials. Harry Reichenbach again was placed in charge of an elaborate national publicity and advertising campaign. New York, London, Paris, Algiers and the African coast were publicized as the locations for the action which included: a fight between Tarzan and a horde of ruffians; a duel between Tarzan and a jealous husband; hand-to-hand fighting between Tarzan and a crowd of fanatics; a ship afire at sea; lifeboats filled with tortured derelicts; fights between Tarzan and wild beasts.*

The cast included Gene Pollar† as Tarzan, Karla Schramm as Jane and Estelle Taylor (later married to Jack Dempsey), as the Countess De Coude. The film was directed in six reels by Harry Revier.

Moving Picture Herald

Ever since the good impression was made with the novel and fantastic *Tarzan of the Apes*, the sponsors have tried to duplicate it.... Whether the fault lies with Edgar Rice Burroughs in subordinating his fantastic search for unreal melodrama we cannot say [but the] effort to make Tarzan cultured in maturity somehow fails to be convincing. An exaggerated note of hectic melodrama is introduced in taking the hero out of the jungle and giving him taste of civilization. The spirit of the story is not conveyed until three or four reels have passed, when the onlooker is thankful that Tarzan is back with the birds and beasts. And even then Gene Pollar's impersonation fails in its psychology. He appears to be as contented away from the jungle as in it.... Picture-goers who remember *Tarzan of the Apes* will probably reflect that the novelty is lost in the latest release.[1]

Motion Picture News

Seriously, have you the least idea of what to do, if you should come face to face with a lion in the jungle? No, you haven't. Well, in the first place, you glare steadily at him, the while you shift from one foot to the other to distract his attention. Then you maneuver until you are either able to get in back of him or in a tree above him. This accomplished, the rest is comparatively simple. Leaping suddenly upon the animal's back, you apply what the wrestlers know as the body scissors by winding your legs around him and at the same time place both thumbs directly back of his ears. Then you frown fiendishly, and press the thumbs nearer and nearer the base of the ears.... In a moment the animal's struggles are over. The tickling of the thumbs so amuses him that he just naturally laughs himself into a state of coma, where you leave him until the next reel. The adventures of Tarzan are all exciting.... The thrills are carefully staged and guaranteed and the acting and directing are as good as need be....[2]

On April 3, 1920, an announcement in *Motion Picture News* read that Jack Hoxie, "who has become one of the leading serial stars through his work in 'Lightning Bryce,' is to be starred in 'Son of Tarzan,' screen rights purchased by the National Film Company.... Henry M. Rubey, president of National, said work will begin immediately on an Isle in the Pacific, with L. V. Jefferson doing the continuity from the original version of 'The Son of Tarzan.'"

It so happened that "Lightning Jack" did *not* get the part, nor did Jefferson do the continuity, but Pioneer (for National) did get away first on the initial Tarzan serial. The first chapter was shot on March 15, 1920, and the fifteenth and final chapter on January 27, 1921, with the chapters released as soon as they were ready. (Chapters were two reels each, except for the first, which was three reels.)

Pioneer officials released a statement

---

*Many of the animals were filmed at the Weiss Brothers Zoo in Los Angeles.
†Real name, Joseph C. Pohler. Pollar, according to the Trade ads, was a "silent serial star." However, Burroughs fan Vernell Coriell says Pollar was no serial star but a member of the New York Fire Department.

in January, predicting "this serial will break every previous record not only in the history of Pioneer but also that of any other concern that has ever distributed a serial to exhibitors in New York City, State, Northern New Jersey, or any other territory. Never before," said Pioneer, "has so much money been spent on the production of a serial equal to that which has been spent by Mr. Howells [producer David P. Howells] in the making of the jungle attraction." The announcement also pointed out that moving picture theatre owners had booked it for fifteen weeks on the strength of its drawing power.

The serial starred P. Dempsey Tabler* as Tarzan, and Karla Schramm again played Jane. Hawaiian actor Kamuela C. Searle portrayed Tarzan's son as a young man, and Gordon Griffith played Tarzan's son as a lad. Scenario was credited to Roy Sommerville and Harry Revier again directed. Tarzan's role was secondary to that of his son, and Searle received top billing. But it was the young man's last picture. He died from injuries received during the filming and was replaced with a double in the final scene.

The second fifteen-chapter serial, *Adventures of Tarzan*, was first released October 1, 1920 (re-released in 1928). Like the previous serial, each chapter was two reels except for the first, which ran three. This was to be bigger in every way than the Pioneer-National serial. Not only did it have the jungle know-how and experience of the Weiss Brothers behind it (*Return of Tarzan*), but Elmo Lincoln was signed for the starring role with Louise Lorraine, star of many a serial adventures, as Jane.

Actual production was in the hands of the Great Western Producing Company, sponsored by Julius Stern, president, and Oscar and Louis Jacobs. They owned a large and modern studio in Hollywood and had produced such successful serial films as *The Flaming Disk*, *Elmo the Mighty*, and *Elmo the Fearless*, all of which had served as leading vehicles for their star.

For the purpose of exploiting and marketing the serial, The Adventures of Tarzan Serial Sales Corporation was formed, with offices in New York, and they immediately announced sale of the first foreign rights to Australasian Films, Ltd. A deal subsequently was made with Universal, giving the latter exclusive rights to market the serial in South America, Mexico, Central America, Panama, Cuba, Puerto Rico and the West Indies.

Directed by Robert F. Hill, the serial was made from the concluding chapters of ERB's story, *The Return of Tarzan* (plus some imaginative adaptation by Hill and Lillian Valentine). When another film company circulated rumors to the effect that *Adventures* was not a new production but a rehash of old films, Louis Weiss issued a statement in which he said, and correctly, that Elmo Lincoln had never before appeared in a Tarzan serial of any kind. "Those interested in the production of 'Adventures of Tarzan,' including myself, naturally have a tremendous financial investment in this special production and I wish to nail now all rumors concerning this serial and to state that vigorous legal prosecution will follow any misleading statement regarding 'Adventures of Tarzan.'"[3]

In the first few chapters, a wild tribe of the interior of Africa and wild animals supply most of the thrills. Principal characters besides Tarzan and Jane are his arch-enemy, the bolshevik Rokoff (Frank Whit-

---

*From Tennessee, Tabler was an all-around athlete, particularly in track and as an amateur boxer. He studied for the operatic stage in Leipzig, Germany, and later produced several films. Tabler had starred in a few of Thomas H. Ince's Triangle productions and it was after a long absence from the screen that he returned to play the role of Tarzan.

son), and Clayton (played by Percy Pembroke), pretender to Tarzan's title as Lord Greystoke. Tarzan has a busy time keeping Rokoff from the fabled jewels of Opar as well as fighting off the attention of his beautiful queen, La (Lillian Worth), who is in love with the ape-man. One episode ends with Tarzan alone on a rock. Two lions crouch above him on either side. As the picture fades out, the lions make a flying leap from their respective cliffs and pounce upon the ape-man. What happens to our hero? For the next thrilling episode come back next week!

2. SELLING THE APE-MAN

In a Special Service Section of the *Motion Picture News*, theatre owners received these tips on how to exploit the *Adventures of Tarzan* serial:

1) The serial is, of course mostly thrills and action, and it should be circus stunts that predominate in exploitation. This does not mean any extravagant use of real animals, but the lobby can be made attractive by means of cut-outs. A florist can supply a good substitute for jungle foliage so that your lobby will resemble, in a general way, the opening shot of the serial, which is a dense tropical growth.

2) It is even possible to build a wooden cage and place in it a man dressed as near as possible like the bull ape in the picture. A reputable costumer can provide a realistic make-up.

3) For street displays a camouflaged motortruck looks like the best bet. Drape it with creeping vines. Palm trees and native plants could well be used. Hide the chassis and wheels with huge banners announcing that the first episode of *Tarzan of the Apes* will be seen on such and such a date. It would be even better to use several men inside the truck, dressed in monkey costumes, who could distribute throw-aways at the busy street corners.

4) If you do not like the cage idea for the lobby, set aside one corner of it and erect, in a rustic fashion, parallel bars or cross bars. Obtain a gymnast, not necessarily a professional, put him in the monkey costume and let him delight the crowd with his antics. A man with some originality and cleverness, coupled with ability on the bars, will help immeasurably.

5) It is important to get the children interested. This simply amounts to spreading the news until every youngster in town knows that the serial is to be shown. It would be worth special ads for children in newspaper and posters.[4]

In addition to dispensing promotional ideas, the producers also made available to exhibitors a fantastic amount of advertising supplies, including posters from one to twenty-four sheets in black and white and assorted colors, from 11 × 14 to 22 × 28 inches. Exhibitors were offered heralds, windowhangers, window cards and even oil paintings, as large as 40 × 60 inches. Moreover, each episode was being syndicated in local newspapers. Also available were series of animal drawings (one for each episode) and miniature animal sets.

Going to the cinema for the *Adventures of Tarzan*? Who wouldn't? Who *didn't*?

There were no Tarzan films between 1921 and 1927. The National Film Corporation ran into tax difficulties with the government which resulted in their assets being confiscated, and it did not outlive the *Son of Tarzan*. The Weiss Brothers continued as independent producers for several years but never made another Tarzan picture.

ERB might have missed the opening of the first Tarzan film to appear in six years—*Tarzan and the Golden Lion*. He flew to Salt Lake City (in February of 1927) to see his daughter Joan, who was playing with a stock company in Ogden. Then when Ed returned home there followed an attempt to break into the safe at his office on Avenida Oriente. However, the would-be burglar succeeded only in hammering the hinges off the safe and the gold from the jungle treasures remained untouched.⁵

The new film was produced in 1926 for release the following year by F.B.O. (Film Booking Offices—later RKO), of which that financial wizard, Joseph P. Kennedy,* was president and chairman of the board. There was also a new Tarzan—James H. Pierce. Burroughs must have thought as well of Pierce the man as of Pierce the Tarzan, for he later became the author's son-in-law. ERB remarked at this time: "If you would like to see the personification of Tarzan of the Apes as I visualize him, see the film *Tarzan and the Golden Lion* with Mr. James Pierce as Tarzan. Pierce should interest university men in particular, because he himself is a university graduate, Indiana, a member of Phi Delta Theta, and a former All-American center."⁶

From the book of the same title, the new Tarzan film† had the usual quota of adventures: wild animals, native fighting, search for a mysterious city of diamonds and a thrilling climax when Tarzan and Jad-bal-ja, his golden lion, rescue a girl who is about to be sacrificed to another lion. A review called it "pretty far-fetched; however, it has a rather new order of thrills and atmosphere that might prove distinctly attractive."⁷

While Edna Murphy is usually mentioned as the Jane of this production, it actually was Dorothy Dunbar who played the Big Bwana's lady. Miss Murphy portrayed the pretty blonde heroine and her boyfriend was played by Harold Goodwin. Direction was by J. P. MacGowan, scenario by William E. Wing and photography by Joseph Walker. A bit player: Boris Karloff.

In 1928 and 1929, Universal produced two highly successful Tarzan serials, *Tarzan the Mighty* and *Tarzan the Tiger*. Frank Merrill‡ played the ape-man in both of the films, and Natalie Kingston also appeared in both, but as "Jane" only in the second. *Tarzan the Mighty* was an original scenario, not based on any of Burroughs' stories, but the second serial was taken after *Tarzan and the Jewels of Opar*.

In *Tarzan the Mighty*, Black John, the villain, is ruler of a village of pirates. He attempts to pass himself off as the real Tarzan when the ape-man's uncle comes from England to look for the rightful heir to Lord Greystoke's fortune and title. Black John (played by Al Ferguson) is successful in his scheme and he is about to wed young Mary Trevor (Natalie Kingston) when the real Tarzan arrives in England and the jig is up. The serial was directed by Ray Taylor and Jack Nelson

The second fifteen-chapter serial, *Tarzan the Tiger*, was released by Universal in January 1930. It is of particular interest in that it was the first Tarzan movie to be made both in silent and sound versions. Thus, it is Frank Merrill to whom credit goes for the first Tarzan yell. Tarzan's familiar yell was the product of M-G-M's sound department and not perfected—as we know it today—until 1934. They laid four or five different sound tracks over each other (bleat of a camel, howl of a hyena, growl of a dog, pick of a violin

---

*The father of the late president made no great splash during his thirty-two months as studio head (producing mainly Westerns) although he reportedly made about two million dollars in a stock deal when he bowed out of the industry.

†William S. Campbell filed suit against ERB in July 1929, for $500,000, claiming half the profits of the screen rights of *Tarzan and the Golden Lion*. Campbell contended that he contracted with Burroughs to market the motion picture rights of the novel and that he sold the scenario to F.B.O.

‡Merrill had played in several films prior to his Tarzan role, and also acted as a double and stunt man. He was a champion gymnast and after films became a Los Angeles Park Commissioner.

G-string), timing it so that each of the sounds played a fraction of an instant after the preceding one. Weissmuller and, later, Lex Barker, learned to imitate the sound.

The story of *Tiger* followed an oft-repeated Burroughs pattern. Tarzan is suffering from amnesia and cannot distinguish friend from foe. Al Ferguson again appears as the villain, this time posing as a friendly scientist. After Tarzan's plantation is raided and Jane sold into slavery, all trails lead to the treasure vaults of Opar. Tarzan regains his senses and in the final three episodes—"Human Sacrifice," "Tarzan's Rage" and "Tarzan's Triumph"—he bests the villain and succeeds in recapturing Jane. Direction was by Henry McRae, adaptation by Ian McClosky Heath.

In 1931, Metro-Goldwyn-Mayer announced a forthcoming Tarzan picture to be released the following year. It was to be the biggest, most colossal jungle epic seen to date (even bigger than the studio's *Trader Horn*, which was packing them in). Studio boss L. B. Mayer assigned Irving Thalberg, his top producer, to the new project. All they needed was the ideal leading man. Would the real Tarzan please step forward!

XIV

Tarzan of the World 1920–1929

"What brings my children so far from their own country?"
"Oh, Bwana, it is well that you have come.... Your children need you."
Tarzan's Quest, 1935

1. REVOLUTION KILLED THE FAIRIES

Burroughs' jungle flourished wildly in the mid and late twenties and Tarzan stories and Tarzan sales spread vinelike throughout the world, snaring any and all who strayed out of their civilized habitat. A Scottish journal reported the phenomenon thusly:

> Mainly through the influence of the cinema, Tarzan dominates millions of British minds. There is no escaping talk of him; in smoke rooms, railway carriages and boarding houses and quite nice gentil women thrill to the suggestion of his rippling muscles and indomitable courage. Of the books I can say little that is respectful. Mr. Burroughs has an imagination and nothing more. He cannot be trusted to write grammatical English; style is no concern of his; words are only a convenient (but yet inadequate) vehicle for his exhuberances.... As a literary man he simply does not count.... He writes directly for the Cinema....[1]

Dispatches from Russia in 1924 reported that the most surprising literary phenomenon in the 1920s was the immense popularity of Edgar Rice Burroughs.

The Reds pay no royalty for they are not a part of the world copyright laws but if they did, Burroughs would become a second millionaire.... Anyone who reads reads Burroughs—soldiers, peasants, intellectuals—it [is] impossible to locate a single bookstore [not] prominently displaying the Tarzan books.... Printed in cheap paperback issues at sixty cents each, the Tarzan books [are] read in offices, factories—and read to the peasants by one of the educated villagers....[2]

The New York Times' man in Moscow, Walter Duranty, relayed this dispatch:

"We are being defeated on the literary front," writes one Moscow newspaper today. "We publish books and pamphlets about Marxism and our great revolution. We encourage young authors to interpret its spirit and inspire the masses. We even issue cheap editions of the Russian classics. But the public reads—what?—'Tarzan.'"

Six books of Tarzan adventures have already appeared here and been eagerly snapped up in a cheap paper edition at the price of sixty cents a piece to the number of 250,000. "Yet the supply is far inferior to the demand," a representative of the publishing house told the Soviet reporters. "We could easily sell a million.... Go to the villages and you find the educated young soldier reading 'Tarzan' to a circle of peasants with mouths agape."

This is no exaggeration. Next in popular favor come O. Henry, H. G. Wells, Jack London, Conan Doyle and Upton Sinclair. No Russian author, old or new, is within miles of them. Why? asks the Soviet newspaper, and answers its own question: "Because old Russian literature is out of date, and the new dry, dull or too subtle for mass comprehension."

Perhaps a truer explanation would be that the newly emancipated Russian nation represents the average cultural level of the American schoolboy between 11 and 16.

The astonishing vogue of "Tarzan" is further explained [by Axionof, a sophisticated Russian poet]:

"Our revolution killed the fairies, just as education killed them in Western countries. But if you dress up Jack the Giant Killer in a sufficiently modern guise to give him at least a semblance of probability the masses will love him as did their fathers and grandfathers. And to that fact 'Tarzan' takes his readers away from strenuous, complicated modern life and you get the secret of his success.

"In my opinion this alone proves the necessity for some dictatorship over the proletariat. On the other hand it appears that 'Tarzan' is also extremely popular in America—but comparisons are odious."[3]

Duranty's dispatch led to this 1924 "Tarzan" editorial of *The New York Times*:

JUST LIKE THE TIRED BUSINESS MEN

Running a government that pays no attention to the peculiarities of human nature, including those of liking to accumulate property and to own the products of one's labor, is not an easy task, and difficulties accumulate ... [such as] refusal of the Russian masses to be interested in plays and movies based on and inculcating Marxian doctrines and on their eagerness to see others that have no relation either to socialism or communism....

Those adventures [of Tarzan] have become immensely popular in the villages as well as the cities of the Bolshevist realm. The Moscow paper regretfully ascribes the popular neglect of "sound" doctrine to the dullness with which it is presented, but the Times correspondent, in his dispatch on the subject, offers the more plausible explanation that the great majority of the Russians are at the stage of mental development that makes fairy stories the most enjoyable of all literary forms, and Tarzan, being merely a fairy prince in modernized guise, is just what they might be expected to demand and enjoy.

But it is not necessary to go to Russia to find great numbers of people of about the same mental age—people who lack ... the forms of literature and drama. Sometimes they call themselves "tired business men" and so admit that their delight in trivial pleasures needs excuse, but oftener they are content to let an expression of contempt for "highbrow stuff" be the only defense of their choice of books and plays.

Oh, well, grown-up children anywhere might be worse employed than in following Tarzan through assorted wilds. It is a little surprising, however, that Sovietism doesn't supply sufficiently exciting material to satisfy all demands for the incredible and the sensational. Hangings and shootings have abounded, and for mingled pathos and humor surely no more could be found than in the recent experiences of the intellectuals and the aristocrats.

An old university professor selling shoelaces on the street or a duchess waiting in a restaurant should inspire the communistic playwright to his best efforts in either comedy or tragedy, and he could make it all "sound," too, if he had skill and ingenuity.[4]

2. GUJARATI BUT NOT SESUTO

Writers of news stories and feature articles about the jungle lords invariably state that Burroughs' stories have been translated into fifty-six or fifty-eight languages. However, a closer look reveals that while the jungle tales may have been *read* in that many countries, they actually have been published in thirty languages and dialects,[5] thirty-one, counting Esperanto. Tarzan also has been published in Braille editions. One additional language could have been added in 1951 when a South African agent offered to translate Tarzan into the Zulu or Sesuto tongue, but Burroughs, Inc. did not follow through at the time. Umgawa!

1. Afrikaans
2. Arabic
3. Chinese
4. Czechoslovakian
5. Danish
6. Dutch
7. English
8. Finnish
9. French
10. German
11. Greek
12. Hebrew
13. Hungarian
14. Icelandic
15. Indonesian
16. Italian
17. Japanese
18. Norwegian
19. Polish
20. Portuguese
21. Rumanian
22. Russian
23. Spanish
24. Swedish
25. Turkish
26. Yugoslavian

And in these Indian dialects:

27. Assamese
28. Gujarati
29. Marathi
30. Urdu (or Hindustani)

While Methuen Ltd. of England in 1917 was the first to reprint Tarzan outside of the United States, rights for the first foreign language reprint were sold to Hasselbalch of Copenhagen, Denmark, on July 5, 1918, for *Tarzan of the Apes*. The following June, the same publisher also bought Danish and Norwegian rights for *The Return of Tarzan* and *The Beasts of Tarzan*. Assorted Tarzan titles subsequently were reprinted in Dutch in 1919, Swedish and Russian in 1920 and for English readers on the Continent (by Tauchnitz of Leipzig) in 1921; Arabic, Hungarian, Icelandic and Italian in 1922; Finnish, French, German, Polish, Rumanian, Spanish in 1923; Urdu in 1924 and in Czechoslovakian five years later. By 1929, Tarzan was being read in seventeen languages and in that year of the stock market crash Tarzan, appropriately seventeen years old, was decidedly "bullish."

XV

The Mid-Rancho Period 1922–1929

====

While he appreciated the intellectual superiority of man over other creatures, he harbored contempt for him because he had wasted the greater part of his inheritance. To Tarzan ... contentment is the highest ultimate goal of achievement, and health and culture the principal avenues along which man may achieve this goal.
　　　　　　　　　　　Tarzan and the City of Gold, *1932*

1. Business as Usual

In the mid-twenties, Edgar Rice Burroughs led the quiet, dignified life of the Lord of the Rancho. He was also proving his business acumen little more astute than in his prewriting days. Ed started ranching on a major scale, importing pedigree cattle and fancy-bred swine and branding all dairy animals with the Tarzan label (after the animals in his jungle adventures). The venture flopped when the wells ran dry and the lord discovered that it cost more to bring in water than the animals were worth.

In 1922, Burroughs announced the creation of *Tarzana*—"an artistic colony on high-class residential acres [open to all] who expressed artistic desires through the medium of pictures, flowers, or vegetables, furniture, drugs, plumbing, poetry or the screen — but artists, each in his own field, and each a lover of the beautiful. The mere desire to join this art colony will not in itself be sufficient unless you also have the artistic urge." Ed coined the motto for his colony — "live and let live"— and laid down the law that the inhabitants would be expected "to respect the rights and privileges of their neighbors, and mind each his own affairs."[1] The project flopped.

These were days of rising taxes, when "to be poor assures one an easier life than being rich,"[2] so Edgar Rice Burroughs became Edgar Rice Burroughs, Inc. The corporation, chartered under California law on March 26, 1923, listed ERB as president and owning one-quarter of the stock, and his daughter and two sons each owning a one-quarter interest.

On April 15, 1925, the corporation petitioned the California State Department for permission to sell $200,000 worth of 7 per cent first mortgage bonds, with proceeds from the sale to be loaned to the El Caballero Country Club for purchase and improvement of 120 acres of land north of Ventura Boulevard. When the private club was organized,* included in the purchase was the Burroughs' Mil Flores residence plus other building son the immediate property.

With the stock market crash and the ensuing depression, the country club was forced into receivership and ownership of the club and golf course reverted to Burroughs. He announced that he would operate it as a public golf course and the name of El Caballero was dropped. But this never did come off and shortly after assuming proprietorship, ERB offered to sell his Tarzana ranch to the city for use as a mountain recreation park. This was to include 315 acres plus the 18-hole golf course. Valuation placed on the property was $500,000, but the deal fell through.

ERB also became the principal stockholder of the Apache Motor Company of California, established to manufacture a new airplane engine (named Apache Devil from the story of the same name), said to be capable of developing more than 300 horsepower. This venture flopped.

2. Master Mind of Mars

The planet Mars made the headlines all over the world in 1926, for in that year Mars was supposed to be in a more favorable position for radio reception to and from the earth than in the previous one hundred years. Everyone was waiting for a message, for signs of life, for authentic information about the "Red Planet" and Burroughs, who already had had five books published in his Martian series, was willing to oblige:

> The surface of Mars was formerly physically identical with the earth, and, as similar conditions doubtless still prevail on both planets, there is no reason to question a like evolutionary development of fauna from identical life spores. Clouds, winds, snow and marshes that astronomers have discovered on Mars indicate an atmosphere. Vast reclamation schemes by means of intermediate aqueducts presuppose that there are rational inhabitants highly developed in engineering and agriculture, and naturally suggest further considerable culture.
>
> The enormous waste spaces on the planet, combined with our knowledge of human nature, postulate nomadic, war-like, predatory border tribes. The constant battle for survival has rendered the Martian merciless al-

---

*In 1926, a suit was filed against the corporation for $10,000 as part of a commission on an asserted deal to organize a country club for this purpose. Plaintiffs said they were to receive compensation of $40,000 for organization of the club which, according to them, purchased the 120-acre tract for $280,000.

most to cruelty, and ages of military service against the apaches of the Martian deserts have made him loyal, just, fearless, and self-reliant. I visualize the Martian of the dominant race in Mars as distinctly of human type, with strong features and intelligent expression, a large chest and slightly less pronounced muscular development than ours, owing to the rarer air and lower form of gravity on Mars. The Martian might fairly resemble the intellectual spiritual composite of Spencer, Caesar, de Lesseps, and Geronimo.[3]

Ed would have been delighted to learn that data relayed back to earth by Mariner 4 in July 1965 approximated what he had said about Mars all along: "frozen polar caps—probablly snow or frost—seasons ... clouds and even severe storms ... and an atmosphere, even if very thin by terrestrial standards."

3. MODESTY PREVAILS...

When the private country club was organized, the Burroughs family moved to an English cottage at the foot of the hill, intending it as a temporary residence. In 1927, ERB built a beach house at Malibu, where many of the movie colony had summer or year-round homes. He later added a studio and moved there in 1931.

The new residence in Tarzana had its share of gardens and pools, both of which were a "must" with the author, throughout his life, a lover of the out-of-doors. "A garden is a place to enjoy living, not just a place to rest in," he was quoted as saying. "It must be informal—as big as possible, and have pools and many trees. Include, if you can, as a sort of annex, a rolling countryside—you don't have to own it—where you may ride, explore, and on which you may gaze with a far-away look. A garden is the greatest sport in the world."

The house stands near the center of a green velvety lawn interspersed by trees, ponds, shrubs, and plots of flowers. On the one side a driveway runs from the front wire gate to the barnyard gate ... extending for about twenty-five feet is an S-shape pool, rather two pools with a slender stream connecting them.... Trees, pampasgrass, and Japanese Papyrus reflect their shimmering feathery leaves in the mirrored water. Frogs, fish—a host of varieties—dance thru the sunlight.
[The residence contains] a jungle of tropical plants ... barns for old cars, trucks, tractor, road scraper and other farm equipment ... stalls and saddle rooms (for four horses) ... a riding ring ... flowers of vivid colors (marigolds, purple iris, pink hollyhocks, yellow lilies, blue stocks) ... countless variety of trees (Oregon Blue Cedars, Monterey Pine, junipers, deodars, Acacia, redwood, Bull Pine, Australian Beefwood).... A matchless picture....[4]

This "matchless picture" seemed anything but that, in the author's reply to a sketch of himself by columnist Jack Casey that appeared in the *Chicago Daily News*.

Like most Americans, I dislike any ostentatious show of wealth,* and I would not make a show of it even if I had it, which I have not.
Aside from the fact that I was never a bookkeeper for Sears, Roebuck & Co., and that I remained in Chicago and wrote many stories there after I left Sears, Roebuck and before I came west, and that I do not own any Arabian horses, and that there is no such thing as an "Arabian thoroughbred," and that the horse I do ride would probably bring, at the outside, a hundred dollars if I

---

*But ostentatious he was when it came to cars, the author's long and lasting love. His sports cars were known throughout Southern California, according to his daughter Joan. They usually were the open touring Packards and Cords. Joan Burroughs recalled a Packard that was painted a bright maroon, "and it stood out high, wide and handsome in those days. One day Dad told me his car might be considered too flashy and the next time I saw it, it was a startling canary yellow!"

had to sell him, and that in almost every other respect the article is incorrect, I am not worth $2,000,000.

I live in a very modest cottage.* I have been driving the same roadster for over eight years and I have to work hard and continuously to keep my head above water. But if the reverse were true and I was worth $2,000,000, I know that I should live the same simple life as I do now and that I should not confide the fact of my wealth to any interviewer.[5]

The author still maintained his vast hilltop acreage — site of the defunct country club — but he had a complaint to register to the Los Angeles County Board of Supervisors:

For ten years I have been running hunters off my property in the Santa Monica mountains, without authority and without assistance. A week ago a drunken man with a gun ran me out. Wild life in this district is a source of pleasure and instruction, if it is permitted to remain. Selfish men from other districts are trying to destroy it. My sons and I have never shot at a deer, quail or dove, and recently we have not been shooting predatory animals, believing that nature strikes her own balance. Recently a high-powered bullet from a deer hunter killed one of my high-powered hogs....[6]

Meanwhile, as Ed wrote to the *Chicago Daily News*, he was working "hard and continuously" — "to keep my head above water."

It took ERB about six weeks to complete a book-length story, working five hours a day, five days a week. At times he would dictate directly to his secretary, but more often he transcribed into a Dictograph. Mildred Jensen, his secretary recalled:

Later on he got into the habit of keeping the machine at his bedside, and when he would awaken during the night he would talk into the machine. Only one draft was needed and very few corrections were made — mostly typographical. Mr. Burroughs did extensive research and worked out his story line and characterizations so well that each character about wrote his own story. He never changed plot or story line once he started to dictate, and usually he was in a pretty good humor while dictating. His memory was fantastic, although he enjoyed telling everyone what a terrible memory he had. I don't recall that he ever forgot a date, or name or place.[7]

Joan Burroughs said:

What was so great was that Dad trusted us completely and gave us our independence as well as allowing us to use our own judgment. I was sixteen when I started going out on dates and he never once told me to be home at such and such an hour or to do this and not to do that. I recall his telling me that he thought I was capable of taking care of myself and that he had confidence in me.

But when he made up his mind on a subject he was stubborn about it and there wasn't anything to be said or done. He demanded one thing from us and he got it; this was *respect*. If we answered smart or stepped out of bounds, Dad would take us to another room and it was across his knee —

Every Sunday our family had a standing box at the Majestic Theatre in downtown Los Angeles and this was a special and exciting event to which we all looked forward. He never tried another *Girl from Hollywood* type of book, but he did try a detective story once called *Marcia of the Doorstep* [1924], but it did not work out and never was published.†

I know that Dad never dictated love scenes. This seemed to embarrass him and all such scenes were transcribed from the Dictograph.[8]

---

*Fox studios selected Burroughs' "cottage" as the English setting for *Daddy Long Legs*, filmed in 1931 and starring Janet Gaynor and Warner Baxter.

†ERB did write several murder mystery story-puzzles in the mid-thirties which appeared in *Script*, a West Coast weekly magazine, since defunct.

4. THE NONSEXUAL 1920S

In the author's "Mid-Rancho" Period, there was little involvement in love scenes, dictated or otherwise. The lords had not yet met anyone who could stir their emotions and in the quintet of stories of this period, Tarzan was highly adventurous, the backgrounds were highly imaginative, the plots were highly entertaining (frequently amusing) and the ape-man was highly non-sexual.

Jane did not appear in *Tarzan, Lord of the Jungle*,* but in the southern extremity of Abyssinia the fun begins when two natives shoot at Tantor and miss the elephant; a low-hung branch trips the ape-man and he lies unconscious before them:

"Billah! Thou missed," exclaimed Fejjuan.
"Gluck!" ejaculated Fahd. "Sheytan guided the bullet. But let us see—perhaps el-fil is hit."
"Wellah! What have we here? I fired at el-fil and killed a Nasrany."
"It is indeed a Christian dog, and naked, too. I will finish him."
"By Ullah, no, carry him back to the menzil."

Translated into the modern idiom:

"Hell! You missed," said Sam.
"Bad luck!" Tom shrugged. "The old devil had it in for me. But—let's have a look. Maybe I hit him."
"Say! What's this? I fired at the elephant and killed whitey."
"You're right, and damned if he ain't in his B.V.D.'s. I'll finish him off."
"By God, no, carry him back to camp."

The story is right out of King Arthur and his Knights of the Round Table. In the fabled Leopard City of Nimmr—resembling a medieval English city—live the descendants of Richard the Lion Hearted. These are the good guys. The bad guys live across the valley in the City of the Sepulcher, and they also are descendants of the good King Richard. How did it start? Back in 1911 two parties sailed from Sicily for the Holy Land and the Great Crusade, but a storm arose the two ships were wrecked off the coast of Africa. The bad guys decided that they had landed in the Valley of the Holy Sepulcher and the Crusade was over. But the good guys insisted this was not so and for nearly seven centuries descendants of the original settlers fought one another.

Meanwhile, we also have good and bad Bedouins, and even a good and bad American. The good, young, rich American falls in love with the beautiful princess and must fight off the competition of the black knight. The climax finds the princess kidnapped but the good American, aided by Tarzan, effects her rescue. Does the young man then take the lovely Guinalda back to America to live happily ever afterward? Nonsense. He goes back to the medieval English city—preferring life in the Middle Ages with the woman he loves.

Tarzan and the Lost Empire† can (and should) be dismissed quickly. From Richard the Lion Hearted and medieval England we traipse across the Continent to find ourselves with Emperor Augustus in Rome! There is this plucky archeologist, young Erich von Harben, who finds himself deep in the mountains of the Wiramwazi, hunting for the Lost Empire. He also finds himself among a race whose people speak ancient Latin and whose soldiers wear the tunics of Caesar's legionnaires—subjects of Validus Augustus, Emperor of the East. But the good guys of the east

---

*First published in *Blue Book Magazine* in six parts, beginning December 1927.
†First published in *Blue Book Magazine* in five parts, beginning October 1928.

(Castrum Mare) are opposed by the bad guys of the west (Castra Sanguinarius). Burroughs catalogues the society of "Roman" Africa in his usual manner: the blacks, who are servants and slaves; the brown men, soldiers and shopkeepers; and the whites, aristocrats or patricians.

The third of the "Mid-Rancho" quintet, *Tarzan at the Earth's Core** shows the master storyteller at his height. The setting is Pellucidar.

> A world within a world, lying upon the inner surface of the hollow sphere which is the earth ... discovered by David Innes and Abner Perry.† After boring five hundred miles downward into the earth's crust [they] broke through the crust of the inner world....

The land and water areas of Pellucidar are opposite to those of the outer crust. In the exact center hangs Pellucidar's sun. There is no night but an endless eternity of noon; with no stars and no apparent movement of the sun, Pellucidar is a timeless world.

Tarzan enters the picture when he is visited by young Jason Gridley of Tarzana (*sic*). Would Tarzan accompany Jason to rescue David Innes (Perry's partner, and the first emperor of Pellucidar), who is languishing in a dark dungeon in the land of the Korsars, "far across ocean and continent from his beloved land of Sari, which lies upon a great plateau not far inland from the Lural Az"? Of course he would. Tarzan and Jason first journey to Germany, where a special cigar-shaped dirigible is constructed for the trip:

> The 0-220 was 997 feet in length and 150 feet in diameter.... Eight air-cooled motors drove as many propellers ... the engines, developing 5,600 horsepower, were capable of driving the ship at 105 miles per hour....

So Tarzan, young Gridley, three ex-officers of the Imperial German air force, a navigator, twelve engineers, eight mechanics, a Negro cook, two Filipino cabin boys and ten fighting Waziris set sail "to the west of Hamburg and out across the North Sea" and through an opening in the North Pole, entered Pellucidar.

When a saber-toothed tiger has Tarzan at his mercy, the ape-man is philosophical about his fate.

> He felt no fear, but a certain sense of anticipation of what would follow after death ... Tarzan of the Apes realized that at last he faced inevitable death, yet even in that last moment of life the emotion which dominated him was one of admiration for the magnificent beast drawing angrily toward him.
> [He] would have preferred to die fighting, if he must die; yet he felt a certain thrill as he contemplated the magnificence of the great beast that Fate had chosen to terminate his earthly career....
> And while he realized that he knew nothing of such matters, he liked to believe that after death he would live again.

Of Jana, the Red Flower of Pellucidar's Zoram:

> Her people had few superstitions, not having advanced sufficiently in the direction of civilization to have developed a priesthood....

Again, Burroughs' incredible imagination is seen in his description of the snakeman, or Horibs.

> The conformation of the Horibs was almost identical to man insofar as the torso and extremities were concerned. Their three-toed feet and five-toed hands were those of reptiles. The head and face resembled a snake but the pointed ears and two short horns gave a grotesque appearance.... The arms

---

*First published in *Blue Book Magazine* in seven parts, beginning September 1929.
†Commander Robert E. *Peary* was the first man to reach the North Pole on September 6, 1909.

were better proportioned than the legs, which were quite shapeless. The entire body was covered with scales, although those upon the hands, feet and face were so minute as to give the impression of bare skin, a resemblance which was further emphasized by the fact that these portions of the body were a much lighter color, approximating the shiny dead whiteness of a snake's belly.... They sat on their grotesque mounts with their toes locked behind the elbows of the Gorobors, anomodont reptiles of the Triassic....

Burroughs had been writing at a furious pace for sixteen years and, apparently, he was starting to wonder and worry about *time*—and its demands. He would be increasingly concerned with this subject in subsequent stories, but it starts with Jason, who has this thought:

> Without time (and there is no time on Pellucidar), there was no accountability for one's act since it is to the future that the slaves of time have learned to look for their reward or punishment. When there is no time, there is no future ... and in that the sense of his responsibility for the welfare of his fellows seemed deadened.

In *Tarzan the Invincible*,* the author takes on one of his favorite villains—the Russians. But this time instead of those stereotyped "heavies," Rokoff and Paulvitch (prominent in the early adventures of Tarzan), we encounter a gang of international communists, gathered together in Africa to stir up trouble.

There are more characters in this story than you could hurl a spear at: La, Queen of Opar; Abu Batn, the crafty swart Arab chief; Wayne Colt, a suspected commie but actually an agent in the employ of the United States Government; Miguel Romero, a swarthy young Mexican; Raghunath Jafar, a swarthy East Indian; Tony, a Filipino; Peter Zveri, the big, smooth-faced commie; several other assorted party members and Zora Drinov, the young and beautiful Russian.

One might suspect that Zora is too beautiful to be a Red. Is she, then, a secret agent? Not on Comrade Zveri's grave. At book's end, she confesses that the scoundrel had killed her mother and father (also an older brother and sister), so she joined the expedition to gain revenge. Which she does by shooting Zveri after the latter attempts to kill Wayne Colt. As might be expected, Colt and Zora are scheduled to live happily ever after.

In this story, ERB has a few unkind words to say about certain American types (bankers, manufacturers and engineers):

> ...who are hastening the day of world communism ... selling their own country and the world to us in the hope of adding more gold to their already bursting coffers. One of the most pious and lauded citizens is building great factories for us in Russia, where we may turn out tractors and tanks; their manufacturers are vying with one another to furnish us engines for countless thousands of airplanes; their engineers are selling us their brains and their skill to build a great modern manufacturing city.... These are the traitors, these are the men who are hastening the day when Moscow shall dictate the policies of the world.†

---

*First published in *Blue Book Magazine* in seven parts, beginning October 1930.
†Burroughs obviously was referring to the first Five-Year Plan of the Soviet Union (1928–32), wherein the Russian Government hired American engineers to supervise the building of dams and machine tool factories. U.S. farm experts also were hired to instruct their counterparts in modern farming methods and in the use of modern machinery. Combines, harvesters and threshers were purchased mainly from the International Harester Company. (Americans were paid in dollars by the Soviet Government and paid very well.)

The significance of *Tarzan Triumphant*,* last of ERB's "Mid-Rancho" quintet, is that it marks the end of tranquility and peace of mind for "The Big Swingers." After this one, life never would be the same for either of the lords. Tarzan and Jane were losing their "togetherness" and so were the author and his wife, but for the time being:

> ...the noted novelist is intensely a family man; in fact, when one leaves him after an interview, he is likely to have many notes about Joan and her baby daughter (the first grandchild), Hulbert's writing and his love of digging for archeological treasures, Jack's art and his gardening ability, Mrs. Burroughs' charm, but few about the father. Modest, sincere, with a great love for his family, for all people, for gardens, and the out-of-doors, he looks at everything with a rare and wholesome sense of humor. He is a real person![9]

Only the name is different in *Tarzan Triumphant*; pull back the jungle foliage and you will recognize its identical twin, *Tarzan the Invincible*.

The cast in *Tarzan Triumphant* consists of Lafayette Smith, the young, handsome American hero; Jezebel, the pretty foreign girlfriend; and Leon Stabuch, the commit villain on assignment from Stalin to avenge the death of Zveri. They replace, in *Tarzan the Invincible*, Wayne Colt, Zora and Peter Zveri, respectively. But while the actors resemble one another, there has been a change in the set design. Instead of Africa, it reverts once again to a "lost civilization" (ERB's favorite haunt), with an exploration of its religious mysticism.

It started in approximately A.D. 67, when Paul of Tarsus visited the ancient Ionian city of Ephesus and made a convert of Augustus the Ephesian. Augustus was already an epileptic and inclined to fanaticism, and the martyrdom of Paul turned him into a maniac. He managed to get to Africa, together with a fair-haired slave girl (apparently it was not *total* mania at this point), and his descendants make up the ancient city of the Midians—peopled mainly by morons. But again separating tribes into the good guys and the bad guys, in this story we also have the *North* Midians, stocky, blond warriors; lusty and primitive and in full possession of their faculties.

The story is not much and, unfortunately, shows Burroughs at a great disadvantage in trying to put *lingua gangstera* into the mouth of a second-rate, albeit sympathetic Chicago mobster. Danny "Gunner" Patrick is on the lam and after he meets Lafe Smith aboard ship, the former figures that Africa might be a good place to lie low for a spell. He questions Lafe about Africa:

> What sort of burg is it? I don't think I'd like being bossed around by a lot of smokes, though most of 'em is regular at that. I know some nigger cops in Chi that never looked to frame a guy.

Danny is prone to refer to the natives as "smokes" and "tar baby," and he confuses Jezebel with his many expressions for money: "iron men," "smackers," "bucks," "jack." But Danny is really an okay guy, and when all is settled (in a great confusion of characters and story line) the former hoodlum and the beautiful (and sane) Midian find they have a great deal in common. As Danny tells Jez:

> I got a few grand salted away, kid, and when we get out of this mess, we'll go somewhere where nobody doesn't know me and I'll start over again. Get myself a garage or a filling station, and we'll have a little flat. Geeze, it's going to be great showin' you

---

*First published in *Blue Book Magazine* ins ix parts, beginning October 1931.

things. Geeze! You don't know what you ain't seen — movies and railroads and boats! You ain't seen nothin' and no body ain't goin' to show you nothin', only me.

If the above sounds somewhat idyllic (and naïve) with a rainbow in the sky and a "they lived happily ever after" ending — label it fiction. An era was over and the beginning of the thirties will show a changing Tarzan and, as well, a changing author.

XVI

The Comic Strip 1928–

...Already am I deathless; already am I omniscient; already, to some extent, can I direct the minds and acts of men. It is the forces of nature that yet defy me. When I have conquered these, I shall indeed be God.
Tarzan's Quest, 1935

1. No More "Balloons"

In 1929, a major newspaper suggested to its readers: "If an election were held to determine America's most popular hero of fiction, Mr. Edgar Rice Burroughs' Tarzan would probably poll as many votes as Herbert Hoover polled for president."[1]

Joseph H. Neebe, of the executive board of the Campbell-Ewald Advertising company, Detroit, held similar thoughts about the drawing power of Tarzan; on a trip to Los Angeles in the early summer of 1928 he contacted Ed Burroughs. Why not put the adventures of the ape-man into comic strip form? Why not, indeed? answered Burroughs, and a contract was negotiated. In July a new syndicate,* Famous

---

*Members of the advisory board included: John Golden, theatrical producer; Oscar Graeve, editor of *Delineator*; Paul Meyer, publisher of *Theatre Magazine*; William B. Stout, president of Stout Air Services; Henry T. Myers, director of sales, Chrysler Sales corporation; William LeBaron, vice president of F.B.O. Productions.

Books and Plays, Inc., headed by Neebe and capitalized at $100,000, was formed in Detroit to handle the Tarzan novels (also a series of aviation articles and one on bridge lessons).

Neebe took Burroughs' first novel, *Tarzan of the Apes*, had it condensed and, in what turned out to be a stroke of genius, hired Harold (Hal) Foster, an advertising artist, to do a sampling of ten weeks' strips. Foster later originated his own strip, *Prince Valiant*, in 1937 for King Features Syndicate. It is still one of their leaders, still illustrated and written by its creator. Foster discarded the then prevalent use of balloons (enclosing the text matter) and initiated a new strip form — using four or five panels in each strip, with text printed *under* the panels. Tarzan thus became the first "running" comic strip story. By discarding the balloons in favor of text below the drawings Foster also made use of the entire drawing area. Hal Foster had brought the illustrator into the comic strip business.

The next step for Neebe was to hire salesmen and promote the new strip. He had no luck, however, and decided to approach an experienced newspaper syndicate. The Metropolitan Newspaper Service* of 150 Nassau Street, New York, was a live-wire outfit with an aggressive leadership. President and General Manager Maximilian Elser, Jr., immediately recognized the potential of a Tarzan strip (as did his associate, Earl Hadley), and a new contract was drawn up among Metropolitan, Neebe's Famous Books and Plays and ERB, Inc.

Working for Metropolitan at this time, illustrating fiction, was Rex Maxon, who immediately followed Foster and continued to draw the daily Tarzan strip. Maxon recalled:

> "Max" Elser saw a good thing in the Tarzan strip. He started advertising it to the trade in November as "The Strip of Thrills," in sixty strips, starting January 7 [1929]. This was to be followed by ten others, each to run from ten to twelve weeks and each to be a sequel of the other. He had set the date and had to come through, but it wasn't easy to sell. Finally, Max made a deal with the North American Newspaper Alliance. If their papers would use the strip for ten weeks and then ask their readers if they wanted the strip continued — then Max would give them the entire ten weeks for what amounted to practically nothing. There was a condition, however. If the same papers were to continue *after* the first ten weeks, they would pay the regular rate.[2]

By April the Tarzan strip was a phenomenal success, appearing in forty-four newspapers across the country — from the *Providence* (Rhode Island) *Journal and Evening Bulletin* to the *Los Angeles Times*. Elser wasted no time in announcing that the second Tarzan story, *The Return of Tarzan*, would be available in strip form for release on June 3.

> Hal Foster had returned to his advertising work and Elser told me to get busy and turn out the next batch of illustrations. George Carlin, who was the syndicate editor, said he thought I would be on this job for a while. He never was so right.† I got *The Return of Tarzan* finished in time for the June 3rd release date, and then I just kept on doing them — from the original stories, until we exhausted them, and then from our own scenarios.[3]

Max Elser maintained a steady barrage of advertising "The Strip of Thrills" in

---

*Organized in 1911, Metropolitan dealt mainly in "second-right" (thirty-installment story) fiction, handling such writers as Mary Roberts Rinehart, Edith Wharton, Edgar Wallace, P. G. Wodehouse and E. Philips Oppenheim. It also syndicated the popular strip, "Ella Cinders."

†Maxon drew the strip for eighteen years.

the newspapers' trade publication, *Editor & Publisher*, by printing the names of papers signing up for the feature as well as quoting from their letters[4]:

Albany Knickerbocker Press

The news that the Tarzan strip is to be resumed is most welcome. Ever since the first ten weeks of Tarzan was completed in the *News*, we have been besieged with inquiries from readers who said: "Give us more Tarzan."

Tacoma News Tribune

Tarzan strip one of the most popular series we ever ran. Scores of readers have been calling up asking when it will be continued. Never ran a strip that took hold so fast and kept up interest so well.

Waterbury (Connecticut) *American*

...On the first night that the first series ended, and we printed the first issue following without Tarzan, our office was deluged with telephone calls from people who thought we had forgotten to put it in and were demanding that it be restored. We found that interested ranged all the way from small children, who had to have the text read to them, up to old people. All human beings are interested.

Birmingham News

At the beginning of the ninth week of the first Tarzan story we printed a two-line footnote asking to know the readers' wishes as to carrying another Tarzan story.... Approximately 1,500 persons [urged] us to carry the sequel.... The most spontaneous and most enthusiastic response we ever had to any feature I recall....

Mainly on the strength of the Tarzan strip (and Ella Cinders), Scripps-Howard (United Press) bought out Elser in March 1930 to complement its newly established United Features Syndicate, which to this day syndicates the Tarzan strip. Elser continued as vice president and Metropolitan retained its own identity but the new guiding light was general manager Monte Bourjaily,* who directed both services.

The Tarzan strip was booming† and Monte — who was a real genius — thought there was a demand for a color page. I did the first Tarzan for the Sunday papers. It was released March 15, 1931. But I was still doing the daily strip, as well, and it was too much work. United Features got Foster back, only we did a switch; he did the Sunday and I stayed with the daily Tarzan. Then when Foster came up with Prince Valiant, Burne Hogarth, a fine artist, took over the Sunday page.[5]

Mrs. Jensen, ERB's secretary, recalled the author negotiating with King Features Syndicate for a Martian strip, based on the exploits of John Carter, but it never came off. A short time later the Hearst syndicate started "Flash Gordon," drawn by Alex Raymond, who had been doing "Secret Agent X-9." The "John Carter of Mars" Sunday strip, drawn by John Coleman Burroughs,‡ was released in December 1941 by United Features and ran until the spring of 1943.

2. MORE THAN 21 MILLION READERS

How many newspapers carried the Tarzan strip at its peak of popularity? A fire at United Features some years ago destroyed most of their records prior to 1939. Rex Maxon recalled the peak as "around

---

*Father of author Vance Bourjaily.
†According to a report (never confirmed by ERB) his income in 1933 from comic strip syndication amounted to $1,200 weekly.
‡The author's youngest son (better known as Jack) also illustrated his father's books, starting from 1937 with *The Oakdale Affair* and *The Rider* and *Back to the Stone Age*.

three hundred in the late thirties." The syndicate shows 1942 as the peak year, with the strip appearing in 141 daily newspapers and 156 Sundays. Rounding this out to 300 and multiplying by 70,000 — following the syndicate's rule-of-thumb for gauging circulation — at its peak the Tarzan strip was read by 21,000,000 families in the United States.

World War II succeeded in making the adventures of the ape-man rather tame as opposed to the pursuits of battle and the strip rapidly lost popularity. It has dropped from 90 dailies and 125 Sundays in 1949, to 65 and 95 in 1959 and down to its present (1966) low of 53 dailies and 67 Sundays.

In foreign lands, the Tarzan strip is carried in 75 newspapers located in 36 countries, having dropped from a post war peak of 55 countries. It appears in most Latin American countries and is more popular in these nations and in Mexico than anywhere else. In major European nations, the ape-man and his friends cavort only in France (Paris), but Tarzan appears in comic book form in Italy as well as France. The strip has run in Iceland from the very beginning, and also appears today in Finland, Greece, Yugoslavia, Egypt, India, Pakistan, Malasia, Mozambique, South Africa and the Philippines.

3. Tarzan of the Workers

An illustration of what happens to an American comic strip before it appears in a foreign-language paper was given by Albert Parry, former editor of *Russky Golos*, a pro-radical but noncommunistic Russian-language daily in New York:

From the start, it appeared unfortunate, for Tarzan was the son of an English lord and lady. We could, of course, allow no such snobbishness in the workers' paper. Accordingly I de-lorded and de-ladied Tarzan's parents, presenting them as modest and democratic Professor So-and-So and his equally un-uppity wife.

By the end of the first month, there was a wedding scene showing Tarzan getting married in a *church* ceremony. Most of our readers being strongly anti-priest and anti-church, I cut out the entire church scene. In the blank space resulting I primly explained that the ape man and his sweetheart were married. The readers took it for granted that it was a civil ceremony.

Later in the story there appeared a villain whom Mr. Burroughs had emerge as a Russian. This was a problem. I triumphed by saying in my text that this particular Russian was a tsarist spy and a White Guard hangman. The Russian Whites in this country (who, as it now appeared, had been surreptitiously reading our newspaper for the Tarzan strip) raised a howl. But our legitimate readers were delighted.

Still later there bobbed up another Russian villain. It would not have sounded like real life were I to make another fiend a White Guard. Yet, his Slavic whiskers and name were unmistakable. So I made him a Pole. My Russian readers, who never liked Poles, were again delighted.

So were my bosses. They could not recall a feature more successful with our readers than the Russianized tree-climber. Not only from various parts of this continent but from the Soviet Union as well, we received our readers' acclaim of the lion's chum. Some of them who wrote did so to inquire the way to the nearest jungle. A few were convinced that Tarzan was a real person....

Edgar Rice Burroughs would not have recognized his own creation had it been translated from my version back to English.[6]

XVII

Two Women 1931–1933

...Had he gone stark, raving mad that he was even subconsciously entertaining such thoughts of this little barbarian..., who went almost naked as the beasts of the field and with all their unconsciousness of modesty? Could it be that his eyes had told this untutored savage that he was harboring love for her?

Tarzan at the Earth's Core, *1929*

1. HIGH, WIDE AND HANDSOME

In the autumn of 1931 Ed Burroughs added a study to his Malibu beach house and, with Emma, moved to that popular summer and weekend ocean retreat of the movie colony. Shortly thereafter the Jungle Lord was elected to Malibu's highest political office, that of "Mayor"—an honorary title—for a one-year term. Burroughs was elected at a town meeting and assumed "office" September 13, 1933. He obviously fared much better than fellow Republican Herbert Hoover who, in trying for a second term as president, was soundly trounced by Franklin D. Roosevelt and his "New Deal" program. In the breadlines of the early thirties, the gold mines of Burroughs' were flourishing as never before. Tarzan was king—and everyone paid homage.

Signal Oil of California featured Tarzan gasoline with "go" power. More than twenty million loaves of Tarzan bread were sold in a four-month period "to make kids grow up as big and strong as Tarzan." There were Tarzan ice cream cups, Tarzan games, Tarzan coloring books, Tarzan toys (wooden toys, rubber toys, game toys); Tarzan balloons, Tarzan stationery, Tarzan bubble gum, Tarzan belts, Tarzan jungle maps, Tarzan hunting knives, Tarzan bow and arrow sets; sweat shirts, blouses, shirts, license plates, masks, candy, baseballs, helmets, movie cards, 8 and 16 mm Tarzan films...

Radio audiences, too, could thrill to the adventures of their favorite adventurer in three separates series of programs,* consisting of 364 fifteen-minute episodes. The first serial was an all-family affair with daughter Joan as Jane and son-in-law James Pierce re-creating his motion picture role as the ape-man (*Tarzan and the Golden Lion*, 1927). The programs were prerecorded and sold to sponsors and stations throughout the country.

There was even a "Tarzan Special" drink,[1] which stemmed from a contest held in 1933 at Carmel, California, sponsored by the National Association of the Advancement of the Fine Arts of Drinking. Well-known persons were asked to give their favorite concoctions and ERB made the claim that after two of his specials, "you will beat yourself on the chest and go roaring into the jungle."

Tarzan Special
2 ounces bourbon
1 ounce water
5 drops angostura bitters
2 tsp. simple syrup
1 cube ice

Pour into old-fashioned glass and stir; squeeze lemon peel over top and garnish with thin slice of orange and a maraschino cherry.

Entering his "Late Rancho" period, everything was coming up roses for ERB. He had fortune, fame and was in the best of health. There was a constant market for the Tarzan stories—now appearing in newspaper syndication, comic strips, comic books, magazines, books, radio and films. At fifty-seven, ERB had learned to fly; he was riding almost daily and his tennis game was improving. He was Lord of Plenty in the Land of Plenty—"plenty" for the likes of Edgar Rice Burroughs, to whom had been given "the fruits and the nuts and the roots.... All that He asks is that we be strong enough or cunning enough to go forth and take it."† The author had everything—everything a man could want, or even dream of.

2. ENTER, THE QUEEN

Tarzan and the City of Gold‡ begins like any good serial should. Abyssinia is the background and there is the usual bitter rivalry and warfare between the author's usual "lost cities"—this time, Athne and Cathne—closely following plot and setting of *Tarzan, Lord of the Jungle*.

Enter, the Queen of Cathne.

That she was marvellously beautiful by the standards of any land or any time grew more apparent to the lord of the jungle as she came nearer to him, yet her presence exhaled a subtle essence that left him wondering if her

---

*Twenty years later Tarzan reappeared on radio; first, regionally, in 1951, over some forty stations in the western states, and on March 22, 1952, the Tarzan series made its debut over the coast-to-coast CBS radio network, sponsored by General Foods' Krinkles. The series, which replaced *Hopalong Cassidy*, was beamed from Hollywood on prime time—Saturday nights, 8:30–9:00, EST. It lasted sixty-five weeks.
†*Jungle Tales of Tarzan*
‡First published in *Argosy* magazine in six parts, beginning March 12, 1932.

beauty were the reflection of a nature all good or all evil, for her mien and bearing suggested there could be no compromise — Nemone, the Queen, was all one or all the other.

Tarzan's eyes were fixed upon Nemone. She fascinated him.... He only knew that few women ... had ever so wholly aroused his interest and his curiosity.

When the Queen first comes into sight:

> A narrow diadem set with red stones encircled her brow.... Covering her ears, a large golden disc depended from the diadem; while from its rear rose a slender filament of gold that curved forward, supporting a large red stone above the center of her head. About her throat was a simple golden band that held a brooch and pendant of ivory in the soft hollow of her neck. Upon her upper arms were similar golden bands supporting triangular, curved ornaments of ivory. A broad band of gold mesh supported her breasts, the band being embellished with horizontal bands of red stones, while from its upper edge depended five narrow triangles of ivory....
> A girdle about her hips was of gold mesh. It supported another ivory triangle the slender apex of which curved slightly inward between her legs and also her scant skirt of black monkey hair that fell barely to her knees, conforming perfectly to the contour of her body.... Her movements seemed to Tarzan a combination of the seductive languor of the sensualist and the sinuous grace and savage alertness of the tigress.

Tarzan and the Queen find they are drawn to each other, as witnessed by their initial meeting in her quarters.

> ...She fascinated him; she seemed to exercise a subtle influence, mysterious; hypnotic.... He could feel the warmth of her body close to his; the aura of some exotic scent was in his nostrils; her fingers closed upon his arm with a fierceness that hurt....

The ape-man feels weak, but whatever might have happened never does. They are interrupted by an old hag, a Negress, who seems to exercise some kind of spell upon the Queen, and Nemone follows her out of her chambers.

> Tarzan shook himself as might a lion; he drew a palm across his eyes as one of whose vision has been clouded by a mist; then he drew a deep sigh ..., but whether it was a sigh of relief or regret, who may say?

They meet a second time:

> "You should not try to make it so hard for me to be nice to you. Why do you not meet me half-way? Why are you not nice to me, Tarzan?"
> "I wish to be nice to you, Nemone, but not at the price of my self-respect.... I wish you to like me; you would not like me if I cringed to you."

(Can this be the same Tarzan who, during the past twenty years as Lord of the Jungle, sooner would be found pierced by a thousand arrows than admitting he wants a woman to like him?) Nemone continues:

> "Everyone cringes until the sight of it disgusts me; yet I am angry when they do not cringe. Why is that?"
> "[Because] you are not quite sure of yourself. You want this outward evidence of their subservience that you may be constantly reassured that you are the Queen...."
> "They would not understand; if I were generous and merciful they would think me weak; then they would take advantage of me; and eventually they would destroy me. You do not know them."
> "I am ... shocked that one so beautiful may at the same time be so heartless. Were you are a little more human, Nemone, you would be irresistible."
> "Oh, Tarzan, what magic have you exercised to win such power over me! In here [her chambers] alone together, you shall teach Nemone how to be human!"

But, again, they are broken up by the old hag who has such a hypnotic power over the Queen. That same evening, after dinner, Tarzan and the Queen retire to her room.

It seemed incredible [to Tarzan] that this sweet and lovely woman could be the cruel tyrant that was Nemone, the Queen. Every soft line and curving contour spoke of femininity and gentleness and love; and in those glorious eyes smoldered a dreamy light that exercised a strange hypnotic influence upon him, gently pushing the memories of her ruthlessness into the oblivion of forgetfulness.

She leaned closer to him. "Touch me, Tarzan," she whispered softly.

Drawn by a power that is greater than the will of man he placed a hand upon hers. She breathed a deep sigh of contentment, and leaned her cheek against his breast; her warm breath caressed his naked skin; the perfume of her hair was in his nostrils.... "Take me in your arms," she breathed faintly.

He pressed a palm across his eyes as though to wipe away a mist, and in the moment of his hesitation she threw her arms about his neck and covered his face and lips with hot kisses.

"Love me, Tarzan!" she cried passionately. "Love me! Love me! Love me!"

She slipped to the floor until she knelt at his feet.... "God of gods ... How I love you!"

The lord of the jungle looked down at a queen grovelling at his feet, and the spell that had held him vanished; beneath the beautiful exterior he saw the crazed mind of a mad woman ... all that was fine in him revolted.

"And yet [Tarzan admitted] I am drawn to you. I cannot understand it. You are attracted to me in spite of wounded pride and lacerated dignity; and I to you though I hold in contempt your principles, your ideals, and your methods. It is strange, isn't it?"

When Tarzan spurns the love of the Queen he is condemned to death at the jaws of her pet lion. Nemone has a fetish about her lion — believing that she will die when her lion does. As her pet is about to leap upon Tarzan, "a tawny body streaked past the ape-man..., a fury of talons and gleaming fangs, a great lion with a golden coat and black mane — a mighty engine of rage and destruction." Yes, it is Jad-bal-ja, the Golden Lion, who bests the lion of the Queen, whereupon Nemone ends it all by plunging a dagger deep into her heart. Tarzan buries her himself and "beneath the soft radiance of an African moon he stood with bowed head beside the grave of a woman who had found happiness at last."

The ape-man's involvement with the beautiful and seductive Queen certainly is departure from the traditional Tarzan tale. Prudish and priggish, with as much ardor as an amoeba; narcissistic, nonsexual to the point of completely masking his virility since the first two Tarzan stories, *Tarzan of the Apes* and *The Return of Tarzan*, where he showed some emotional stirrings, first, with Jane, and then with the Countess Olga de Coude —*suddenly*, after twenty years, Tarzan seems hypnotized by this desirable and alluring temptress. He is seized with foreign desires and passion. His puritanical shield is in danger of being pierced at the point of widely conflicting emotions. Should he or shouldn't he — On one hand:

> Women would contaminate us. We are not allowed to have them. If we were to weaken and succumb to their wiles, we should live in torment forever.... Man may only attain godliness alone. Woman weakens and destroys him.
>
> *But*— I should like to keep you as you are. And why not? Am I not almost a God? And may not God do as he chooses? And the God of the Kavuru seized her and drew her to him.*

In attempting to read the author's jungle hieroglyphics, "Cathne" could be construed as meaning "Cine" or "Cinema." The "Queen" of Cathne, therefore, could be translated as "movie Queen," with the "City of Gold" representing Hollywood. Is it then the movie industry to which the beautiful Queen is referring

---

*Tarzan's Quest.

when she says that she must be cold and heartless ... she must be strong ... she must be constantly reassured that she is the Queen, for otherwise:

> If I were generous and merciful they would think me weak; then they would take advantage of me; and eventually they would destroy me. You do not know them.

Now, for the Queen: "...there could be no compromise — Nemone, the Queen, was all [good] or all [evil]. She fascinated him.... He only knew that few women ... had ever so wholly aroused his interest...."

The name "Nemone" itself is a derivation of nemesis, Queen of Retribution or Vengeance in Greek mythology. But is she fiction or fact? Probably a combination of both. After Burroughs separated from his first wife and before he married again, he was said to have been infatuated with actress Thelma Todd.*

3. AFTER TWO YEARS

Tarzan and the City of Gold was closely followed by *Tarzan and the Leopard Men*.† The final installment of the former appeared on April 16, 1932, and the first part of the latter serial in August of the same year.

Principal characters are Old Timer, age thirty, and a Yale graduate (so he can't be *all* bad); The Kid, who is about twenty-two, and *Kali*, a beautiful American girl, trekking bravely through the jungles of Africa in search of her brother (who had run away from a sad love affair).

The Kid and Old Timer have been together for about one year — poaching ivory. Each has been secretive about his past and even after the year together, they do not know each other's real name. The Kid acknowledges that the only reason they have gotten along so well together was because neither one asks any questions. As he says:

> People who ask questions should be taken gently, but firmly, by the hand, let out behind the barn and shot. It would be a better world to live in.... There are some things that a fellow just *can't* talk about — to anyone.

This causes Old Timer to admit:

> It was a woman with me; that's why I hate 'em.... I hate the sight of a white woman. I hope to God I never see another one as long as I live.

When Old Timer first meets up with Kali, she is dirty, perspiring and covered with blood.

> How beautiful she must be when properly garbed and groomed he dared not even imagine. He had noticed her blue-grey eyes and long lashes; they alone would have made any face beautiful. Now he was appraising her hair, confined in a loose knot at the nape of her neck; it had that particular quality of blondness that is described, today, as platinum.

(Florence Gilbert Dearhold — later, Burroughs' second wife [see Chapter XX] — recalled that she wore her hair just this way at the time she first met ERB, although her hair was golden blonde and not platinum.[2])

---

*Thelma Todd, the "ice cream blonde," was found dead under mysterious circumstances on December 16, 1935. The beautiful and zany comedienne, who starred in many Hal Roach films, was found in her sports car, parked in the garage of a movie director near Malibu. Los Angeles police were baffled — murder or suicide? Officially, her death was listed as "due to carbon monoxide asphyxiation," but her clothing was disarrayed, there was blood on her lips and witnesses claimed to have seen the actress riding in her sports car the day *after* police claimed she had died!

†First appeared in *Blue Book Magazine* in six parts, beginning August, 1932.

It had been two years since Old Timer had seen a white woman.... The moment that his eyes had beheld hers, her beauty had recalled all the anguish and misery that another beautiful girl had caused him ... arousing within him the hatred of women that had nursed and cherished for two long years.

(Florence Dearholt recalled that when she first met ERB he was in a low state of depression, that he had been estranged from his wife, that she felt he could do something desperate.[3])

When Old Timer says to Kali that he will direct her back to his camp, she stubbornly refuses and he snaps:

> It's too much to expect you to have a heart. You're like all the rest — selfish, inconsiderate, ungrateful ... cold, calculating, hard.

But the following day he cannot keep his mind off the girl.

> All day he had tried to rid his mind of recollection of that lovely face and the contours of her perfect body, but they persisted in haunting him. At first they aroused other memories, painful memories of another girl. But gradually the vision of the other girl had faded until only the blue-grey eyes and blonde hair [of Kali] remained....
> What have women ever done for him? "Made a bum of me ... ruined my life.... This girl would have been lost but for me. She owes me something. All women owe me something for what one woman did to me. This girl is going to pay the debt.
> "God, but she's beautiful. And she belongs to me. I found her, and I am going to keep her until I am tired of her. Then I'll throw her over the way I was thrown over. See how [she] will like it!"

In all of his other works, ERB never wrote passages such as the following:

> "Gad, what lips! Tonight they will be mine. She'll be all mine, and I'll make her like it. It's only fair. I've got something coming to me in this world. I'm entitled to a little happiness; and, by God, I'm going to have it...."

> ...Forgotten was the girl whose callous selfishness had made him a wanderer and an outcast.
> The picture of her that he had carried constantly upon the screen of memory for two long years had faded. When he thought of her now he laughed; and instead of cursing her, as he had so often done before, he blessed her for having sent him here to meet and know this glorious creature who now filled his dreams....
> ...He realized that no other woman had ever aroused within him such an overpowering tide of emotion.... He could see her only dimly in the darkness; but in his mind's eye he visualized the contours of that perfect form; the firm bosom; the slender waist, the rounded thigh; and again passion swept through him.... His desire to take her in his arms was almost maniacal....

After her rescue, the beautiful blonde Kali makes this confession:

> I am so happy. I didn't expect ever to be happy again. It must be because I feel so safe with you.

Old Timer is furious at her remark:

> What right had she to say that. She was *not* safe with him.... Had he not saved her life at the risk of his own? Did not all women owe him a debt for what one woman had done to him?

Kali takes a second look at Old Timer:

> Through the unkempt beard she saw strong, regular features.... [He] was handsome in spite of the dirt and the haggard look caused by deprivation and anxiety.... "You are tired," she said, soothingly, her voice like the caress of a mother's hand; "You have been through so much, and all for me...."

Old Timer, shaken by the touch of her hand, "covers her lips with his in a brief, hot kiss of passion," she gets all upset, after which he confesses his love for her, and she her hate for him. But it all ends well as Tarzan enters the scene in the nick of time, Kali (who turns out to be Jessie Jerome) finds her brother—The Kid (Jerry Jerome)—and Jessie says that Old Timer is coming home with them. "What makes you think so?" he asks. "Because I love you, you will come," she replies.

Several other points are worth noting in *Tarzan and the Leopard Men*. The tribe of the Leopard Men, a secret order, likely was patterned after the Ku Klux Klan—"Their rites and practices are viewed with contempt by even the most degraded of all tribes." Then, as author Burroughs similarly had described in other works, the heroine (in this instance, Kali) is stripped and "prepared":

> Two young women proceeded to anoint her with a vile-smelling oil ... rubbed in by rough hands until her flesh was almost raw; then a greenish liquid, which smelled of bay leaves and stung like fire, was poured over her; and again she was rubbed until the liquor had evaporated....

But white supremacy also is accounted for:

> ...Now [Tarzan] seemed suddenly clothed in the dignity of power and authority. The change was so subtly wrought that it was scarcely apparent and was due, doubtless, to the psychological effect of the reawakened mentality of the white man over that of his black companions.

A comment is made on the foibles of human nature. As the fate of Kali is being decided—the pygmy chief and the native chief are discussing what to do with her.

> No one once addressed her, just as no one would have addressed a cow he was arranging to stable. She recalled the plaints of American negroes that they were not treated with equality by the whites. Evidently it all depended upon which was the more powerful and had nothing whatsoever to do with innate gentleness of spirit or charity.

There was partying:

> The priestesses placed many cuts of meat in the cooking pots, while the priests returned for gourds and jugs of native beer.... As the men drank they commenced to dance ... pausing only to take long drinks from the beer jugs.... The tempo of the dance steps increased, until the temple floor was a mass of howling, leaping savages.... The drinking and the dancing worked the savages into augmented fury.... [Old Timer] trembled to think of what excesses they might commit when they had passed beyond even the restraint of their leaders; nor did the fact that the chiefs, the priests and the priestesses were becoming as drunk as their followers tend but to aggravate his fears.... Already the black priestesses were mingling freely with the excited, drunken warriors; presently the orgy would be in full swing. After that it was possible that no one could save [Kali]; not even the high priest, [who] lay in a stupor....

> The effects of the native beer wore off almost as rapidly as they manifested themselves in its devotees, with the result that in a few hours the warriors commenced to bestir themselves. They wished more beer; but when they demanded it they learned that there was no more, nor was there any food. They had consumed all the refreshments, liquid and solid.

> The head Leopard Man had never had any of the advantages of civilization (he had never been to Hollywood)*; but he knew what to do under the circumstances, for the psychology of the celebrators is doubtless the same in Africa as elsewhere. When there is nothing more to eat or drink, it must be time to go home.

---

*Parentheses are ERB's.

XVIII

The One and Only 1932–1943

How much like a lion he was, in his strength, and dignity, and majesty, and with all the quiet suggestion of ferocity that pervaded his every act.
Tarzan the Invincible, *1930*

1. WANTED: A TARZAN

Johnny Weissmuller, a scrawny and sickly-looking kid from Chicago,* was told by a doctor that in order to fight off a withering sickness he should build himself up and it was suggested that he might consider swimming. Following instructions, the lad attended one of the city's YMCA pools (Larrabee and North avenues) and proved to be a patient after any doctor's heart by becoming the fastest swimmer in the world—a gold-medal winner for the U.S. Olympic Teams of 1924 (Paris) and 1928 (Amsterdam); holder, at one time, of more than fifty swimming records (several of which were not broken for twenty years). When he retired in 1929, Weissmuller held every free-style record from one hundred yards to the half-mile and in

---

*He was born in Windber, Pennsylvania, on June 2, 1904.

1950 was named in the Associated Press National Poll as "the greatest swimmer of the past fifty years." But this scrawny weakling who developed into a six-foot-three, 190-pound champion athlete, achieved even a higher measure of immortality by playing the title role in *Tarzan the Ape-Man*, the first full-length Tarzan feature in sound.*

Sol Lesser, producer of sixteen Tarzan movies, said:

> Weissmuller not only had the physique but he had that kind of face — sensual, animalistic and good-looking — that gave the impression of jungle ... outdoor life. Undoubtedly, Johnny was the greatest of all Tarzans.[1]

Metro-Goldwyn-Mayer's first choice for the role of the ape-man was not Weissmuller, however, but Herman Brix, a weight-lifting star at Stanford University (and winner of the shot-put title at the 1932 Olympic games held in Los Angeles). But Brix had suffered a slight injury while making his first film (*Touchdown*), and the role of the ape-man went to Weissmuller. Brix subsequently became the eighth Tarzan, chosen by Burroughs himself; he later changed his screen name to Bruce Bennett.

After the great success of its African adventure film *Trader Horn* (1931) starring Harry Carey, Edwina Booth, Duncan Renaldo and C. Aubrey Smith, M-G-M was ready for Tarzan. But was Tarzan ready for M-G-M? According to Mrs. Jensen, Burroughs had been trying to sell another film (the last feature, *Tarzan and the Golden Lion*, had been produced in 1927) but was having little success.

Ralph Rothmund, the corporation's general manager, swung the sale on his own,† and Mr. Burroughs celebrated by buying five cars the following day, one for each member of his family. Rothmund was driving an old Ford at that time but he got nothing.[2]

Studio czar Louis B. Mayer assigned Irving Thalberg, his top producer, to the project, and Thalberg immediately selected W. S. Van Dyke to direct. A protégé of D. W. Griffith, Van Dyke was one of the studio's ace directors and had won his jungle spurs by directing *Trader Horn* (supervised by Thalberg).

The jungle was to be the Toluca Lake area of North Hollywood, then a sparsely settled region already thick with vegetation and brush, and boasting its own "jungle river." Truck loads of tropical plants and lush vegetation were brought in to create the proper atmosphere: Gigantic tropical orchids and fruit trees of all sizes and shapes, fleshy-leaved plants of the lily family from South Africa and shrubby, herb-like plants all were hurriedly planted. The roars of jungle animals (carted in from Hollywood's jungle compound) brought equally fierce roars from nearby residents, but the production got under way.

Jane turned out to be a brilliant bit of casting. Thalberg chose a lovely, twenty-year-old newcomer to the screen. Fair, dark-haired, curvaceous, delicate and as feminine as Weissmuller was masculine, Maureen O'Sullivan proved a perfect counterpart to the dark, moody and uncommunicative Tarzan. Born in Ireland May 17, 1911, Miss O'Sullivan was brought to Hollywood in 1929 by director Frank Borzage. After the first Tarzan film she achieved world-wide fame as Jane, portraying Tarzan's mate six times, the last in 1942.

The filmed story bore little resemblance to the novel, *Tarzan of the Apes*,

---

*Tarzan the Tiger, made both in silent and sound versions in 1929–30, was a serial.
†Rothmund confirmed that it was he who first thought about the M-G-M possibility and negotiated the deal.

which had been more or less faithfully followed in the original Tarzan silent film of 1918. Cyril Hume, who did the adaptation, wove the story about an aged English trader (C. Aubrey Smith) and his young partner (Neil Hamilton) who are about to leave their African trading post in search of the elephants' burial ground (and the tuskers' ivory). They are joined by Jane (the trader's daughter), Tarzan appears to whisk Jane away to his tree-top abode, allowing dialogue writer Ivor Norvello to be credited with one of the most popular lines ever to come out of the film capital — "Me Tarzan, you Jane." (However, the "immortal" line in the film was simply *Tarzan-Jane*. There was no "me" and no "you.")

Scheduled for release at the end of March 1932, the opening was in danger of postponement when two weeks before screening there occurred one of the major personal tragedies of the century — in which the public was deeply and emotionally involved — the Lindbergh kidnapping.*

The film received very favorable reviews, such as in the "Show Biz" trade:

Variety
A jungle and stunt picture, done in deluxe style and carrying large draw possibilities.... Tricky handling of fantastic atmosphere, a fine, artless performance by the Olympian athlete ... and the nationwide interest that attaches to the printed original looks like sure-fire boxoffice.
...Footage is loaded with a wealth of sensational wild animal stuff. Suspicion is unavoidable that some of it is cut-in material left over from the same producer's "Trader Horn."
The idyllic side of the story has been shrewdly handled and fortified by romantic settings and pictorial beauty.... Sequence of the young people splashing about a forest pool, for instance....

Some of the stunt episodes are grossly overdone, but once more the production skill and literary treatment in other directions compensates for exaggerations.... Some of these incidents involved a mild giggle, but ... the athletic star Johnny, in short, makes Tarzan believable, because he does with seeming ease and naturalness the things that Tarzan would do.
The wild-animal stuff is remarkably well managed [and] picture has its thrills.... Miss O'Sullivan acquits herself well in a difficult role, while the performance of Weissmuller really makes the picture.... He's a smash.[8]

2. THE LION ROARS

M-G-M immediately made plans for a second film, after being reassured by the exhibitors that the ape-man and his mate were bringing in the customers. But the studio had to contend for the rights with producer, exhibitor and showman Sol Lesser, who recalled:

Even before the first Weissmuller film was released or marketed — I've forgotten which — a friend of mine brought me a contract and asked if I would be interested in acquiring rights to a Tarzan picture. It had been acquired from an individual whom I did not know — James Pierce — and I learned that Mr. Burroughs had given the rights to make a Tarzan picture to Mr. Pierce as a marriage gift when he married ERB's daughter.
Date for the payment required to be made to Mr. Burroughs, at the time production commenced, had lapsed but Jules Goldstone, a lawyer, said that legally the contract was enforceable, for the requirement under law was that the party in question [ERB] had to notify the one who was in default and no notification had been received.
The thing to do was to tender the payment called for, which amounted to $10,000. I gave Mr. Goldstone the money — ten one-thousand dollar bills — and he went to Mr. Burroughs' house in Malibu.

---

*The two-year-old son of Colonel Charles and Anne Morrow Lindbergh was kidnapped from his crib at the home of his parents near Hopewell, New Jersey, and later found slain.

As Mr. Goldstone explained it to me at the time, a gentleman opened the door, identified himself as Edgar Rice Burroughs, after which he immediately was tendered the ten one-thousand dollar bills. Mr. Burroughs said, "What's this for?" and Mr. Goldstone replied that it was in payment for the rights to make a Tarzan picture which the author had made with James Pierce and which we had acquired. Burroughs said the contract had lapsed and he threw the money back. It was a windy day and Mr. Goldstone had quite a time chasing after the bills.[4]

A suit was filed in declaratory relief by Lesser for the courts to decide if the contract was valid. Meanwhile, Metro's attorney asked Lesser if he would delay any production of a Tarzan film until they had released *Tarzan the Ape-Man*.

> Metro asked for about a year, I think, and I agreed. This made a bit hit with Ed, who was in a spot because in his contract with M-G-M he had alleged there were no outstanding rights.* We worked out an amiable contract all around, with M-G-M, Burroughs and my own producing company. Metro had an option for a second Tarzan film and, meanwhile, I worked out a contract with ERB for five Tarzan pictures, at the rate of one a year.[5]

Once *Tarzan the Ape-Man* was released, Lesser was under no obligation to wait any longer and, armed with his five-picture contract, he moved quickly to produce his own Tarzan film. But first he needed a Tarzan! Where to find one? Weissmuller was under contract with M-G-M and the giant Culver City studio was not about to release their jungle lord. But — why not another swimming champ? Buster (Clarence Linden) Crabbe, winner of the 400-meter contest in the Olympics held in Los Angeles was an ideal choice for the role. Not only did his feats (and physique) resemble those of Weissmuller, but he had just completed a jungle film for Paramount, appropriately called *King of the Jungle* (Philip Wylie was credited with screenplay and dialogue, along with Fred Niblo, Jr.).

Tarzan the Fearless was released in March 1933, the same month that Franklin Delano Roosevelt was inaugurated as thirty-second president, with the reviewers unanimous that "no one in the cast gets a chance with the material on hand."

Jacqueline Wells (who later changed her screen name to Julie Bishop) co-starred with Buster Crabbe and Mischa Auer played the High Priest of Zar. Directed by Robert Hill from a story by Basil Dickey and George Plympton, with dialogue by Walter Anthony, the film was produced by Sol Lesser both as a feature and a serial. The idea was for the exhibitors to show the first chapter as a sixty-minute feature, with eight additional two-reel installments to follow in succeeding weeks. That was the idea, but in many movie houses nothing was said about the "continuation" and as the feature left many things unresolved the film received poor reviews.

Perhaps a Tarzan comedy — which Lesser almost produced in lieu of *Tarzan the Fearless*— would have attracted more favorable reviews. After Lesser had bought the contract to produce a Tarzan film, he discovered that a clause therein called for the appearance of ex–Tarzan and Burroughs' son-in-law James Pierce to play the title role.

Lesser recalled:

> I had met Pierce while he was training at the Hollywood Athletic Club, but he had put on considerable weight and I told Burroughs that I didn't think he would be right for the

---

*No doubt an honest error. Burroughs might have forgotten he gave a film right to Pierce, or else considered the contract invalid.

part. Burroughs answered that it was a matter between myself and Pierce and I said that if he [Pierce] insisted on playing the role I would have to treat it as a comedy, and if I did the character of the Tarzan picture would be lost. Burroughs said he didn't think anything could hurt the character of a Tarzan picture, and if I wanted to make a comedy to go ahead and do it. So I engaged Corey Ford to do a travesty in which Jane was the strong one and she would do things like boosting Tarzan up a tree. It was actually written this way except that Pierce, realizing that he couldn't get his weight down, released me from that clause in the contract—for which I paid him a substantial sum of money—and then I hired Buster Crabbe.[6]

Meanwhile, back at M-G-M, work had been continuing on their second Tarzan movie and in mid-April 1934 *Tarzan and His Mate* was released, again co-starring Johnny Weissmuller and Maureen O'Sullivan (considered by aficionados the best Tarzan film ever made). The story by J. Kevin McGuiness, as adapted by Howard Emmett Rogers and Leon Gordon, opens with two of Jane's Mayfair friends paying a visit to her jungle home. They are after that fortune of ivory, still up for grabs in the elephants' burial ground. Battles with gorillas and natives ensue and there is a wing-ding of a fight between a crocodile and rhinoceros. But all this is par for a jungle thriller. What made *Tarzan and His Mate* an outstanding production was a combination of the right qualities: beautiful photography (cameramen were Clyde De Vinna and Charles Clarke), the warm antics of the elephants and chimps in some delightful sequences (like when Tarzan is given medical assistance at a monkey first-aid station), fast-paced and continual action throughout the film, fancy swimming on the part of Tarzan, and one more thing—two beautiful young people who managed to capture their roles of a still-primitive man and his mate.

Lesser agreed:

Maureen O'Sullivan was an ideal Jane with a figure that is greatly revealed in the second Metro picture ... but done so beautifully that it couldn't be criticized.* As I recall the situation she is standing on a tree limb with Tarzan. He tugs at her garment, dives in the water and she dives in after him. Then she comes up from the swimming scene with her breast exposed. It was done in such good taste.... I think that a kind of snobbishness developed afterwards with Miss O'Sullivan from her role as Jane. Maybe the public kidded her too much ... or maybe she thought it wasn't good acting. I don't know ... but I do know the movie audiences worshipped her.[7]

3. Filmland Gold

In the early thirties, the Tarzan movies consistently out-grossed any other motion picture, American or foreign, in the overseas market. Whether it was Cairo, Shanghai or Bombay, the Sol Lesser Tarzans broke the record of every picture ever released by RKO† (and RKO released such box office draws as all of the early Fred Astaire–Ginger Rogers musicals). In some Asiatic countries, the Tarzan films opened with all the trappings of a Hollywood premiere—even to evening gowns and white tie and tails.

Lesser recalled:

Commencing with my era of producing the Tarzan films, Burroughs not only had an advance payment but also a participation in

---

*M-G-M *did* come in for criticism (by certain groups and individuals) for allowing Jane to wear as little as she could get away with, and the result was that Miss O'Sullivan's figure was never again shown off to such advantage. Tarzan also had to bow to the conventions of the "puritan thirties": starting with the next film his brief covering gradually lengthened into regular shorts.

†Most of the Sol Lesser films were released through RKO Studios.

the profits.* That is where ERB, Inc. took off in catastrophic figures—catastrophic to the extent that it invaded the earning power of distributor and producer. Burroughs' deal with M-G-M, I believe, called for an outright sale per film which averaged between $25,000 and $50,000.⁸

After Metro made its second film and discovered there was gold in the jungle — although each of the productions cost more than $1,000,000 — they negotiated with Lesser to buy three of his five story rights. Subsequently Lesser acquired from M-G-M the unfinished portion of Weissmuller's contract.

Joan Burroughs remembered:

Dad found it hard to reconcile himself to the movie versions of the Tarzan stories, and never did understand the movie Tarzan. He wanted Tarzan to speak like an educated Englishman instead of grunting. One time we saw a movie together and after it was all over, although the audience seemed enthusiastic, my father remained in his seat and kept shaking his head, sadly.⁹

Lesser said:

As far as I know Ed liked the Tarzan pictures.... At least, he always seemed delighted and often expressed his amazement at the ingeniousness of the writers assigned to these movies.¹⁰

The Lesser productions were stingy with the vocabulary they gave Tarzan, usually limiting his speech to no more than 100 to 150 words.

Tarzan is an international character† and about 75 per cent of the film grosses came from foreign countries during the period when I was producing these films. Their demands were for action, not words. Too much dialogue would only serve to slow up a Tarzan picture and weaken its strongest appeal to the foreign theatregoer — the universal understanding of action and pantomime.¹¹

Tarzan was considered an important propaganda weapon by our government and a message to this effect was made known to Lesser.

It was during the early part of World War II and the State Department was *most* anxious to see that there was no material in a Tarzan film that was inimicable to the best interests of democracy. The department made it clear to me that there was no greater potential vehicle that could reach the minds of people with a message than that contained in a Tarzan picture.¹²

Lesser, thereupon, based an entire film on that principle. In *Tarzan Triumphs*, the ape-man starts out playing the supreme isolationist. (The film was released in January 1943, with Johnny Weissmuller as the ape-man and Frances Gifford as a desert princess. Johnny Sheffield played Boy.)

Tarzan was the epitome of what the American mind was at that time, and when the Nazis came into the jungle and Tarzan was asked to help he merely said, "Nazis go way." The princess, in the story, replied something to the effect that "you don't know the Nazis. Once they conquer us, they'll despoil everything you stand for." After a while, they did. Tarzan seemed to get the message, for he came through with this one line: "Now Tarzan make war." The audience literally got on its feet and cheered.¹³

Tarzan Triumphs was Lesser's biggest earner and he said that it realized ERB, Inc. "more than a quarter of a million dollars."

But thereafter each one of my Tarzan pictures made less and less money — although

---

*Lesser estimated that the sixteen Tarzan films which he produced paid ERB, Inc. between $2,500,000 and $3,000,000.
†A Chinese film, *Adventures of Chinese Tarzan*, appeared in 1940.

they all realized a profit. Sometimes it was because of increasing costs; other times because of world conditions. The total gross of the Tarzan films is hard to calculate.* One picture often played four and five times in the same theatre, and Tarzan films were shown in Arab village tent theatres, African bush theatres and in pampa settlements down Argentine way.[14]

---

*Figures from the Sol Lesser office indicate that since 1918 Tarzan films may have grossed more than $500 million and been seen by more than two billion people.

XIX

On Location in Africa 1933–1934

> *When I was a little girl I saw Rudolph Valentino on the screen; and, ah, brothers, sheiks was sheiks in them days!*
> Tarzan and the Lion Man, *1933*

1. THE REAL THING

What Ed Burroughs thought of the morals of Hollywood was evident in his story *The Girl from Hollywood* (see Chapter XII), which first appeared in 1922. Eleven years later, with publication of *Tarzan and the Lion Man*,* the author saw fit to express his thoughts about jungle film-making. The cover blurb (presumably written by the author, as the book was published by ERB, Inc.) read:

> We have assiduously sought to avoid exaggeration in describing the books we have published. We have never said, "This is the greatest novel ever written by Edgar Rice Burroughs," although we came darn near slipping up on the jacket of the first book

---

*First published in *Liberty Magazine* in nine parts, beginning November 11, 1933; as a novel, September 1, 1934.

that appeared under our imprint, *Tarzan the Invincible*.*

To make amends for that, we are going to tell you that Mr. Burroughs believes this to be the poorest Tarzan novel he has ever written.

At that point however there is a difference of opinion. The editors of LIBERTY† magazine say it is the greatest, and thousands of their readers agree with them. Now what is your opinion?

ERB might have figured he knew something of movie-making when the idea came to him for *Tarzan and the Lion Man*. After all — hadn't ten Tarzan thrillers already been produced, including two talkies, *Tarzan the Ape-Man* and *Tarzan the Fearless*? In addition, Buster Crabbe had starred for Paramount in a Tarzan carbon copy, *King of the Jungle* (1933), and there was the classic *Trader Horn*. So these films are fresh in his mind as the cast of characters step into the clearing:

Milton Smith	production chief of BO (*sic*) Studio.
Tom Orman	veteran director with drinking problem.
Major White	big-game hunter and technical advisor.
Stanley Obroski	the "lion man" — a champion marathoner.
Naomi‡ Madison	female lead — obnoxious Hollywood star.
Gordon Z. Marcus	her father, a white trader.
Rhonda Terry	Naomi's double and a peach of a kid.
Bill West	chief cameraman, in love with Rhonda.
Pat O'Grady	assistant director.

The story moves swiftly — but only physically, as cast and crew journey from Hollywood to their African location, assured by BO's production chief that the film is "bound to be a knockout; no synthetic jungle, no faked sound effects, no toothless old lions.... This will be the real thing."

It is. The Hollywood group is ambushed by natives, Major White is killed, Orman accepts the blame and swears off drinking, two of the Arab guides kidnap Naomi and Rhonda with plans to sell them to the highest bidder, Stanley is captured by a tribe of cannibals and Tom Orman and Bill West hightail it after the girls. Considering their plight, the girls are plucky:

"I'm as about as cheerful as a Baby Star whose option hasn't been renewed."
"They must have paved this saddle with bricks."
"The black sultan that gets me is goin' to be out of luck."

Then Naomi has a change of heart and says to Rhonda:

"I don't see how you can be so decent to me. I used to treat you so rotten. I acted like

---

*Burroughs did slip. On the jacket of *Tarzan the Invincible*, the first novel to be published by ERB, Inc. (November, 1931), the cover blurb read: "And when you have turned the last page you will say that this is the greatest Tarzan story that Edgar Rice Burroughs ever wrote."

†The editors of *Liberty* said: "Here he is — Tarzan. His fame is world-wide. He appears in *Liberty* for the first time in the greatest of all his stories. Thrills, drama, comedy, romance — all the mystery and lure of the jungle that have made him as well known as Sherlock Holmes.... *Liberty* has yielded to a persistent demand of popular appeal, and whether you have or haven't met Tarzan before, you will be surprised and gripped by the startling chain of circumstances that carry this novel to a dramatic conclusion" (November 11, 1933).

‡"Naomi," Queen of the Cinema, sounds remarkably similar to "Nemone," Burroughs' "Queen of Cathne" in *Tarzan and the City of Gold*.

a dirty little cat.... I just want you to know—that's all."

Does Rhonda forgive the star?

"I understand. It's Hollywood—we all try to be something we're not, and most of us succeed in being something we ought not to be."

Meanwhile, Tarzan appears in the nick of time to save Stanley, the "lion man," from being cooked for dinner. Amazing—the two bear an uncanny resemblance to each other (another look-alike was the Spaniard Esteban Miranda of *Tarzan and the Golden Lion* and *Tarzan and the Ant Men*). Rhonda manages to escape from her Arab captors, but she is soon taken by gorillas who speak English, live in buildings with towers and ramparts, till fields and bear names like "Cardinal Wolsey," the "Duke of Buckingham" and "Henry the Eighth." The reader also gets to meet God:

> It had the face of a man, but its skin was black like that of a gorilla. Its grinning lips revealed the heavy fangs of the anthropoid. Scant black hair covered those portions of its body that an open shirt and loin cloth revealed. The skin of the body, arms and legs was black with large patches of white. The bare feet were the feet of a man; the hands were black and hairy and wrinkled, with long, curved claws; the eyes were the sunken eyes of an old man—a very old man....
> "I am God!" it cried.

God explains that after he was graduated from Oxford in 1855 he was traveling in Austria and met a priest "who was working along lines similar to mine."

> His name was Mendel* ... we exchanged ideas. He was the only man in the world who could appreciate me, but he could not go all the way with me.

God tells Tarzan and Rhonda that he has learned to control heredity through the transfer of genes from one individual to another. He succeeded in gaining access to the tombs in Westminster Abbey and "from the corpses of former kings and queens of England and many a noble lord and lady I extracted the deathless genes." He then shot the gorillas with anesthetized arrows, removed their "germ cells" and substituted the "human cells" which he had brought from England:

> ...I taught [the gorillas] agriculture, architecture, and building, among other things. Under my direction they built this city, which I named London, upon the river that I have called Thames. We English always take England wherever we go....
> With the body cells from you two I shall not only insure my youth but I shall again take on the semblance of man.

Enter Balza: ("Golden Girl" in the language of the great apes)

> Swinging downward toward them with the speed and agility of a monkey was a naked white girl, her golden hair streaming out behind her. From between her perfect lips issued the horrid screams of a beast.

Balza, who speaks English, is not one of the gorilla god's "children." In fact, she used to live in "London" before "they drove me out because I was not like them. My mother kept me hidden for years, but at last they found me out. They would have killed me had I remained."†

---

*Gregor Johann Mendel (1822–84), an Austrian monk and botanist, is considered the father of modern genetics. Experimenting with the common variety of garden peas, he discovered and formulated the principles of hereditary phenomena.
†ERB—in a rare departure from tying together all loose ends—does not explain why Balza was never like "them," why she was kept hidden for years by her mother, and why she would have been killed had she remained in "London." Burroughs also leaves God up in the air; in his final appearance, "The gorilla god breathed a sigh of relief when [Tarzan] had departed."

Tarzan (doubling for Stanley Obroski, who later succumbs to fever) escorts Rhonda and Balza back to camp. Rhonda is wondering about Balza, who is still running about nude.

Of course we're all from Hollywood, but don't you think we ought to rig up some sort of skirt for Balza before we take her into camp?

Tarzan merely laughs at Rhonda's suggestion and says that Balza should "be allowed to keep her naturalness and her purity of mind as long as she may."

Everyone [back at the camp] was staring at Balza with open admiration, Orman with the eye of a director discovering a type, Pat O'Grady with the eye of an assistant director — which is something else again.

The ape-man tells Balza to return to civilization:

Balza, go with these shes. Do as they tell you. They will cover your beautiful body with uncomfortable clothing, but you will have to wear it. In a month you will be smoking cigarettes and drinking highballs; then you will be civilized.... Go with them and be unhappy.

The film is completed and after one year Tarzan decides to see for himself what Hollywood is all about. Upon his arrival in Los Angeles, a huge crowd is at the railroad station awaiting the arrival of a celebrity. "A slip of a girl with green hair alighted ... instantly she as engulfed by reporters ... she stepped to the microphone":

"Hello, everybody! I wish you were all here. It's simply mahvelous. I'm so happy to be back in Hollywood."

Yes, it's BO's beautiful new star — the glorious Balza!
Tarzan, as John Clayton, lunches at the Brown Derby, and is alert to the fact that "each was trying to out-do the others in attracting attention to himself." He attends the premiere at Grauman's Chinese Theatre, where Balza again speaks to her audience:

"Hello, everybody! I wish you were all here. It's simply mahvelous. I'm so happy to be back in Hollywood."

Then Tarzan and two others crash a Hollywood party (Tarzan thought they were coming as guests). It's in the Hollywood Hills and there is a wild scene with booze flowing and someone chasing after the wife of the host. The ape-man is introduced to a producer, after which he "tests" for the role of Tarzan! The production manager decides he is not the right type and Cyril Wayne, a famous adagio dancer, is signed for the role. "John Clayton" is offered a bit part and he accepts. As they are shooting, the lion breaks away and menaces the cast. The play Tarzan runs for his life while the real Tarzan, John Clayton, Lord of the Jungle, leaps onto the back of the charging beast and overcomes him.

An excited man rushed onto the set. It was Benny Goldeen, the production manager.
"My God! ... You've killed our best lion. He was worth ten thousand dollars if he was worth a cent. You're fired!"
The clerk at The Roosevelt looked up. "Leaving us, Mr. Clayton.... I hope you have enjoyed Hollywood."
"Very much indeed, but ... what is the shortest route to Africa."

(So, dear readers, what is your opinion? Do you go along with Mr. Burroughs, who believed *Tarzan and the Lion Man* the poorest Tarzan novel he ever had written — up to and including 1934 — or do you stand with the editors of *Liberty* — and thousands of their readers — who agreed it was the greatest?)

XX

New Adventures 1934–1938

> ...It is not so much peace and security that I want as freedom. You know, all my life I have been a prisoner.... Perhaps you can imagine then how much I want freedom, no matter how many dangers I have to take along with it. It seems the most wonderful thing in the world.
> Tarzan the Magnificent, *1939*

1. FICTION AND OTHERWISE

Filmed in Guatemala towards the end of 1934 and the early months of 1935 was the Burroughs-Tarzan Enterprise production of *The New Adventures of Tarzan*.* Starring Herman Brix (personally selected by Burroughs) as Tarzan and featuring Ula Holt as Ula Dale, it proved to be a mediocre story and ended up a mediocre film. A review said, in part, "Film handicapped

---

*A serial was released simultaneously with the feature film. The first two chapters of the 12-episode serial was a résumé of what had happened in the 71-minute feature. *Tarzan and the Green Goddess*, released in May 1938, was a 72-minute feature taken from the last chapters of the serial.

here by serial story tempo, acting, plot development and direction. Whole sequences in which hardly a word is spoken. Maybe that's for the best since the dialogue is pretty corny."[1] Production manager of Burroughs' independent production was Ashton Dearholt, a silent-screen actor who became associated in business with ERB in the summer of 1935, after having been acquainted several years beforehand.

The new enterprise had another plot going simultaneously with the film. Principals were Burroughs, his wife Emma, Dearholt, his wife Florence, and a strong supporting cast led by Joan Burroughs Pierce.

Florence Dearholt said:

> My family in Chicago were friends of both the Burroughs and the Hulberts, and it was natural that I look them up in California. He had left his wife before our meeting — it was one of the "depressions" he was fighting ... but he enjoyed his kids.[2]

Joan Burroughs recalled:

> Florence and I became very good friends, and she was over at our house frequently ... which made what happened worse for everyone concerned.[3]

What happened was that on March 30, 1934, Florence filed divorce proceedings against her husband, Ashton Dearholt. Shortly thereafter Dearholt, who had been named production manager of Burroughs' new film company, left for Guatemala, to spend the next several months making *Tarzan in Guatemala* (later released as *The New Adventures of Tarzan*). On December 4, the following appeared in the newspaper: "It is understood that Emma Burroughs will name a woman correspondent in the divorce action — which she files today."[4]

December 5: "A divorce suit charging his wife with extreme cruelty was filed in Las Vegas today by Edgar Rice Burroughs, author of the Tarzan books. Mr. Burroughs, who lives near Hollywood, came here six weeks ago, ostensibly to collect fiction material. At that time he denied he was establishing residence with the idea of divorce. Counsel by Mrs. Emma Hulbert Burroughs said in Los Angeles after the suit was filed that she would not contest the case and that a property settlement, understood to be several hundred thousand dollars, had been arranged."[5]

December 6: "Edgar Rice Burroughs divorced his wife of 34 years standing in Las Vegas. She did not contest the suit. A property settlement was arranged, giving her half of the estate, estimated at several hundred thousands of dollars."[6]

December 12: "Mrs. Florence Gilbert Dearholt (who has an interlocutory divorce from her husband, a production manager) said: 'I am still married and I think it would be highly unbecoming for me to announce my engagement until my divorce is final, March 30, 1935. I regret the whole matter has been brought up but as long as it has I won't deny that I might marry Mr. Burroughs. I want to make it clear, however, that we did not seek our divorces in the same year with the intention of marrying. That was a coincidence.'"*[7]

Joan Burroughs recalled:

---

*More a coincidence: Florence Gilbert's first picture, *The Desert's Price* (1926), starring Buck Jones, was directed by the same W. S. Van Dyke who did *Tarzan the Ape Man* in 1932. Of her performance, a reviewer in *Variety* said: "Florence Gilbert as the Starke girl is new to this reviewer and, if new to pix, looks like a pretty miss who'll go a long way before long...." In the same year, Florence appeared in *Johnstown Flood*: "George O'Brien is good but Janet Gaynor, a newcomer and a corker, wins the lion's share of everything. Florence Gilbert is pretty in all her scenes."

We all tried to talk Dad out of the divorce, but he was stubborn and wouldn't be talked out of it. It was obvious why she married Dad — after all, they were thirty years apart....[8]

Mrs. Jensen:

Mr. Burroughs hated the thought of growing old and always surrounded himself with young friends....[9]

Florence:

Ed was the life of every party.... he seemed ageless, and the fact that he was almost thirty years older than I never bothered me nor did it interfere in our pursuits. He never seemed his age.[10]

Meanwhile, reporters were trying to track down rumors of the "impending wedding."

March 28: "I called ERB tonight [Thursday] at Mrs. Dearholt's home, Hempstead 2579, and he sounded a little drunk and asked me to quit disturbing his sleep. He said he didn't know when and where they would be married. This probably means this will be done at the Yuma or some other out-of-state marriage license bureau at the crack of dawn tomorrow, the first day they are eligible to be married, I understand. We'd better check this date to be certain. Her decree is due to be final on it.

"They're both hard to get hold of late. They leave their homes and offices before I get down there at three and I have been trying unsuccessfully for a week to reach them. Somebody should check them early today. He refused to make an appointment. I asked to speak to her and he said she wasn't there."[11]

March 29: "ERB was not at home at Mrs. Dearholt's house, 1446 Queen Road ... Hempstead 2579. The garage was empty and there were no servants at home. Made three stops at different times to make certain.

Learned that Mrs. D. moved on March 20 to 806 North Rodeo Drive, Beverly Hills. Did not learn phone number. Learned from butler that Burroughs generally spends evenings there, has dinner with Mrs. D. around 6:30. Then he returns to Queens Road place.

"Also discovered that they have a big party planned for Sunday at Beverly Hills place. Maybe they plan to be married tomorrow, Saturday, and celebrate Sunday.

"Gardener, who also acts as chauffeur tipped us he was to be on duty early tomorrow, Saturday.

"Mrs. D. was there this afternoon having a luncheon for a gang of women and wouldn't see us because she was 'too busy at time.'"[12]

It was a good job of sleuthing by the reporters — but this was no *ordinary* person with whom they were dealing. The passing years had witnessed slight diminution of the mighty powers that had made him the invincible Lord of the Jungle — this was Tarzan, son of Kala the she-ape, and the Times men were forced to whisper "ka-goda"* as Burroughs and Florence glided swiftly and silently out of sight. They were married in Las Vegas on Thursday, April 4, 1935, by Judge William E. Orr (the same judge who had granted ERB his divorce four months previously), and on the sixth, the couple sailed aboard the Matson liner *Lurline* for a forty-day Hawaiian honeymoon.

Mrs. Jensen recalled:

Mr. Burroughs was penny-wise and pound-foolish" in many things he did. For instance, he brought back paper clips from Hawaii and instructed me to use them — although they were rusted from the sea voyage.

---

*"I surrender" in Burroughs' ape language.

I kept them on my desk and discarded a handful every day. On the other hand, he spent money in large amounts and he gave substantial loans to friends.[13]

Ed and Florence returned to live in Beverly Hills, where they were popular hosts to frequent parties—providing an ample amount of proper party ingredients: entertainment, food and drinks.

Florence recalled:

Ed loved to entertain and give parties even though he realized that people came not because he was Edgar Rice Burroughs but because there always was plenty to eat and drink. At these parties he kept urging me to have another and another—as if I had to catch up with him. He never seemed to care what his friends thought or did. This didn't seem important. He was interested only for the moment and that was all. Ed never trusted many people but he had several large personal loans outstanding—some for ten thousand dollars. After we were married, he told me that he didn't have a great deal of money—that it was all in the corporation. He must have spent tremendous sums for his family. After his divorce, Emma got a good settlement, I know, and the kids always had everything they wanted.[14]

Joan Burroughs:

Dad was a free enough spender when it came to dishing out for the family. He always seemed to anticipate our desires and it was rare when any of us had to ask for anything—even a car.[15]

Ralph Rothmund recalled:

Burroughs trusted his friends too much and he went wild on occasions ... like the time he went out and bought two huge "land yachts"—even equipping them with electric brakes, which was a tremendous added expense. They cost ten thousand dollars and he only used them for one trip—to Oregon. (The second trailer was stuffed with servants and commissary supplies.) I got rid of them several years later. One, I managed to sell for fifteen dollars and the other I just had to give away during the depression. Later, I had to put a tight rein on his spending. He was a great one for detail—he indexed and cross-indexed everything. He wasn't a great businessman but had a great asset in that he was very honest, and considered that a foremost quality. If he ever discovered that someone had lied to him—no matter how insignificant the matter—it was the end of that particular relationship.[16]

Mrs. Jensen recalled:

The corporation was having a hard time financially, in the late thirties. Business was not good and everything seemed to be going downhill. Mrs. Burroughs was getting a personal allowance of several thousand dollars a month and the parties they were hosting cost a lot more. Finally, toward the end of 1939, Mr. Rothmund "ordered" them to Hawaii, with the idea that it would be less expensive. It really wasn't until the mid-forties that the corporation started to come back, financially.[17]

The author's production in 1936–37 was at an all-time low. His writing consisted of three Tarzan stories, one in the Venus series and a fourth published only in magazine format.* M-G-M's third Weissmuller-O'Sullivan film, *Tarzan Escapes*, released in November 1936, proved to be a dud and elicited such comments as: "While at first the sight of Tarzan doing everything but playing pinochle with his beast pals was a novelty, it's all rather silly now. Derisive laughter greeted the picture too often at the Capitol [New York] and it probably will run into similar difficulty most everywhere...."[18]

Ed sold his ranch to the Rateree Land

**Tarzan and the Magic Men*, *Tarzan and the Elephant Men* (combined in the novel, *Tarzan the Magnificent*); *Tarzan and the Forbidden City*, *Carson of Venus*, and a magazine story, *The Resurrection of Jimber-Jaw*.

Company for thirty thousand dollars, and on August 20, 1938, with Florence, he sailed again to Hawaii. Interviewed upon his arrival, the author confessed he would like to cast Tarzan in a Hawaiian or another setting but he said his public would not stand for it. "They don't want him different."[19]

XXI

Monkey Business 1935–1950

=====

...while those who work hard and accumulate property have only their labor for their effort, since the government takes all from them in taxes.
Tarzan and the Ant Men, 1924

1. THE DEPRESSION

Ed and Florence returned from their Hawaiian honeymoon at the end of May 1935, and several days later came a letter from an old friend from whom Ed had received no news (and no checks) for some time: Joseph Bray, president of A. C. McClurg:

Joseph Bray to ERB
June 10, 1935

It is a long time since I wrote you, and I hope you are well and happy.

My immediate reason for writing is, I wrote Grosset & Dunlap several days ago asking whether all the plates they had on hand belonging to us were likely to be used for further printings. These are *The Moon Maid* and *The Mad King*. I am wondering whether you would care to purchase these plates from us. There is nothing, as far as I can see, that we can do with these books, but your corporation is very ingenious, and might possibly be interested....

The book business is pretty dull at present. It was the last, I believe, to be affected by the depression [and] will be the last to improve. I am glad to say there has been, during the past year-and-a-half, a distinctly upward tendency. As a matter of fact, however, we were down so low that we could not possibly go any lower....

Some of the financial prophets are predicting an upward tendency in business for 1936. I cannot persuade myself that this is profitable.... It will be a campaign year, and the next campaign* is going to be one which may leave its scars upon this country. It will be one of demagogy, in my opinion, and this share-the-wealth cry, which is a favorite idea of the present regime at Washington, is likely to raise hell.

Ed replied that he was well and happy and he hoped his old friend was wrong in his prophecy of little improvement in business conditions—especially in the book trade. Ed disclosed that with two radio programs going, Burroughs, Inc. was netting more than from the sale of all their books, and perhaps this was the new way people were taking their fiction.

Joseph Bray to ERB

June 20, 1935

I was very glad to get your letter. I did not know that there were many happy people in this greatly disturbed world. Most of us are wondering (and perhaps worrying just a little bit) what the Communist regime to which we are hastening will do to us.

As near as I can gather, if we make any money it will be taken from us, and punished, perhaps, for not having more. It seems to be assumed that practically all business men, with the exception of good Democrats, are crooks.†

I am very much inclined to think that next year is going to be a very trying period in the history of this land of the free. We are going to have demagogues roaring all over the place. Demagogues are pretty cunning. They realize that the way to get support of the crowd is to promise anything if it serves to secure votes. I am told that the average voter has good sense. Maybe he has, but he certainly conceals it.

To return to business. If you should buy the plates of the two books (*The Moon Maid* and *The Mad King*),‡ I do not think that you could do anything with the plates at this time.... The plates are listed in our inventory at $50.00 each ... supposed to represent their earning power....

Burroughs then suggested that inasmuch as McClurg had already been able to charge off the cost of the plates several times over, they might consider just "giving them to us."

Joseph Bray to ERB

June 28, 1935

Yes, you can have the plates, binding dies, and all other manufacturing paraphernalia of the two books ... together with all rights ... for $100.000 F.O.B. New York. You say you had a pain, and yet you tell me you are still happy.§ Evidently I don't know much about you, Ed, because most people that I have met, when they have a pain, are decidedly unhappy. As a sale this is a loss of course, but we have become so accustomed to losses that an extra one or two does not count so much....

---

*In one of the most bitter presidential campaigns ever seen in this country—with the Republicans attacking Roosevelt's New Deal reforms and "planned economy"—FDR won a smashing second-term victory over GOP candidate Governor Alfred M. Landon of Kansas by carrying every state but Maine and Vermont. (The election also made a mockery of the so-called power of the press: 75–80 per cent of the newspapers favored Landon.)

†No doubt referring to the New Deal reforms of Franklin Delano Roosevelt and the upcoming (1936) election; also referring to the 1935 "Soak the Rich" Revenue Act then before Congress which would levy heavier taxes on the wealthy, on large inheritances and on corporation incomes. (Congress passed the tax bill in August.)

‡Both novels were published by McClurg in 1926.

§Probably referring to Burroughs' divorce and remarriage.

In the same month, McClurg's agent in Europe, Curtis Brown Ltd., with home office in London, advised that Methuen (original Tarzan publisher in England) was contemplating the reissue of several Tarzan titles at 2/6d net, with an offer of 2¼d per copy to McClurg. This no doubt prompted Bray to write to ERB on July 22: "I don't believe we care to dispose of the Tarzan books at this time."

The confusion was starting: Methuen, the original English publisher of the Burroughs' titles, had begun to reprint Tarzan and non–Tarzan titles both in half-crown and shilling editions. While most of these titles were controlled by ERB, Inc., others were held by McClurg. Curtis Brown Ltd. suggested that since the mix-up in royalty payment seemed to rest on a genuine mistake on Methuen's part, that McClurg allow the English publisher to carry on in the present form, with royalties of five cents on the half-crown edition and one cent on shilling novels. McClurg accepted.

Bray wrote another letter to ERB, in which he announced that he had moved up to chairman of the board, preparatory to retiring:

Joseph Bray to ERB
July 22, 1935

...I am getting pretty old, Ed, seventy-three in the Fall, and while I think my head is just as good as it ever was, the physical part of me is waning all the time. There is nothing for you to worry about. The same ideals which General McClurg ingrafted onto the firm will be retained. The institution will stand as it has always stood, for honorable dealing, truth and integrity.... I don't believe we care to dispose of the Tarzan books at this time. As far as I know, they are all in print.

Again, in 1938, upon his return from a Hawaiian vacation, Burroughs took up the matter of his obtaining rights and plates of the non–Tarzan books which were out of print and "evidently as dead as a doornail." Ed suggested to McClurg's that because they had realized many more thousands of dollars on the stories than they had anticipated (making, he said, such an excellent profit), they could easily afford to turn back all rights instead of his paying fifty dollars per title for same.

McClurg checked with their reprint house, Grosset & Dunlap,* and the two firms agreed that there was not likely to be any more demand for the two titles in question. On April 11, 1939, for the sum of eight hundred dollars, ERB, Inc. regained all rights (plus text and wrapper plates, dies, binding stamps and illustrations) to these sixteen titles:

The Eternal Lover	*At the Earth's Core*
A Princess of Mars	*The War Chief*
The Gods of Mars	*The Cave Girl*
The Warlord of Mars	*The Outlaw of Torn*
	The Monster Men
The Chessmen of Mars	*Thuvia, Maid of Mars*
The Master Mind of Mars	*The Bandit of Hell's Bend*
The Mucker	*Pellucidar*
The Land that Time Forgot	

2. Rothmund

It was about this time (March 1939) that Ralph Rothmund, a rather dour Scotsman with a penchant for business

---

*McClurg had been nothing more than a middle man since 1929, when it last published a Burroughs book under its own name. However, the Chicago firm retained rights to the titles it originally published and therefore was able to make its own deals with reprint houses. McClurg and Grosset & Dunlap enjoyed a harmonious relationship for more than thirty years in reprinting the works of ERB.

anonymity—after "ordering" Burroughs and his new bride to Hawaii in an economy move*—assumed control of the Jungle empire. He was outranked in corporate hierarchy by Joan, Hulbert and Jack Burroughs, aged thirty-one, thirty and twenty-six respectively, but he was oldest from point of service and had been handling the day-to-day business for twelve years.

Rothmund recalled:

> We first met in May of 1927 when I was already a resident of the San Fernando Valley. Burroughs advertised for a secretary and I applied, thinking it was the Burroughs Business Machine company. I talked to Mr. Burroughs and he said that he would let me know about the job. About one week later he pulled up to my house in a big, open Packard. I was up on a ladder, painting, and he yelled: "How soon can you come to work?"[1]

If there was one characteristic of Rothmund's which did not endear him to eastern publishers (and, as well, to foreign publishers interested in reprint rights), it was that Rothmund either was negative to their proposals or simply ignored their letters.

In 1940, Grosset & Dunlap first suggested to McClurg that they issue the Tarzan books in their new Madison Square fifty-cent edition. McClurg passed the proposal on to Rothmund but nothing ever came of it. In February 1942—two months after Pearl Harbor†—Grosset made another attempt. Their Madison Square lines were booming, but the Tarzan books had been in a steady decline. (Grosset & Dunlap's 1942 catalog failed to show a single Tarzan title for the first time since before 1918). Now, Grosset was willing to guarantee a cash advance and suggested *Tarzan of the Apes* as a starter. McClurg immediately passed along the offer. When no answer was forthcoming after nearly eight months, a second letter was dispatched to Tarzana.

Again, there was no action from ERB, Inc. E. C. Ketcham, secretary and one of the directors of Grosset & Dunlap, mailed McClurg a memorandum to the effect that the plates for the Tarzan books had not been used since June 1939 and (under government orders) might have to be melted down for the war effort. This Chicago firm tried once more ... waited another month and then dispatched a telegram to Rothmund: "Grosset shortly required by Government destroy plates Tarzan books unless reprinted. Must have word from you relative to our proposals." This struck home! Which titles, Rothmund asked, did Grosset & Dunlap propose publishing? McClurg replied: the first eleven Tarzan titles (to which they owned publishing rights).

Now, a very shrewd counter-proposal was made: ERB, Inc. would accept Grosset & Dunlap's proposition to reprint fifty thousand copies of each of the eleven Tarzan titles *if* McClurg would relinquish their rights, including the manufacturing plates, to Burroughs without the corporation having to pay anything for them.

McClurg would *not* relinquish the rights at this time but the deal, after several more exchanges of letters, went through in April with Grosset & Dunlap contracting to publish 50,000 each of eleven Tarzan titles (550,000 assorted). Time limit on the contract was for three years.

---

*Another illustration of Rothmund's economy: ERB, who personally handled all business correspondence until the spring of 1939, used a heavy-weight, high rag content gray stationery with engraved lettering; Rothmund, an inexpensive, light-weight, printed white stock.

†ERB was living in Hawaii and had been there during the Pearl Harbor raid (December 7, 1941). Florence Burroughs was back in California to obtain a divorce.

In 1944, ERB, Inc. gave permission to the Armed Services Editions, Inc. to publish three Tarzan books for distribution exclusively to the American armed forces overseas (these were distributed free to libraries, hospitals, etc.). The titles were *Tarzan of the Apes*, 106,722; *Return of Tarzan*, 126,275; *Son of Tarzan*, 5,000. The rights to these titles, however, belonged to McClurg and after an inquiry to the publisher (which had not been consulted in the transaction), Rothmund suggested they split the royalty fifty-fifty.

3. To Each His Title

The next order of business took fully three years to be resolved. In February 1945 McClurg and Grosset & Dunlap discussed the possibility of a low-priced (49 cents) edition of those Tarzan titles in which the Chicago firm held the interest. However, ERB, Inc. had the right of approval on all price changes and the corporation preferred to continue releasing its own Tarzan titles* in original editions at two dollars, with reprints at one dollar. Their thinking was that a lower selling price than one dollar would harm the sale of the original edition two-dollar books; meanwhile, if McClurg would want to include *their* eleven† Tarzan titles in the Burroughs dollar reprint editions, this could be a happy arrangement. Then Rothmund struck a solid note when he said that if the prices could be held at two dollars for original editions and one dollar for reprints, it might be advantageous to consider a cheap edition to sell for twenty-five cents.

McClurg and Grosset & Dunlap now were applying pressure on Burroughs, Inc. to the tune of a substantial royalty payment (if Rothmund would approve printing the eleven Tarzan titles in Grosset & Dunlap's Madison Square 49¢ retail edition) but Rothmund was too canny to take the bait. Business was improving and the company was selling off some of its extensive real estate holdings in the San Fernando Valley, so there was no immediate press for cash.

Ed Burroughs had been home from the wars for six months but it is not clear how much of an active role he was taking in the current negotiations. All corporation correspondence was signed by Ralph Rothmund, and he took the long-distance telephone calls as well. Regardless, Burroughs, Inc. was still negative to the McClurg–Grosset & Dunlap proposition. McClurg continued pressing Rothmund and continued to get nowhere — through January, February and on to July.

On July 24, McClurg suggested to Grosset: "If you wish us to proceed on the Bantam Books independently of Grosset & Dunlap reprints on the basis of the $5,000 advance ... believe in this case Burroughs will sign. Up to this time I have indicated to Burroughs that you were unwilling to make a Bantam agreement independently...." Grosset & Dunlap concurred and on September 4, in anticipation of Burroughs' okay, McClurg entered into a contract agreement with Bantam for publication of a 25-cent reprint of *Tarzan of the Apes*. Terms of the agreement‡ were airmailed to Rothmund on the 10th. On the 21st, the word came from Tarzana: *No!*

---

*Which started with *Tarzan and the Lost Empire*, published in September 1929.

†The eleven Tarzan titles originally published by McClurg were the most popular of the ape-man series, giving the Chicago publisher a decided advantage in wheeling and dealing with Burroughs, Inc.

‡On Bantam's part, the agreement was signed by its president, Ian Ballantine, who was more successful in 1962 when an agreement was signed with Burroughs, Inc. for publication of the complete Tarzan series, plus other titles, in Ballantine's fifty-cent paperback editions.

The Bantam deal never was negotiated, and when it came to the offer of McClurg and Grosset to reprint the Tarzan books for less than one dollar, Burroughs, Inc. would not budge from its unyielding stand which it had maintained for three years. Grosset & Dunlap, meanwhile, was running out of Tarzan titles. They had listed none at all in 1946 and only three titles in 1947, the last of their Madison Square line—*Jungle Tales of Tarzan, Tarzan the Untamed, Tarzan and the Jewels of Opar*. One year later, McClurg tried again—passing along Grosset & Dunlap's offer regarding possible reprinting of the Tarzan books at a $1.00 retail price.

> *McClurg to Rothmund*
> November 24, 1947
>
> For some months we have been talking and corresponding with Grosset & Dunlap, regarding possible reprinting of the Tarzan books on $1.00 retail basis. Now, for the first time, we have an offer to proceed with 5,000 copies of each of three titles as a test to see if the public will accept them on this retail price basis.... Your share of the royalty would be 5¢ per copy. Grosset & Dunlap are reserving an allotment of paper and printing facilities until we can advise them.... Please wire us your approval....

When no immediate reply was received, McClurg wrote again on December 8, "thinking our letter of November 24 may have gone astray." This was followed up by a hurried phone call after McClurg had been tipped by Grosset & Dunlap that Burroughs, Inc. was planning to reprint its own one-dollar series.

Grosset & Dunlap was right about ERB's plans to reprint the later titles.* They would publish themselves, beginning in March, ten Tarzan titles, nine Martian titles and three Venus titles. Rothmund's reasoning (certainly sound) was that the list of Burroughs books was getting too unwieldy, that the trade would stock only a few of each series, that if only the Tarzan titles were published as reprints, it would tend to kill ERB's other series of stories, and that there was little enough profit in other than the Tarzan series.

A counter-move was called for and there was little time to spare. After McClurg heard that Burroughs, Inc. had "finally decided" to publish themselves, the Chicago book wholesaler — still undecided if this were a bluff or not — wrote to Grosset: "Don't know just how far Edgar Rice Burroughs, Inc. has gone in the way of making definite commitments for the newer Tarzan books...."

John O'Connor, Grosset & Dunlap president, made it his business to find out. As a result of his investigation, McClurg was told that Rothmund meant business. In fact, the new Burroughs books were actually in the process of manufacture— more than 160,000 books to retail at one dollar. Grosset & Dunlap suggested several alternatives to McClurg: because they had the best titles (the early ones) and because of their greater ability to blanket the trade, they could sit it out, or Grosset & Dunlap and McClurg could go ahead on the eight of the eleven titles that could be reprinted without Burroughs' permission (as long as the latter received the royalty payments called for in the original contracts). The sales staff of Grosset & Dunlap thought the Tarzan books would move well if they were

---

*McClurg and Grosset & Dunlap both may have been feeling too sorry for themselves. Grosset & Dunlap had been reprinting Burroughs' titles since 1918—thirty years—and naturally they were unhappy in foreseeing the end of a long and profitable relationship. McClurg, too, had been companion to the apeman and his friends for thirty-four years, and considering that their last original Tarzan book had been published in 1928, the trail had been most fruitful. McClurg and Burroughs shared equally all monies received from Grosset & Dunlap on the eleven Tarzan titles controlled by McClurg.

placed into their new series—Books for Boys and Girls—to sell for seventy-five cents or one dollar as a series for boys.

Grosset & Dunlap selected three titles with which to kick off their one-dollar Tarzan reprint: *Tarzan the Untamed*, *The Return of Tarzan* and *Tarzan, Lord of the Jungle*. The contract with McClurg, signed March 18, called for five thousand copies each of the three titles, with a May shipping date. Grosset & Dunlap's president anticipated that Burroughs and Rothmund would get the surprise of their lives. The new run would be on good quality, free sheet paper, with cloth (not paper) over board binding and with the jackets modernized. O'Connor also was convinced that his people would sell rings around the other sales force.

R. Kalivoda, vice president of McClurg & Co., left for California in mid–March to "beard Papa Tarzan in his den." Grosset & Dunlap suggested that Kalivoda should try to get general permission for McClurg to license dollar reprints on all titles that they controlled. From the San Fernando Valley, Kalivoda reported on his meeting to D. H. Sparks, president of McClurg:

Kalivoda to Sparks
March 31, 1948

Arrived here yesterday noon. Called on Mr. Rothmund where I received a rather chill reception. Rothmund talked to me briefly in the outer office, but wouldn't invite me to his private office. I asked about Mr. Burroughs; the answer was that he is very sick, bad heart, and couldn't be seen.

Rothmund said he talked to you several times on the phone and you understand their feelings…. He also was rather uncomplimentary about Mr. Bray.* Finally I persuaded Rothmund to have lunch with me today. After a few arguments and his insistence that a contract was a contract … he agreed to talk things over with Mr. Burroughs and let me know before I left…. Rothmund agreed to let me talk to Mr. Burroughs if he is not too weak. The outfit appears prosperous and I am sure a few thousand dollars royalties is no inducement…. I am keeping my fingers crossed until tomorrow.

Upon his return to Chicago, Kalivoda wrote Rothmund: "It is with some delight that I think back of the royal treatment I received from you and the pleasant hours you, Mr. Burroughs and myself spent during my third conference in your office…."

4. No Relations

From this point, relations only worsened between the "partners" of more than thirty years' standing.

Encouraged by Grosset & Dunlap and discouraged by ERB, Inc., McClurg entertained thoughts of returning the rights to their Tarzan titles to Burroughs (if the price were right), and so mentioned this possibility to Grosset. The latter immediately dispatched a long telegram to McClurg urging them to hold on in anticipation of greatly increased long-term sales. The Tarzan titles should be able to earn over ten thousand dollars annually in royalties year after year if properly developed, McClurg was told. Meanwhile Grosset & Dunlap requested permission to reprint *Tarzan and the Golden Lion* and *Tarzan the Terrible* in July to keep the campaign rolling.

It all appeared to be a game—with each of the three contestants applying pressure to gain maximum leverage. Grosset then decided the moment was propitious for a long and strong agreement and on May 20, 1949, entered into a five-year con-

---

*Joseph E. Bray, president of McClurg until his retirement in 1935.

tract with McClurg to publish eight Tarzan titles with a retail price between $1.00 and $1.49. Up to the time of Burroughs' death (March 19, 1950) the McClurg–Grosset & Dunlap team was publishing eight Tarzan titles; ERB, Inc. was publishing ten additional Tarzan titles, but neither was publishing the most popular Tarzan title, *Tarzan of the Apes*, or two other excellent titles: *The Beasts of Tarzan* and *The Son of Tarzan*. Monkey Business!

XXII

Search for the Fountain of Youth 1935–1937

> ...*If this was a sleep adventure, what then was reality? How was he to know the one from the other? How much of all that had happened in his life had been real and how much unreal? ... No, he did not know what was real and what was not....*
>
> Jungle Tales of Tarzan, *1916*

1. Post-Rancho Stories

Way back in 1922 (*The Girl from Hollywood*), Colonel Pennington, of wealth and good family, owner of the Rancho del Ganado, insisted that youth was a physical and mental attribute, independent of time: "If one could feel and act with the spirit of youth, one could not be old"—Ed Burroughs' philosophy in a nutshell.

In *Tarzan and the Lion Man*, we already have witnessed the figure of "God," who sought to bring back his youth by transplanting body cells of young gorillas into his own body. In *Tarzan's Quest*,* written in the "Post-Rancho" period im-

---

*First published in *Blue Book Magazine* in six parts, beginning October 1935.

161

mediately before and after the author's first divorce, it was now an all-out search for the tree of immortality. Jane is back in this story—the first time in eleven years*—and there is good reason for her return. How could the Jungle Lord assume immortality and leave his mate behind? In fiction, this would never do.

The story of *Tarzan's Quest* gets under way at the Savoy in London, where Lady Greystoke chances to run into several friends, one of whom is Kitty Krause, a wealthy widow, who is now married to someone young enough to be her son, Prince Alexis Sborov. Kitty and the prince have heard tell of a witch doctor in Africa who knows the secret of a formula for renewing youth and inducing longevity. This is not Jane's cup of tea but she is on her way back to the estate and it is agreed that they will drop her off at Nairobi.

Meanwhile, Tarzan is trying to track down a rumor to the effect that young native girls (between fourteen and twenty) seem to be vanishing into thin air. But it seems to be little more than a rumor until Buira, daughter of Muviro, chief of the Waziri, disappears. "Oh, Bwana," says Muviro, "your children need you." Will the big Bwana help his children? Of course he will.

The private plane, hired by Kitty and her prince, crashes in a storm. There are some lengthy passages of interplay among the occupants of the fallen plane (besides Jane, Kitty and the prince, there is Brown, a "gangster type," who is the pilot, Annette, the French maid, and Tibbs, the butler). Kitty is found dead, the prince tries to pin the blame on Brown, and then both Annette and Jane mysteriously disappear.

Jane is brought before the king and god of the Kavuru, a beautiful man with the divine face and figure of youth. How old is he? Maybe a thousand, maybe several hundred years, he has no way of knowing. Then he asks Jane if she believes in God. When she answers yes, he discloses his philosophy:

> ...There is no such thing—not yet, at least. That has been the trouble with the world. Men have imagined a god instead of seeking god among themselves. They have been led astray by false prophets and charlatans.... God should be a leader, and a leader should be a tangible entity—something men can see and feel and touch. He must be mortal and yet immortal.... Already I am deathless; already I am omniscient; already, to some extent, can I direct the minds and acts of men.

When Jane asks to be set free, the king tells her:

> You can serve the only purpose for which women are fit. Men may only attain godliness alone. Woman weakens and destroys him.... We are all celibates ... it would be death for [us] to succumb to the wiles of a woman.

The king reveals the secret of deathless youth.

> It lies in an elixir brewed of many things—the pollen of certain plants, the roots of others, the spinal fluid of leopards, and principally, the glands and blood of women—young women.

But then the king proves himself a mere mortal.

> I should like to keep you as you are. And why not? Am I not almost a God? And may not God do as he chooses?

Jane refuses the tempting offer of eternal youth and eternal beauty although the king tells her this time it is different:

---

*Not since *Tarzan and the Ant Men*, 1924.

I love you. I have never known love before. No living creature has ever affected me as you do. I will keep you here forever; I will make you high priestess; I will keep you young throughout the ages; I will keep you beautiful. You and I will live forever. We will reach out ... we shall have the world at our feet ... we shall be deities—I, a god, you, a goddess.

Realizing that Jane will never be his, the king decides to kill her, but in the nick of time enter Tarzan and the pilot Brown (the prince has long since been disposed of). Jane greets her mate with a cry, "Tarzan! Tarzan of the Apes." However, despite an absence (albeit fictional) of eleven years, the Jungle Lord deigned no reply (and, in fact, does not address her once during the remainder of the story, although Brown and Annette are emotionally choked up at their own reunion). Buira, the daughter of Muviro, is also all choked up. "The Big Bwana! At last I am saved," she cries.

Three weeks later, a party of six are gathered in Tarzan's bungalow: he and his mate, Brown and Annette, Tibbs (the loyal manservant) and little Nkima, the monkey. Brown wants to know what to do with the secret of perpetual youth (in the form of black pellets the size of peas). Jane reminds the pilot of his former statement that the pills would be worth a fortune in the States. But Brown is hesitant:

...The more I think of it, the less I like my scheme. Most everyone lives too long anyway for the good of the world—most of 'em ought to have died young. Suppose Congress got hold of 'em?—just think of that! Not on your life.

But he divides them into five equal parts and then, prompted by Jane, makes it six—including Nkima.* "He's sure a lot more use in the world than most people," Brown agrees.

2. BLACK AND WHITE

Tarzan the Magnificent† is quite similar to *Tarzan's Quest*, in addition to bearing a strong resemblance to other jungle tales. The Queen of the Kaji, an all-woman tribe, is said to be the most beautiful woman in the world. "One moment she is all womanly compassionate and sweetness, and next she is a she-devil." (She resembles Nemone, the beautiful but mad queen of *Tarzan and the City of Gold*.)

The Kaji have strange occult powers, by which they lure white men to their country (exact opposite of *Tarzan's Quest*, where an all-male tribe lures young girls to their country, also through mysterious powers). Of particular interest are the author's comments on the natives and the relationship between natives and the whites:

Originally [the Kaji] were blacks who wished to turn white; so they married only white men. It became part of their religion. That is why they lure white men to Kaji—and frighten away the blacks.... [Now] there is no unmixed black among them.... If a baby is born black, it is destroyed, and male babies are destroyed. They believe the color of the skin is inherited from the father.

---

*On September 27, 1962, Skippy, age thirty-four, the chimpanzee cinema co-star of Tarzan, died at the Griffith Park Zoo in Los Angeles. When he passed away (he refused his breakfast although he did not appear to be in any pain), he was the oldest chimpanzee of its kind in the United States, equivalent to one hundred years in the life of a human. Skippy retired in 1939. He never married and there were no survivors, nor was there a funeral. (Records do not show if anyone from ERB, Inc. shed a tear at his death.)

†The first half of this novel was initially published in *Argosy* in three parts, beginning September 19, 1936. The second half in *Blue Book*, also in three parts and beginning November 1937. The *Argosy* story was entitled "Tarzan and the Magic Men"; in *Blue Book*, "Tarzan and the Elephant Men."

An American writer of travel articles, Stanley Wood, falls in love with Gonfala, Queen of the Kaji. Later, Tarzan is told more of this by one of Wood's guides:

> Wood has a crush on Gonfala, the Queen; and it looks like Gonfala was sort of soft on Wood. That'd be bad, too; because she's a Negress.... She's whiter than you, but look at these dames here [in Kaji.] Ain't they white? They look white, but they all got Negro blood in 'em. But don't never remind 'em of it. You remember Kipling's, "She knifed me one night 'cause I wished she was white"?* Well that's it; that's the answer. They want to be white. God only knows why; nobody ever sees 'em but us; and we don't care what color they are....

When Wood's second guide also is captured:

> ...I never knew it to fail that you didn't get into trouble with any bunch of heathen if you start mixin' up with their women folk — especially niggers. But a guy's got it comin' to him that plays around with a nigger wench.

Tarzan gives the great emerald of the Kaji to Wood, in trust for Gonfala and Wood tells her that with the proceeds from the great stone she will be a very rich woman:

> You will have a beautiful home, wonderful gowns and furs, automobiles and many servants and there will be men — oh, lots of men.... They will want you, for yourself and for your money.

Stanley obviously is worried about the type of men his bride-to-be will encounter:

> ...you have never known men such as you are going to meet. You may find someone who ... you'll like better than you do me.... You haven't the slightest idea what you're going to be up against ... in the civilized world....

Gonfala feels that she will only bring unhappiness to Stanley so she runs away. Tarzan finds her wandering in the jungle, brings her to his estate "where his wife welcomed and comforted her" (the only reference made to Jane), Wood enters and the first half of the novel ends when Gonfala shows Tarzan a letter (she cannot read) revealing that she is not a "nigger wench" at all, but the true daughter of an English lord!

The second half of the story opens with Gonfala getting captured by the two former guides. Tarzan goes to her rescue, making his way to a range of hills to the north:

> ...It was a scene of peace and loveliness. The beauty was not lost upon the ape-man, whose appreciation of the loveliness or grandeur of nature ... was one of his chief sources of the joy of living.
>
> In contemplating the death that he knew must come to him as to all living things,† his keenest regret lay in the fact that he

---

*The same couplet is used in Burroughs' final novel, *Tarzan and "The Foreign Legion"* (written in 1944 and published in 1947), about an air force gunner who falls hard for a brown-skinned Eurasian. The quotation is from Kipling's *Barrack-Room Ballads*. The poem is entitled "The Ladies," and the particular stanza reads:

>   Then we was shifted to Neemuch
>   (Or I might ha' been keepin' 'er now),
>   An' I took with a shiny she-devil,
>   The wife of a nigger at Mhow;
>   Taught me the gipsy-folks' *bolee* [slang];
>   Kind o' volcano she were,
>   For she knifed me one night 'cause I wished she was white,
>   And I learned about women from 'er!

†The lords are in conflict; while Burroughs established in *Tarzan's Quest* that the ape-man would be immortal, in this, the following work, he has second thoughts about "immortality."

would never again be able to look upon the hills and valleys, and forests....

Stanley also goes to the rescue, taking another direction. Everyone winds up getting captured, but, somehow, all is righted by the story's end, at which time Tarzan, Stanley and Gonfala have a discussion abut life and civilization. Wood comments upon a bloody fight he has witnessed between husband and wife:

> ...I imagine there are a lot of married couples who would like to do that to one another if they thought they could get away with it. [But, he assures Gonfala,] We're different; these people are beasts.

Tarzan corrects Stanley with the reminder that they (the fighting couple) are merely behaving like human beings. He adds that he does not envy civilization with its accidents, robbers, kidnappers, war and pestilence. The African jungle has its own share of pitfalls, Wood adds, and Gonfala makes her speech.

> Neither one of you paints a very pretty picture. You make one almost afraid of life. But after all it is not so much peace and security that I want as freedom. You know, all my life I have been a prisoner.... Perhaps you can imagine then how much I want freedom ... [even love has no point] without freedom.

3. LIFE AND DEATH

Tarzan and the Forbidden City appeared as a novel one month after Ed and Florence, now married three years, sailed to Hawaii for a short stay. It was written one year earlier, in the latter part of 1937, and appeared first in magazine form under the title of *The Red Star of Tarzan.**

An old friend reappears, Captain Paul D'Arnot of the French navy, after a leave of twenty-five years (it was D'Arnot who taught Tarzan his first spoken language in *Tarzan of the Apes*). He asks Tarzan if he would help a friend. It seems that Brian Gregory has disappeared while hunting for the mysterious city of Ashair, where he went to search for "The Father of Diamonds." Would Tarzan help? Of course.

Helen Gregory, Brian's sister, is a nineteen-year-old vivacious blonde as "cool and inviting as the frosted glass before her." Unfortunately, this work is neither "cool" nor "inviting." In Brian Gregory, the author re-creates Tarzan's third look-alike†; we find again the two rival cities, but there is little else to sustain the story and the last fifty pages are almost impossible to wade through.

Two passages are worth noting, one reflecting the author's increasing concern with death:

> Tarzan had no fear of death.... To avoid it was a game that added zest to life. To pit his courage, his strength, his agility, his cunning against death, and win — there was the satisfaction. Some day Death would win, but to that day Tarzan gave no thought. He could fight or he could run away; and in either event preserve his self-respect, for only a fool throws his life away uselessly; and Tarzan had no respect for fools....

The second passage — likely, Ed's feeling about his new wife:

> [She] was, despite her flair for adventure and her not inconsiderable fortitude, essentially feminine. She was the type that stirred the deepest protective instincts of men; and, perhaps because of that very characteristic, she subconsciously craved protection,

---

*Argosy magazine in six parts, beginning March 19, 1938.
†Other two Tarzan "twins": Esteban Miranda, *Tarzan and the Golden Lion*, *Tarzan and the Ant Men*; Stanley Obroski, *Tarzan and the Lion Men*.

though she would have been the last to realize it....

Less than two years after the above was written, a new manuscript would be in the works, more fact than fiction. Burroughs would put his courage on the line and he would have other feelings about his new wife.

The world's first picture of Tarzan, painted by Clinton Pettee for the premiere publication of "Tarzan of the Apes" in *The All-Story Magazine*, October 1912.

First hardback edition of *Tarzan of the Apes*, published June 17, 1914, by A.C. McClurg & Company, Chicago.

Top left: Elmo Lincoln (Otto Elmo Linkenhelt) was discovered by D.W. Griffith, who cast him as a blacksmith in *The Birth of a Nation*. In 1917 when the United States entered World War I, the actor who had been signed to play "Tarzan of the Apes" (Stellan S. Windrow) left to join the army and was never heard from again, so Elmo replaced him as the first movie Tarzan. *Top right:* Tarzan No. 1: Elmo Lincoln, 1918–1921. *Bottom:* Elmo Lincoln and Louise Lorraine in *The Adventures of Tarzan*, 1921. She was only 15 years old when filming began.

Advertisement for the premiere of *Tarzan of the Apes*, which opened on January 27, 1918, at the Broadway Theatre. It was an overnight sensation and earned more than a million dollars at the box office.

Top: Tarzan No. 2 — Gene Pollar, 1920, with the famous acting orangutan "Joe Martin" in *The Revenge of Tarzan*. After this one film, Pollar went back to his job as a New York City fireman.

Left: Tarzan No. 3 — P. Dempsey Tabler, 1920. He wore many hats as actor, film producer and opera singer.

The Son of Tarzan, 1920, placed Tarzan (P. Dempsey Tabler) and Jane (Karla Schramm) in relatively minor roles. Here they ham it up for the camera with Eugene Burr, the villain "Paulovich."

Top left: Hawaiian actor Kamuela Searle starred as *The Son of Tarzan*, 1920. He was injured by an elephant during filming and was replaced in the final scene by a stand-in who never showed his face to the camera. Searle died three years later of cancer. *Top right:* Tarzan No. 4 — James H. Pierce, 1927, All-American center at the University of Indiana and star of *Tarzan and the Golden Lion*. *Bottom:* James H. Pierce with his leading lady, Dorothy Dunbar, in *Tarzan and the Golden Lion*, 1927.

Top: Tarzan No. 5 — Frank Merrill, 1928–1929. Last of the silent film Tarzans, Merrill taught Johnny Weissmuller how to swing on vines. *Bottom:* Frank Merrill and Natalie Kingston star in *Tarzan the Mighty*, 1929.

Top: Edgar Rice Burroughs with director J.P. McGowan on the set of *Tarzan and the Golden Lion*, 1927. Joe Kennedy (father of President Kennedy) was the producer, while Boris Karloff played a native chieftain (he became famous four years later as the Frankenstein monster). *Bottom:* ERB and his three children, Joan, Hully and Jack, on the set of *The Son of Tarzan*, 1920.

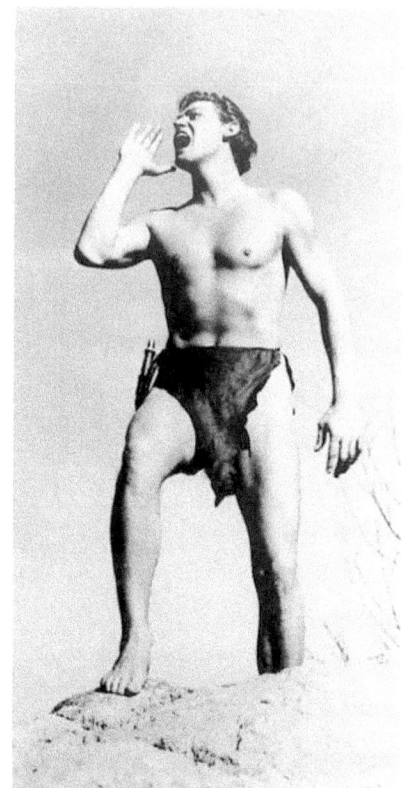

Top left: ERB, center, introduces Tarzan actor Weissmuller to director Woody Van Dyke on the set of MGM's *Tarzan the Ape Man*, 1932. *Top right:* Tarzan No. 6 — Johnny Weissmuller, 1932–1948. Olympic swimming champion Weissmuller was voted greatest athlete for the first half of the twentieth century. *Bottom left:* The best known and easily the most popular Tarzan and Jane were Johnny Weissmuller and Maureen O'Sullivan, shown here in *Tarzan and His Mate*, 1934. He made 12 Tarzan movies and she made six. *Bottom right:* Johnny Sheffield stars as "Boy" in *Tarzan Finds a Son*, 1939.

Top: And Jiggs makes four… Johnny Weissmuller, Maureen O'Sullivan and Johnny Sheffield star in *Tarzan's New York Adventure*, 1942. *Bottom:* Hollywood created the perfect jungle family when it introduced Johnny Sheffield as the adopted son of Tarzan and Jane. He played in eight different Tarzan films before leaving to play "Bomba, the Jungle Boy."

Top left: Tarzan No. 7 — Buster Crabbe, 1933. He starred in only one Tarzan film but made a great success as "Flash Gordon."

Top right: Buster Crabbe first saw jungle service in the non–Tarzan *King of the Jungle*, produced in 1933. He is shown here with actress Frances Dee. Later that year, Sol Lesser signed him to play the leading role in *Tarzan the Fearless*.

Left: Tarzan No. 8 — Herman Brix, 1935, 1938. An Olympic champion in shot put, Brix later changed his name to Bruce Bennett to avoid being typecast as Tarzan. Here he is in *The New Adventures of Tarzan*, 1935.

Top: Tarzan No. 9 — Glenn Morris, 1938. Winner of the decathlon at the 1936 Olympic games in Berlin, Morris made one Tarzan movie opposite swimming champion Eleanor Holm: *Tarzan's Revenge*, 1938. *Bottom:* Glenn Morris and "Cheeta" exchange views on the Stanlislavsky acting method, on set of *Tarzan's Revenge*, 1938.

Top left: Tarzan No. 10 — Lex Barker, 1949–1953. Shown here in *Tarzan and the She-Devil*, 1953, Barker married two of Hollywood's leading ladies, Lana Turner and Arlene Dahl. *Top right:* Lex Barker and Vanessa Brown with "friend" in *Tarzan and the Slave Girl*, 1950. *Bottom:* Lex Barker, Tarzan No. 10, rides into cinematic history in *Tarzan and the She-Devil*, 1953.

Top left: Tarzan No. 11 — Gordon Scott, 1955–1960. Here he hurls an opponent in *Tarzan and the Lost Safari*, 1957. *Top right:* Gordon Scott with producer Sol Lesser on the set of *Tarzan's Hidden Jungle*, 1955. *Bottom left:* Tarzan No. 12 — Denny Miller, 1959. Denny and a jungle friend are shown here in *Tarzan, the Ape Man*, using the same script as the 1932 film starring Weissmuller and O'Sullivan. *Bottom right:* Denny Miller in *Tarzan the Ape Man* making a spectacular leap into the camera.

Top left: Tarzan No. 13 — Jock Mahoney, 1962–1963. Stunt man and cowboy actor Jock Mahoney made two Tarzan films; he is shown here in ***Tarzan Goes to India***, 1962. *Top right:* Tarzan No. 14 — Mike Henry, 1966–1967. A former linebacker for the Pittsburgh Steelers and the Los Angeles Rams, Mike Henry starred in three Tarzan films. Here he is in ***Tarzan and the Valley of Gold***, 1966. *Bottom left:* Mike Henry with Nancy Kovack in ***Tarzan and the Valley of Gold***. *Bottom right:* Tarzan No. 15 — Ron Ely, 1966–1968. The first television Tarzan, Ron Ely filmed weekly episodes with such stars as Julie Harris and Diana Ross and the Supremes. Note Ely's simian friend; even though Burroughs did not create a chimp companion for Tarzan, the character has become indispensable in the movies and television.

XXIII

Pre-Pearl Harbor 1938–1941

The trouble with the world [is that] men have imagined a god instead of seeking god among themselves.
                                        Tarzan's Quest, *1935*

1. TO HAWAII AND RETURN

On May 27, 1938, *Tarzan and the Green Goddess* came to the screen — a Burroughs-Tarzan Production, released by Dearholt,* Stout & Cohen. Taken from the latter chapters of *The New Adventures of Tarzan* serial (released in 1935), it proved short of even the limited possibilities of an independent production ... seldom impresses or even proves exciting...."[1] Ed had no comments to make, at least not publicly, but this was to end his attempts at producing Tarzan films.

He and Florence sailed again to Honolulu on August 20, looking forward to a two-week stay at the home of Wayne and Mary Pflueger† in Niu. Interviewed by

---

*Ex-husband of Florence Burroughs.
†*The Deputy Sheriff of Comanche County*, published as a novel September 13, 1940, was dedicated to Mary Lucas Pflueger.

Ray Coll, Jr. of the *Honolulu Advertiser*, Ed said that he was still actively writing Tarzan stories, and disclosed that Johnny Weissmuller had signed up for five new features "since Sol Lesser released his rights to the stories for a paltry half-million to M-G-M."[2]

No Tarzan movie was playing in Honolulu but there was a gorilla roaming about the celluloid screen—*King Kong* (co-starring Bruce Cabot and Fay Wray); also an Arab chieftain (Ramon Novarro) playing the title role in *The Sheik Steps Out*.

The couple returned to the mainland in November, after he had completed *The Synthetic Men of Mars*.* In January 1939 he directed the coup against his former publisher, A. C. McClurg, regaining all rights and publishing paraphernalia to sixteen non–Tarzan novels for the fantastic price of fifty dollars each. In February, Ed surprised his wife by exhibiting his new novel, *Carson of Venus*,† dedicated to Florence Gilbert Burroughs.

2. The Clan

In the spring of 1939 Ed attempted a novel experiment which, if it had been initiated a half-dozen years earlier, might have rivaled the Boy Scouts—both in size and enthusiasm. This was the formation of the Tarzan Clans of America, where for only one dollar every red-blooded American boy would receive his membership card, the *Official Guide* and an autographed Burroughs book. The *Guide* was published in May by ERB, Inc. and contained thirty-two pages (including a dictionary of the ape language). Its contents included:

How to Form a Tarzan Clan
Duties of the Medicine Man
Girls
What to Do at Meetings
Tarzan Pledge
What Tarzan Stands For
Clan Songs
How to Make Weapons
Punishments
Demoting a Chief

However, with the European conflict erupting into World War in September, sufficient enthusiasm in the Tarzan Clans could not be mustered and the project failed.

3. Setting the Record Straight

While living in Beverly Hills with his wife, Ed knocked out two quick Tarzan novelettes, a Western serial, and his twenty-first Tarzan novel was published September 15.‡

Late in 1939, on a visit to Chicago, Ed was interviewed by the *Daily Times*. There was one thing the author wanted to get straight:

So many people have written that I was a failure in business before I began writing that most people take for granted the statement's true. Contrary to that belief I never was fired

---

*First appeared in *Argosy* magazine in six parts, beginning January 7, 1939; as a novel, March 15, 1940.
†First appeared in *Argosy* magazine in six parts, beginning January 8, 1938.
‡*The Terrible Tenderfoot* first appeared in *Thrilling Adventures* in three parts, beginning March 1940; subsequently in novel form as *The Deputy Sheriff of Comanche County* in September 1940. *Tarzan and the Champion* appeared complete in the April 1940 issue of *Blue Book Magazine*; *Tarzan and the Jungle Murders*, complete in the June 1940 *Thrilling Adventures*. The two stories appeared with a third novelette, *The Quest of Tarzan*, in both hardcover and paperback editions in 1964–65. ERB also wrote two juvenile novels: *The Tarzan Twins* (October 10, 1927; Volland) and *Tarzan and the Tarzan Twins with Jad-bal-ja, the Golden Lion* (March 9, 1936; Whitman Publishing Company, Racine, Wisconsin).

from a job. If Sears, Roebuck & Co. records go back far enough,* I'll bet they show I was a good departmental manager for them.³

Two years later, Ed again tried to set the record straight (that as a young man he had been a potential executive with great promise in the business world). In the summer of 1941, Miss Helen Sharpe, then personnel director of Sears' Seattle store, came to Honolulu to direct the training of personnel preparatory to the opening of the company's new retail outlet. When a story about the Sears' school appeared in the *Honolulu Advertiser*, the author suddenly materialized out of the treetops to confront Miss Sharpe:

> After reading the interview with you which appeared in this morning's *Advertiser*, it occurred to me that a recountal of my experiences as an employee of Sears might prove inspirational to those just enrolled with you.
>
> About 1906 or 07 I had a very nice position as office manager for a construction company† in Chicago when I took into my head that I wished to learn the mail order business; so I applied for and got a job as a correspondent at Sears.
>
> I was there only a few months when I was made assistant manager of the stenographic department; and when, shortly after, the manager was let out, I became manager of the department which employed some one hundred fifty stenographers, dictaphone operators (I think we called them phonograph operators in those days), multigraph operators and typists.
>
> With each advance I was given a boost in salary; but, having been inoculated with the get-rich-quick virus, I resigned my position after about a year and went into business for myself; with disastrous results.
>
> I then got a position as manager of a small mail order business; and about a year after I had left Sears they sent a man to see me, asking me to return and enter a merchandise department with the purpose of training to become assistant manager.
>
> Had I accepted, I should probably have eventually become the manager, for that was Sears' policy over thirty years ago, as it evidently is today — to promote from within. Also, had I accepted, Tarzan of the Apes would never have been created, for which many parents would have been thankful.
>
> Let me add that I did not know a single person connected with Sears when I joined; so my advancement was in no way the result of favoritism. I never worked for a finer organization than Sears, and I can assure any present or prospective employee that if he will work intelligently and loyally he may be certain of advancement.⁴

Before returning again to Hawaii, Ed wrote a letter to the *Los Angeles Times*, addressing himself to the police commissioner. The author suggested that plainclothesmen be forbidden to shoot except in self-defense or in the defense of others:

> ...My interest in the matter was aroused by an experience that one of my sons had with a couple of highly intelligent, courteous and efficient bully boys of the L.A. Police Department.... He was accosted, insulted and manhandled on a lonely street in Bel Air ... accused of being the "Phantom Burglar." His first and natural reaction when he saw two men leap from a car and come for him was to run — It seems to me that something should be done about this shooting of men simply because they run away from an imaginary danger. ... If it is a capital crime to run, give us a fair trial and an opportunity to kiss our loved ones good-bye....⁵

4. Aloha

The couple, "ordered" back to the Islands by Rothmund, arrived early in May 1940, accompanied by Florence's two children from her previous marriage, Lee and

---

*They don't.
†1905–06, "expert accountant" with the T. J. Winslow Company.

Caryl Lee. Interviewed in the *Advertiser*, Ed remarked that he found his Lanikai home a nice place in which to work. His workshop was sort of a makeshift affair: a cubbyhole of about three paces across and five in length, located in the back section of his garage, with a large packing crate serving as his desk. "I work just the same as any manufacturer. Sometimes I get disgusted with myself. When you've written a book about a character and told all you can about him and then have to write about twenty more it gets to be a chore. I'd rather write along different lines ... historical novels, for instance, but I've been typed!" Ed always liked to say in his early interviews and stories that he wrote "to escape being broke," but now he admitted: "I guess I've always wished I could do the things Tarzan does, but now it's too late in life...."[6]

A grandfather in his own right, Ed tries to soft-pedal the status of the Jungle Lord as a like senior citizen. "It's all Bob Davis'* fault that Tarzan is a grandfather," Burroughs was quoted as saying. "He's the one who suggested that Tarzan have a son."[7] (Although Ed admitted at this point in his career that it was a mistake for Tarzan to have married, his wry comment at this *particular* time obviously was intended to amuse the same Bob Davis, a current Island visitor.)

Through midsummer and fall Ed, who had turned sixty-five on September first, worked at a pace reminiscent of his early days (when he wrote "to escape being broke"). He was pounding out 20,000 words weekly (about seventy typewritten pages, double-spaced), had completed two 20,000-word novelettes† during the first part of the month and had started his third‡ on September 16! His average work day began at nine o'clock, when he would take care of his correspondence. Then from 11 A.M. to 4 P.M. Ed worked on his stories; a hunt-and-peck typist, he wrote about 330 words (one typewritten page, double-spaced) in twenty minutes.

When Ed was interviewed in the *Advertiser*, besides confessing that Tarzan never should have married he also acknowledged that he had come to think of Tarzan as a real person, whereas his other characters were thought of as purely imaginary sorts.

5. Like Carson

If Carson Napier was not as real a person to the author as Tarzan, the plight and thoughts of Carson, in the Ziff-Davis novelettes, seemed to be remarkably reminiscent of those of the author.

As the story opens, Carson and his mate, Duare, are zooming over Venus, while engaging in quite profound conversation:

> "I love my people; I love my country; but I may never return to them. That is why I am sad, but I cannot be sad for long; because I have you, and I love you more than I love my people or my country—"
> "You must be very lonely sometimes, so far from your own world and your friends."
> "Quite the contrary. I have you; and I have many good friends ... and an assured position...."

And the process of ageing was not lost on Carson (as it was not lost on Ed Burroughs):

> ...while I live I shall never admit the possibility of death. Somehow, it doesn't seem to

---

*Fiction editor of Munsey's magazines.
†The first parts, respectively, of *Llana of Gathol* and *Savage Pellucidar*.
‡Part two of *Escape on Venus*. (The first part had been written before May and July 1940.)

be for me — at least not since Danus injected the longevity serum into my veins and told me that I might live a thousand years.

But there are second thoughts:

One must die eventually, even though he has been inoculated with the longevity serum as I have; so if he has no one dependent upon him, he might as well crowd all of the adventure and experience into his life than he can....

ERB had a heart attack in Hawaii and was visited by his son Hulbert. Carson of Venus is also crippled — having been drugged. He, too, is greeted by a visitor from home, and is told that all is forgiven — the ruling family reviewed their findings on Duare and discovered they had made a mistake in condemning her. Carson says: "We seem to come to grief wherever we go — even in beautiful Havatoo."

In the third part of the Venus novelettes, the story finds Carson, Duare and the visitor from home all in the same position — paralyzed from the neck down, and hanging for exhibition purposes in the local museum of natural history. How will they get out of this predicament? One of the creatures who visits the museum returns several times. He apparently has a liking for Carson's mate. Duare suggests that she make the repulsive creature believe she love shim and then he might free her. Carson reassured himself that his wife loved him. He admittedly was jealous when anyone looked at his wife.

I am inclined to believe that every one as much in love as I am with Duare waxes silly occasionally. Of course, I knew that Duare loved me; I knew that I could trust her to the ends of the world — but! That is a funny thing about love — that *but*. The thought that some pussy, amoebic neuter was in love with her, or as nearly so as the thing could understand love, and that it was going to be with her for an indefinite time, while I hung on a wall, dead from the neck down, got my goat. If you are a man and if you are in love, you will know just how I felt.

The last eighty pages of the Venus series are dull and never seem to get anywhere. What is interesting, however, is Burroughs' description of what certainly must have been an aerial observation and then a visit to several ships of the U.S. Fleet based at Pearl Harbor* (plus his comments on the mingling of sailors and the natives):

I circled above ... and dropped down to about a thousand feet above [the fleet].... The largest units were between seven hundred and eight hundred feet long, with a beam of over a hundred feet; and they rose to a height of at least thirty feet above [the water], with lighter superstructures rising another thirty feet or more above the ... upper decks.... The smaller units were ... cruisers and destroyers.... The little scout ships [torpedo boats] to me would be the most interesting ships to command. They are amazingly fast and maneuverable and the busiest things I ever saw, daring in to launch a torpedo, zig-zagging out again at terrific speed....

When the fleet is in — be it New York, San Francisco, Shanghai or Honolulu — does the scene differ much from what ERB described his Venus novelettes:

...Along the entire route we encountered crowds of drunken warriors, singing and dancing with ... girls.
I turned back toward the main avenue which led toward the center of the city ... evidence of the hospitality [of the natives] multiplied, the visible effects of which had

---

War on Venus (the fourth of the novelettes making up the novel, *Escape on Venus*) appeared in *Fantastic Adventures*, March 1942, three months after Pearl Harbor. (ERB had completed it a year earlier, November, 1940.)

degenerated into nothing less than a drunken orgy....

A great many ships of our fleet were ... packed in without military order, their decks filled with ... girls and drunken ... warriors.

While the boys in the fleet were whooping it up and record crowds were pouring into the New York World's Fair (nearing completion of its second season), Germany was overrunning Holland, Belgium and Luxembourg, already having conquered Denmark and Norway. The British Expeditionary Force miraculously managed its withdrawal from Dunkirk, France was forced to submit to Hitler's armistice terms and England's new prime minister, Winston Churchill, took personal charge of the Battle of Britain. The United States took its first major step toward preparedness when President Roosevelt signed the bill providing the first peace-time compulsory military service program in the history of our nation. Two days later, Ed Burroughs roared his approval:

The moral back of Tarzan is that the youths of the land should strive for physical fitness and preparedness [but] preparedness for defense is not enough. The U.S. is surrounded on all sides by people who do not like us. They call us dollar mad, plutocrats, imperialists and worse. They want our trade and our money. If we are only ready to defend what we have, that is not enough. If we prepare for invasion, be sure they will let us alone.[8]

On the lighter side, Ed chided the Honolulu Rotarians (at whose luncheon he was guest speaker) to loosen up and wear slacks and comfortable clothing in their offices and downtown. "Tarzan, my meal ticket, doesn't wear long-sleeved shirts and a necktie."[9]

6. SEPARATE WAYS

On March 18, 1941, after ten months in Hawaii (and six years of marriage), Florence separated from Ed and returned to the mainland. She filed suit for divorce* (July 23) on the grounds of "mental cruelty" without setting forth any specific allegations in her complaint. (In Honolulu, Ed feigned surprise: "Any divorce action by my wife is news to me."[10])

Florence said:

He preferred to live alone. Ed regretted the marriage and felt that we would be much happier if we went our own ways.[11]

In the novelettes that first appeared in *Amazing Stories* (and later as *Llana of Gathol* in book form), ERB tells of his need for solitude:

No matter how instinctively gregarious one may be there are times when one longs for solitude. I like people. I like to be with my family, my friends ... and probably just because I am so keen for companionship, I am at times equally keen to be alone. It is at such times that I can best solve the knotty problems of government in times of war or peace. It is then that I can meditate upon all the various aspects of a full life such as I lead; and, being human, I have plenty of mistakes upon which to meditate.

When I feel that strange urge for solitude coming over me, it is my usual custom to take a one-man flier and range the dead sea bottoms and the other uninhabited wilderness.... Sometimes I am away for weeks on these glorious adventures in solitude. Because of them I probably know more of the geography and topography of Mars than any other living man....

That Ed Burroughs was conscious of what others would think about the twenty-nine-year difference in age between he and Florence is seen in this passage:

---

*A property settlement was arranged and Florence was granted the divorce May 4, 1942, in Juarez, Mexico.

It may seem strange to you denizens of Earth that [she] could have been infatuated with a grandfather, but you must remember that Mars is not Earth, and I am unlike all other Earth-men. I do not know how old I am. I recall no childhood. It seems to me that I have always looked the same ... a man of about thirty.

There is a pretty girl in the *Llana of Gathol* novelettes, who is deceived by John Carter to get her help. When he apologizes for the deception she, too, confesses that she had deceived him:

> I admired you, John Carter, tremendously, but I never loved you. ... I was most unhappy ... I would have sold my soul to have escaped, and so I tried to make you love me so that you would take me away. I thought I had succeeded, and I was very much ashamed of myself. You can never know how relieved I was when I found out that I had failed, for I admired you too much to wish to bring unhappiness to you.

7. Peace—War

By April 1941, World War II was nineteen months old and only the United States, of all the great powers, had not directly committed itself. But it was inevitable. And soon! In May, President Roosevelt had proclaimed an "unlimited national emergency." In June, Germany had invaded Russia; in July, U.S. troops had been landed in Iceland; in August, the Atlantic Charter had been signed, stating the postwar aims of our country and that of Great Britain. No matter if only four days later, the House voted on the extension of Selective Service passed by one vote—203–202. No matter. On September 1, the glow of sixty-six candles shone brightly on the stern-set visage and the ever-trim figure (heart attack or not) of the Jungle Lord. He was ready. Tarzan was ready. A great adventure—this time for real!

XXIV

The Great Adventure 1941–1945

Something told him Fate may have ordained that he was to serve his country quite as well naked [as Tarzan] as uniformed. Else why had Fate plunged him thus into an enemy stronghold?
                    Tarzan and the Foreign Legion, *1947**

1. COVERING THE WAR†

Oliver R. Franklin,‡ Captain and Bombardier of Headquarters, VII Bomber Command, lived in a beach home across the Island from Honolulu.

Franklin recalled:

I first met Ed when he stopped at my beach to watch the high waves that were rolling in during a storm. He was living at the Niumalu Hotel between Fort De Russy and Waikiki at the time. We talked of many

---

*Written in 1944.
†See Appendix C for additional wartime columns of ERB not included in this chapter.
‡Franklin was retired at the end of the war for permanent combat disability with rank of lieutenant colonel, Air Force. Subsequently, he built houses in Florida.

things—I remember his joking about the doings of Tarzan in the newspaper strip. He explained that he was behind several weeks on reading what the syndicate was doing to Tarzan, and explained the agreement whereby they could keep Tarzan working, but he had to be extra good and do nothing out of line, remain true to Lady Jane, and kill only very "bad guys." I asked him about the gentle kidding of ritualistic religion in his Mars books, and he told me a little of his philosophy of living—a gentle sort of idealistic agnosticism, if you have to pin a label on it.[1]

Ed Burroughs' long career was nearing an end. The breakup of his second marriage had hit him hard, but the war was his golden opportunity to go out fighting—as deemed a Lord of the Jungle. (Tarzan had no fear of death. "To avoid it was a game that added zest to life. To put his courage, his strength, his agility, his cunning against Death, and win—there was the satisfaction."*)

When the "day of infamy" hit Pearl Harbor, Brigadier General Kendall J. Fielder† was Chief of Intelligence, under the Commanding General of the Army in Hawaii (Lieutenant General Walter Short later was relieved of his duties).

Fielder recalled:

> I was responsible for all security and censorship. Subsequently, all correspondents had to be accredited to my office. Ed Burroughs was one of them and quite proud of his special uniform and arm band.[2]

Kendall Fielder did not know ERB but, of course, had heard of him.

He first reported to my office on December 7 and volunteered his services for anything we desired. The situation was pretty grim in Honolulu just after the war started and one day Ed asked me how I felt about his writing humorous stories for the *Advertiser*. This he did…. He joined the Business Men's Training corps, a semi-military home guard, composed of men too old for military service. They were issued weapons, given target practice and, in general, received basic military training. Many of Ed's stories were about his experiences on hikes, guard duty and so forth. The public and particularly the military loved them.

I think his stories were more of a free-lance type, not syndicated and written when he was in the mood. Whether or not he was on anyone's payroll‡ I don't know, but many of his articles were used on the mainland.[3]

Thurston Twigg-Smith, president of the Advertising Publishing Co., Ltd., which includes the *Honolulu Advertiser*, where Burroughs' wartime stories appeared, stated: "Our business office has no record of Burroughs ever being on our payroll. He still might have been accredited by this newspaper, as a number of our accredited correspondents were not on the payroll, writing either on a complimentary basis, or on a space basis."[4]

ERB's first story in the *Advertiser* was prefaced by this Editor's Note: "Edgar Rice Burroughs, Honolulu resident and famous author of the 'Tarzan' books and comic strip, has volunteered his services to the Army and will write a column every day on the lighter side of the war, army authorities announced last night. The first of these columns follows. Watch for others from day to day."

---

*Red Star of Tarzan.
†Retired and living in Hawaii at time of this writing.
‡Most stories tracing Burroughs' career listed him as war correspondent for the *Los Angeles Times* and/or United Press, but he never was officially accredited as a regular correspondent to either organization.

Laugh It Off*

Whatever else the civilian population of this Island of Oahu may lack, it is long on co-operation, guts and a sense of humor. Since the Japanese attack started the morning of December 7th, I have seen more grins and heard more laughter and jokes than ever before in all the time that I have spent in the Paradise of the Pacific. There has been no panic and whatever fear there has been has been beautifully camouflaged. These people, regardless of race, color, or antecedents, are A M E R I C A N S. They make me proud to be an American too....

For two hours during the bombing of Pearl Harbor and Hickam Field, my son and I ate breakfast and went out in front of the hotel on Waikiki Beach, where we were living, and played tennis. Most of the hotel guests congregated there to watch the show. It was the middle of the forenoon before we realized that it was the real McCoy and that we were watching a battle. As the radio then broadcast an order for civilians to remain off the streets, we went on with our tennis, stopping occasionally to watch the anti-aircraft shells burst, the bombs dropping into the ocean. I saw no indication of fright....[5]

Toward the end of February 1944, Ed hitched a ride to Tarawa in the Gilbert Islands. The Pacific campaign was a hop, step and jump from island to island — moving our men and bombers closer and closer to Japan. The Solomons were hell — Guadalcanal took six terrible months, and only a victory by our naval forces (preventing Japanese reinforcements from landing) saved the day; Tarawa was one of the bloodiest engagements in the history of the Marine Corps. Now, Kwajalein in the Marshall Islands had been taken, and as advanced troops moved on to the Marianas and Saipan, landing strips for bombers were pushed forward.

Franklin recalled:

Ed arrived about the time our Bomber Headquarters was packing up to move from Tarawa to our newly built base at Kwajalein. He was the guest of our CO, Brigadier General "Ted" Landon.† I hadn't seen Ed in more than two years and it was a pleasant reunion.

Our Headquarters' B-24, *The Pacific Tramp*, had full luggage racks in the rear bomb bays but as the General wanted to give Ed an idea of precision bombing, I talked the Marines into loading six 500-pound general purpose bombs into the front racks, explaining that our direct route took us over the Jap-held island of Jaluit.

As to flying gear — none was worn except for flack vests while flying over target areas. Ed wore a simple khaki shirt without insignia, khaki slacks, tan oxfords and a baseball cap.

Jaluit had been the administrative headquarters for all the Carolines under the old German mandate, and the three-story frame government house was in use by the Japs for food storage and also housed a few geishas, according to our intelligence reports. There were several operation ack-ack guns, mostly 75 mm, and apparently plenty of ammunition....

We knocked out our gun and placed two bombs through the building. From my position up in the nose I could not see Ed, but as he was stationed at the right-waist gun position, I could hear him over the interphone, calmly calling off the ack-ack bursts: "Right and high ... low and behind us ... Dammit, I lost my cap and the wind pulled out more hair than I grew since the war started."

We flew another mission the next day, knocking out a Jap radio station on an atoll near Bikini, and Ed seemed actually disappointed that there was no antiaircraft fire. Ed really enjoyed the missions, and since he was so excited and enthusiastic about the whole show, we felt that he fitted in with our crew of professionals better than any other newsman who ever flew with us.

---

*No further "Laugh It Off" columns were found in the *Advertiser*'s library. ERB's second story appeared two months later.

†Truman H. "Ted" Landon retired from the Air Force July 31, 1963, as a general. (At retirement, he was Commander in Chief U.S. Air Forces, Europe, and Commander, 4th Allied Tactical Air Force — NATO.)

When we first arrived at Kwajalein, all hands parked our luggage and then went down to the nearby beach to dig foxholes. General Landon is the sort of bird who makes his own bunk and digs his won foxhole, so as his guest, Ed got busy filling sand bags and digging with the rest of us, his sparse grey hair sticking straight up in the air. He joked about joining the bag layers' union.

Yes, he was full of life, rarely serious, joking with all hands, rarely spoke of himself — he had the faculty of making even the most shy and reserved chaps feel important.[6]

General Landon called Ed Burroughs a great morale booster:

He was different from a lot of the well-known correspondents who spent their days with the generals. His time was spent with the men and he was "Ed" to everybody. Ed came to us because there wasn't too much ground action in the Central Pacific at the time. He tried to go on dangerous missions but, because of his age, never quite made it. He seemed to thoroughly enjoy himself on the bombing runs he made with us and was as mad at the Japs as the rest of the men.

Ed knew his geography and history and, in fact, he knew more about some of the islands than a lot of us who were supposed to be in the know.

He never spoke too much of his Tarzan writings but I gathered that he had few friends among the Hollywood crowd. He did tell me that of all the movie people with whom he came in contact, Sol Lesser was one of the honest ones and Ed had a lot of respect for him.

There were some lighter moments with Ed around. For instance, some of my men used to sneak my hard-to-come-by liquor out of my quarters and try to get him loaded. But as far as I remember, no one ever succeeded. Ed was gregarious but he wasn't a back-slapper ... the kind of person who walked around all day telling jokes, but he was always friendly and amiable and liked to talk to people.

The last time I saw him was in Tarzana. It was toward the end of '48 and he was in pretty bad shape.[7]

ERB returned to his beach-type cottage at the Niumalu Hotel in Lanikai. His World War II novel, *Tarzan and "The Foreign Legion,"** was completed in September of 1944 but he had no plans to publish it until after the war.

Kendall Fielder recalled:

We spent many evenings together along with several other residents of the Niumalu. At times he did seem somewhat bitter about his divorced wife and would let a remark slip — but this was foreign to his makeup.

Liquor was in short supply and tightly rationed [so] I habitually took my supply to the gang at the Niumalu, where we would have dinner and an hour or two of cards. Ed looked forward to these parties like a kid does Christmas. He thoroughly enjoyed being with his friends and was usually the life of the party with his ready wit. One day, out of the clear blue sky, he told me he was dedicating *Escape on Venus*† to me. Naturally I was pleased and flattered.

After the war I was ordered to the Pentagon for duty and we never got together again, although we exchanged letters, occasionally. He was one of the finest men I have ever known, with a brilliant mind and fabulous imagination, [able] to discuss any subject intelligently.[8]

Ed had written stories about the army and air force but there was still the navy, and in June and July of 1945 he took care of this phase of his war reporting:

On Board Fleet Oiler

Having just completed the first 4,000 miles of a cruise that may take 18 months and take the ship‡ almost anywhere in the Pacific between Pearl Harbor and China, I have acquired vast respect for oilers.... Although not a combat ship, we are adequately

---

*Published by ERB, Inc. August 22, 1947; dedicated to Brigadier General Truman H. Landon.
†Published by ERB, Inc. in novel form October 15, 1946.
‡U.S.S. *Cahaba*, commanded by Lieutenant Commander Julius Burnbaum.

armed.... However, with our enormous inflammable and explosive cargo we appear to an innocent bystander like this correspondent to be an accident going somewhere to happen.[9]

...We are in a convoy and under escort, and we are to rendezvous somewhere with a task force group and fuel them at sea ... this thing and I will have traveled some 5,000 miles....[10]

According to the file on ERB at the *Honolulu Advertiser*, Ed's final war report (written as he approached his seventieth birthday) appeared in the *Advertiser* only two weeks before Japan was handed an unconditional surrender ultimatum by the U.S., Great Britain and China. Appropriately, the column ended with a touch of humor.

...Being with the Army part of the time and with the Navy part of the time and as civilian all of the time is often quite confusing terminologically. One hesitates while determining whether to ask the location of the latrine, the head, or the john. And by that time it may be too late.[11]

XXV

Last Years 1946–1950

We must die sometime. What difference whether it be tonight, tomorrow night or a year hence, just so that we have lived — and I have lived.
   Tarzan the Untamed, *1920*

1. BACK HOME

Ed returned to California too late to attend the funeral of his first wife, Emma, who died in Los Angeles, November 5, 1944. He also had difficulty finding a place to live and was forced to pay a "war bonus" in order to move into a modest two-bedroom and den house and 5565 Zelzah Avenue, Encino (about ten minutes away from the offices of ERB, Inc. and the former Tarzana Rancho that he had purchased in 1919).

Florence recalled:

I met Ed for lunch shortly after he returned. He was still in uniform and spoke mostly of his war experiences. He looked very well and seemed as vigorous as ever.[1]

But in the late forties, as Tarzan (and the great publishing empire that Tarzan built) was slowing down to a stumbling walk, so was Ed Burroughs.

Joan Burroughs recalled:

Dad contracted Parkinson's* and then he had another heart attack, after which he stayed pretty much at home with a caretaker-nurse. He used to call me every day and say, "It's five o'clock," and I would come over for our private cocktail hour.

We used to watch television — Dad was thrilled with it — especially the wrestling matches. He used to go through all the grunts and groans and then insist that the boys were playing for keeps. We talked some about the war. I reminded him that he took a particular delight in exposing himself wherever he could, and I recalled one letter in which he was particularly jubilant as he described being shot at by a Japanese sniper.

One of Dad's last public appearances was when he visited the set of *Tarzan and the Slave Girl*.†

Mr. Coriell‡ had come to Tarzana to meet and talk with my brother, John Coleman, and then later with Dad. The following morning we went down to the set at RKO Studios. There was quite a flurry of excitement as Dad had not been inside a studio for several years. Mr. Lesser came over to chat and flashbulbs were going off.[2]

On Sunday, March 19, 1950, Dr. Herman Seal of Encino stopped off the see the author on his regular morning call. Ed was having breakfast in bed and reading the Sunday comics when, suddenly, the newspaper dropped from his hands. At age seventy-four, Edgar Rice Burroughs was dead — attributed to a heart ailment and hardening of the arteries. ERB was cremated, his ashes lying at the Chapel of the Pines Crematorium, Los Angeles. Funeral cost was reported to be $194. Private services were held at the home of his son, John Coleman, Tarzana.

There were many tributes to ERB on his passing, but I believe he especially would have enjoyed two of them. One, by the late author and columnist Robert C. Ruark, who wrote: *"There is no doubt in my mind that Tarzan of the Apes was the greatest single fictional achievement of our time."*[3]

The second, an editorial in the *Los Angeles Times* that said, in part:

> If a man's life is judged by the amount of pleasure and entertainment he has given others, Burroughs stands high on the list. Few writers have reached a larger audience, yet he was free of arty pretense. He neither went to college, nor to Africa. He said he was an escapist — that he wrote to escape being broke. But he kept on writing after he had made several fortunes, and we suspect he wrote for the same reason millions of people read him — because it was fun.[4]

Tarzan ... John Carter of Mars ... Carson of Venus ... David Innes and Abner Perry of Pellucidar.... Edgar Rice Burroughs gave to them all the immortality about which he dreamed, for which he strived and which — whether he realized it or not — he finally did attain.

---

*Parkinson's Disease is characterized by muscle tremors, rigidity of certain muscles and some loss of automatic muscular control.

†Starring Lex Barker and Vanessa Brown; released in March 1950. *Time* magazine reported: "With a chest thump and ape warble, Tarzan will start vine-swinging from the lianas for the 26th time next week. In *Tarzan and the Slave Girl*, Producer Sol Lesser is giving the tenth and current Tarzan (Lex Barker) a new mate — probably Vanessa Brown. But the script will hold close to the tried & true line that has enchanted three decades of romantics and grossed around $3,000,000 a picture. Tarzan has been the most durable and successful series in movie history...."

‡Vernell Coriell, founder of the Burroughs Bibliophiles, and editor-publisher of *The Burroughs Bulletin*, an irregularly published "fanzine" distributed to members.

Epilogue

How long will Burroughs live?

On pages 261, 262 and 263 of a new college textbook, *Literature for Composition*,* are reprinted the first eighteen paragraphs of *Tarzan of the Apes*.

At last, sighs Usha the wind; *finally, finally*, trumpets Tantor; *He now belongs to the ages*, shrieks little N'kima, at the same time hurtling insults at Simba. The Burroughs excerpt is preceded by passages from the pens of Swift, Thurber, Yeats and Auden; followed by such as H. G. Wells, Hardy, Pope and Carlyle. Co-author James R. Kreuzer, dean of Queens College of the City University of New York, explained the assignment:

"The idea for this particular section is to demonstrate to English classes how a writer [Swift, Wells, Burroughs] gains credibility with the material on hand. I thought *Tarzan of the Apes* would be an ideal choice."

In England, the august Oxford University Press, London, has published *as a schoolbook* in its education series, "Stories Told and Retold" the first story of ERB, *A Princess of Mars*. In this series, Burroughs' *Princess* takes its place alongside such stalwarts as *Robinson Crusoe, David Copperfield* and *The Prisoner of Zenda*.

What of *Tarzan* in foreign countries? Since Burroughs' death, the ape-man has become a figure of the Cold War. When Hungary banned a number of "bourgeois" books, included were the *Tarzan* stories. In August 1964, *Tarzan* appeared in a Cuban newsreel. As the local commentator rallied against racial discrimination here (while denouncing the principle of white

---

*By James R. Kreuzer and Mrs. Lee Cogan (Holt, Rinehart and Winston, 1965).

supremacy), a clip of an old Weissmuller film was shown where Tarzan battles and kills a number of African tribesmen, then a quick dissolve to racial disturbances and violence in the south.

In the Soviet Union, where Tarzan was the popular fictional hero of the 1920s and early 30s, according to *Pravda*, the ape-man still swings. In December 1953, the official Communist organ criticized Soviet movie distributors for releasing old American movies featuring Tarzan, contending that the ape-man's jungle roars were scaring the chickens and pigs on collective farms. *Pravda* demanded that district and regional Communist party cultural departments give the peasants more culture and the pigs and chickens more restful nights, and described events at the village of Kuzikha, when the *Tarzan* film truck arrived and set up in the livestock area of the collective farm.

"Soon the livestock section of the farm was filled with the sound of war cries of African tribal hunters, the deafening roars of tom-toms. Then a wild lion appears on the screen and such a deafening roar was heard that the spectators became frightened. And then the farm animals set up a squealing and howling that almost drowned out the sound from the screen where Tarzan fought a death struggle with the lion and killed him ... the screeching continued on the screen and off as the ape Cheetah danced and screamed on the screen and the livestock howled in the barns.

"'Nastaya, go and quiet them,' said the farm brigade chief to the swineherd. 'Quiet whom?' she asked. Then finally she understood that she should go and quiet the little pigs who had been frightened by the roar of the king of beasts.

"But Nastaya returned and said to the brigade chief: 'You just try to quiet the pigs while there are a lion and a wild man roaring there.'

"At this the farmers having recovered from their own fright had a good laugh."

(The *Tarzan* films were old ones, having been taken by the Russians as war booty from Berlin.)

Five months later (May 15, 1964), the Soviet newspaper, *Komsomolskaya Pravda* reported that postcards of Johnny Weissmuller in the role of Tarzan had become an under-the-counter item in the market of Yakutsk. The newspaper told of a woman in the market who kept a fat handbag hidden under her coat stuffed with "art" postcards of Weissmuller and other fast-selling items. The newspaper noted (with indignation) that while *Tarzan* was a big seller, no postcards by Soviet artists were to be had in the market.

In the United States, new *Tarzan* films are being regularly produced for worldwide movie distribution, old *Tarzan* films have become a staple of television and a *Tarzan* TV series is continuing the thrilling (but more civilized) saga of the ape-man.

So much for movies and television. In print, the Burroughs titles are being reprinted whenever the supply diminishes. What of the new *Tarzan* stories? The hard core fans, ever since the author's death, have requested that the heirs assign a *qualified* writer to carry on in the Burroughs tradition. But can *anyone* replace the master? When ERB, Inc. did not move to appease the gargantuan appetite of the author's fans, another heard the plea. Charlton Publication, Inc. published six *Tarzan* paperback books, but the fanzines bristled with opposition to the non–Burroughs stories and ERB, Inc. charged the publications as "...deceiving, misleading and confusing the public."* Charlton's

---

*Edgar Rice Burroughs, Inc., et al. *v.* Charlton Publications, Inc., 145 U.S. Patent Quarterly, p. 655 (Federal Court, Southern District, New York, 1965).

motion for dismissal was denied by the court on the ground that the plaintiff's [ERB, Inc.] proof might establish a "state of facts" entitling him to relief. The defendant was forced to remove from sale all its *Tarzan* books.

In Tarzana, California, artists have been asked by the Edgar Rice Burroughs "Foundation," a group of local citizens, to submit sketches and models for a landscaped monument and fountain to honor *Tarzan of the Apes*. Also proposed is a literary and art museum, based on the concept of life from its primitive stages so the present space age, as projected by ERB in his works. An early design created a stir (and later was modified by the artist). It showed Tarzan wrestling with a lioness and the ape-man was nude.

Appendix A

Chapter Notes

Prologue

(1) *Tarzan and the Golden Lion*— A. C. McClurg & Co., Chicago, 1924. (2) *Ibid.* (3) Personal Information. (4) Personal Information.

Chapter I—Formative Years

(1) Personal Information. (2) *New York Sunday World*, Oct. 27, 1929. (3) *Ibid.* (4) *Ibid.* (5) *Ibid.* (6) *The Book News Monthly*, August 1918. (7) *New York Sunday World*, Oct. 27, 1929. (8) *The Book News Monthly*, August 1918. (9) Personal Information. (10) *New York Sunday World*, Oct. 27, 1929. (11) *Ibid.* (12) *Ibid.* (13) *Ibid.* (14) *The Book News Monthly*, August 1918. (15) *The War Chief*, 1927. (16) *Ibid.* (17) *Apache Devil*, 1933. (18) *New York Sunday World*, Oct. 27, 1929. (19) Headquarters, Dept. of the Army; National Archives and Records Service, General Services Administration. (20) *The Book News Monthly*, August 1918.

Chapter II— Search for Adventure

(1) *Tarzan of the Apes*, 1912. (2) *The Son of Tarzan*, 1915. (3) *New York Sunday World*, Oct. 27, 1929. (4) Personal Information. (5) *The Book News Monthly*, August 1918. (6) *New York Sunday World*, Oct. 27, 1929. (7) Yale University, '89 Sheffield *Class Record — History of Graduates.* (8) *New York Sunday World*, Oct. 27, 1929. (9) *Tarzan of the Apes*, A. C. McClurg & Co., Chicago, 1914. (10) *Ibid.* (11) *New York Sunday World*, Oct. 27, 1929. (12) Yale University, '89 Sheffield *Class Record—*

History of Graduates. (13) *New York Sunday World,* Oct. 27, 1929. (14) *Ibid.* (15) *Ibid.* (16) *New York Sunday World,* Oct. 27, 1929.

Chapter III — A Lord's Trial

(1) *New York Sunday World,* Oct. 27, 1929. (2) *Ibid.* (3) *Ibid.* (4) *The Book News Monthly,* August 1918. (5) *New York Sunday World,* Oct. 27, 1929. (6) *Ibid.* (7) *Ibid.* (8) *Ibid.* (9) *Ibid.* (10) *Ibid.* (11) *The Book News Monthly,* August 1918. (12) *New York Sunday World,* Oct. 27, 1929. (13) The Burroughs Papers: "How I Wrote the Tarzan Books," 1937. (14) *New York Sunday World,* Oct. 27, 1929. (15) *The Book News Monthly,* August 1918. (16) *New York Sunday World,* Oct. 27, 1929. (17) *Ibid.*

Chapter V — The Ape-man Cometh

(1) *New York Sunday World,* Oct. 27, 1929. (1A) Personal Information. (2) *The Daily Maroon* (University of Chicago), May 31, 1927. (3) *Tarzan of the Apes.* (4) *Ibid.* (5) *Ibid.* (6) *The Daily Maroon* (University of Chicago), May 31, 1927. (7) *Jungle Tales of Tarzan,* A. C. McClurg & Co., Chicago 1919. (8) *Ibid.* (9) Personal Information. (10) *Tarzan at the Earth's Core,* ERB, Inc., 1930.

Chapter VI — Breakthrough

(1) *New York Sunday World,* Oct. 27, 1929. (2) Author's League *Bulletin,* April 1915. (3) *New York Sunday World,* Oct. 27, 1929. (4) *Ibid.*

Chapter VII — Tarzan and Friend

(1) *Los Angeles Times,* Nov. 20, 1938. (2) *Sleuthing in the Stacks,* by Rudolph Altrocchi, Harvard University Press, 1944. (3) *Tarzan and the City of Gold,* ERB, Inc., 1933. (4) *Jungle Tales of Tarzan.* (5) *Tarzan of the Apes.* (6) *Ibid.* (7) *Tarzan the Terrible,* A. C. McClurg & Co., Chicago, 1921. (8) *The Return of Tarzan,* A. C. McClurg & Co., Chicago, 1915. (9) *Ibid.* (10) *Chicago Daily Tribune,* March 30, 1914. (11) *Op. cit.,* May 31, 1915. (12) Personal Information. (13) *Rudyard Kipling — His Life and Work,* Charles Carrington. London: Macmillan & Co., Ltd., 1955.

Chapter VIII — Those Crazy Moving Pictures

(1) Personal Information. (2) Personal Information. (3) *Moving Picture World,* June 2, 1917. (4) From an unidentified publication, likely 1958. (5) *The Cleveland News,* May 18, 1929. (6) *The New York Times,* Jan. 28, 1918. (7) *Chicago Journal,* May 15, 1918. (8) The Burroughs Papers: article by columnist Kitty Kelly, from an unidentified newspaper, May 14, 1918. (9) *Motion Picture Magazine,* March 1918. (10) *The Book News Monthly,* August 1918. (11) *Overland Monthly & Outwest Magazine,* March 1934. (12) Personal Information. (13) *The Book News Monthly,* August 1918. (14) *Motion Picture Magazine,* January 1919.

Chapter IX — On to the City of Gold

(1) *Army and Navy Journal,* August 31, 1918. (2) *Chicago Daily News,* Jan. 28, 1919. (3) *Good Housekeeping,* February 1926. (4) *Better Homes and Gardens,* August 1931. (5) Personal Information. (6) *Moving Picture Herald,* Oct. 11, 1919. (7) *Ibid.* (8) *Ibid.*

Chapter X — Tarzan bei den Affen

(1) Personal Information. (2) The Burroughs Papers: Press-Clipping Books,

March–June 1925. (3) *Ibid.* (4) *Ibid.* (5) *Ibid.* (6) *Ibid.* (7) *Frankfurter Zeitung,* June 27, 1925. (8) *Buffalo Evening News,* March 21, 1934. (9) *Ibid.*

Chapter XI — King of the Serials

(1) *Los Angeles Examiner,* April 19, 1928. (2) The Burroughs Papers: International Press Bureau, 1925.

Chapter XII — The Girl from Hollywood and Other Romances

(1) Personal Information. (2) The Burroughs Papers: book reviews, September 9, 1923.

Chapter XIII — Tarzan Swings

(1) *Moving Picture Herald,* summer, 1920. (2) *Motion Picture News,* summer, 1920. (3) *Motion Picture News,* July 4, 1921. (4) *Motion Picture News,* Oct. 1, 1921. (5) The Burroughs Papers: unidentified news story, February 1927. (6) *The Daily Maroon* (University of Chicago) May 31, 1927. (7) *Film Daily,* March 20, 1927.

Chapter XIV — Tarzan of the World

(1) The Burroughs Papers: unidentified Scottish journal, 1920. (2) Associated Press dispatch, April 17, 1924. (3) *The New York Times,* April 17, 1924. (4) *The New York Times,* April 18, 1924. (5) *A Golden Anniversary Bibliography of Edgar Rice Burroughs,* Henry Hardy Heins. Donald M. Grant, West Kingston, Rhode Island, 1964.

Chapter XV — The "Mid-Rancho" Period

(1) The Burroughs Papers: unidentified Los Angeles newspaper, Oct. 1922. (2) *Tarzan and the Ant Men,* A. C. McClurg & Co., Chicago, 1925. (3) The Burroughs Papers: unidentified newspaper, Oct. 25, 1926. (4) *Better Homes and Gardens,* August 1931. (5) *Chicago Daily News,* Nov. 16, 1929. (6) *Los Angeles Times,* letter to the editor, Oct. 14, 1929. (7) Personal Information. (8) Personal Information. (9) *Better Homes and Gardens,* August 1931.

Chapter XVI — The Comic Strip

(1) *New Orleans Times-Picayune,* 1929 (exact date unknown). (2) Personal Information. (3) Personal Information. (4) *Editor & Publisher,* May 18, 1929. (5) Personal Information. (6) Quoted in *Comics and Their Creators,* by Martin Sheridan. Hale, Cushman and Flint, 1942.

Chapter XVII — Two Women

(1) The Burroughs Papers: unidentified news release. (2) Personal Information. (3) Personal Information.

Chapter XVIII — The One and Only

(1) Personal Information. (2) Personal Information. (3) *Variety,* March 29, 1932. (4) Personal Information. (5) Personal Information. (6) Personal Information. (7) Personal Information. (8) Personal Information. (9) Personal Information. (10) Personal Information. (11) Personal Information. (12) Personal Information. (13) Personal Information. (14) Personal Information.

Chapter XX — New Adventures

(1) *Variety*, Oct. 19, 1935. (2) Personal Information. (3) Personal Information. (4) *Los Angeles Times*, Dec. 4, 1934. (5) *The New York Times*, Dec. 5, 1934. (6) *Los Angeles Times*, Dec. 6, 1934. (7) *Los Angeles Times*, Dec. 12, 1934. (8) Personal Information. (9) Personal Information. (10) Personal Information. (11) *Los Angeles Times* (memo to city desk), March 28, 1935. (12) *Los Angeles Times* (memo to city desk), March 29, 1935. (13) Personal Information. (14) Personal Information. (15) Personal Information. (16) Personal Information. (17) Personal Information. (18) *Variety*, Jan. 25, 1936. (19) *Honolulu Advertiser*, Aug. 25, 1938.

Chapter XXI — Monkey Business

(1) Personal Information.

Chapter XXII — Pre–Pearl Harbor

(1) *Variety*, May 31, 1938. (2) *Honolulu Advertiser*, Aug. 25, 1938. (3) *Chicago Daily Times*, Dec. 1, 1939. (4) *Sears News-Graphic* (an employee publication of Sears, Roebuck and Co.), July 24, 1941. (5) *Los Angeles Times*, letter to the editor, Jan. 24, 1940. (6) *Honolulu Advertiser*, May 6, 1940. (7) *Ibid.* (8) *Honolulu Advertiser*, Sept. 18, 1940. (9) *Ibid.* (10) *Los Angeles Times*, July 25, 1941. (11) *Los Angeles Times*, May 5, 1942.

Chapter XXIV — The Great Adventure

(1) Personal Information. (2) Personal Information. (3) Personal Information. (4) Personal Information. (5) *Honolulu Advertiser*, Dec. 13, 1941. (6) Personal Information. (7) Personal Information. (8) Personal Information. (9) *Honolulu Advertiser*, June 10, 1945. (10) *Honolulu Advertiser*, July 9, 1945. (11) *Honolulu Advertiser*, July 12, 1945.

Chapter XXV — Last Years

(1) Personal Information. (2) Personal Information. (3) Robert C. Ruark's syndicated column, March 28, 1950, *Buck and Tarzan*. (4) *Los Angeles Times*, March 21, 1950.

Appendix B

99 Days

The *Detroit Daily Journal* [July 22, 1916] "broke" the story of Burroughs' cross-country trip after the author, "...a well set-up chap in a neat business suit presented himself in the editorial rooms and said quietly:

"I am Edgar Rice Burroughs."

As a matter of fact [reported the *Journal*], "the author of endless adventure stories had more adventures getting from Oak Park to Coldwater [Michigan] than Tarzan ever had.

"According to Mr. Burroughs', own statement, he ran this touring car 1,500 miles in reaching Coldwater, a distance of 193 miles from his starting point, and he figures that at the same rate he will travel 229,500 miles in getting to Los Angeles and will complete the journey in 23 years, 3 months and 15 days. [It took 99 days.]

"The equipment includes everything portable from a fireless cooker to a refrigerator, and from a phonograph to an electric break (*sic*) mixer. This equipment was too much for Calamity Jane (a trailer) and Happy Thought (an Overland truck) and one or the other of them broke down at least every three miles.

"The start was made in a pouring rain July 14 and the first camp pitched in a torrent at nightfall at Rolling Plains, Ind. Inasmuch as Calamity Jane had broken down completely a mile away, and as the tentmakers had sewed the long side of the tent floor to the short wall, and as everything else that could possibly go wrong had gone wrong, the site was named Camp Despair.

"However the next stop at Michigan City was so much better that it was called Camp Joy, and at the end of five days the party reached Coldwater, having in the meantime discarded Calamity Jane to her fate and purchased a truck, a transaction which involved Mr. Burroughs traveling from Alma, Mich., to Coldwater by rail, an experience which he does not expect to duplicate, as it required four different trains and 12 hours time, the distance being only about 100 miles.

"It was at Coldwater that they decided to start for California instead of Maine, but whether they ever reach there or not the author of 'Tarzan' will continue to write weird and unusual adventure stories. None of them will be about Calamity Jane or Happy Thought, however, because he has found that he can't write about anything he is thoroughly familiar with.

"'The less I know about a thing the better I can write about it,' says Mr. Burroughs frankly."

Appendix C

War Correspondent

Ed Burroughs was not a war correspondent in the usual sense of this term. He did not file regular reports, he did not follow troops from one post to another nor, as an observer, did he participate in close battle engagements. But as an aroused citizen (as well as a resident of Hawaii at the time of the Japanese attack on Pearl Harbor), the 66-year-old author swung into the fight in the only manner he could.

The following stories appeared in the columns of the *Honolulu Advertiser*, under the byline of Edgar Rice Burroughs, and are reprinted herein through the courtesy and with the permission of Mr. Thurston Twigg-Smith, president and publisher, Advertising Publishing Company, Ltd.

AUTHOR OF "TARZAN"
RIDES FLYING
FORTRESS
[Feb. 27, 1942]

I flew in a Flying Fortress the other day. Six of the great capital ships of the air flew in formation. I was in the sixth, with Jack Price, cameraman for Associated Press. I do not know what altitude we flew; but as I stood between two open gun ports, holding on to both because of the roughness of the air the sea, far below, appeared a solid mass of dark blue ice, flecked with snow....

And then two days later I watched some 1,200 other Americans being trained to serve. They were older men ... clerks, salesmen, business executives, bankers, lawyers. It has been said that comparisons are odious. But it can't be said in this instance, not truthfully. These men are as keen and conscientious and as proud of their organization as are the boys who fly the Fortresses. They are members of the Business Men's Training Corps—the BMTC ... I have attended every

BMTC Gets Training in Shooting Pistols
[March 14, 1942]

The training of the BMTC is constant, careful and never-ending. This is especially true of the care given in instructing the men in the handling and combatant use of the heavy .45 colt automatic pistols with which they are armed....

And they are on the streets nights now, guarding you and your homes ... walking their posts in the cold wind, the rain and the mud. You've got to hand it to 'em — these men who work in their regular jobs all day and then go out and walk their post at night. Why do they do it? For $21* a month? They don't get 21¢ a month for it. They do it because they are swell citizens and real patriots ... the Minute Men of 1942 ... living proof that America is not a decadent nation of conscientious objectors. More power to them.

(Unable to gain a combat assignment because of his age and physical condition, Ed wrote approximately a dozen columns from March through the end of 1942, all of which appeared on the editorial page of the *Advertiser*.)

What Is Sabotage
[March 26, 1942]

...Often we hear criticism of the Army and the Navy. Oftener still, we hear various civilian defense organizations belittled or ridiculed. That, my friends, is moral sabotage. Its authors are saboteurs ... worse than enemy Fifth Columnists and more dangerous. A fool is always more dangerous than a knave....

As a member of the BMTC, I am probably more aware of the moral saboteurs who are deliberately trying to undermine that organization than I am of others. Yet I hear many thoughtless criticism of Civilian Defense and ridicule of Air Raid Wardens. Let's stop it. I know that those who are 100 per cent loyal to America will.

Oahu: Singapore or Wake?
[May 19, 1942]

...Our soldiers, our sailors, our fliers have done and are doing a magnificent job. *But what are we doing?* We're sitting on our fat tails and letting "George do it." We are smugly complacent in our belief that with our tremendous resources, man power and wealth we shall eventually be able to lick the world — when we are ready. Okeh, brother! But before we are ready, we stand an excellent chance of being licked ourselves. Right up to the present moment we have been licked. We have been licked good and proper. We are still being licked....

This is an all-out war. Can't we ever get that through our thick heads? ... Are we making an all-out effort? We are not.

(ERB proceeded to read the riot act to his favorite organization, the BMTC, stating that they were only giving 12½ per cent of their leisure time to war work. He called upon them to give a minimum of at least eighteen hours a week — 33⅓ per cent.)

Other citizens should give as much. Oahu should set an example ... the eyes of the world are upon Oahu as never before since she was lifted from the depths of the ocean. Her place in history lies in our hands. Shall we go down in history as another Singapore or another Wake?

Don't Be Stupid
[July 4, 1942]

Shortly after the battle of Midway, I have heard a man say: "Now we can throw away our gas masks." A remark which exemplifies with some accuracy the stupid complacency of the general public since our decisive defeat of a Japanese Task Force.... Hitler has said that we are stupid. Perhaps Hitler is right. But why risk our lives to prove he is right?

---

*A private's pay during the peacetime draft and early part of the war.

...What I do know, and what everyone else must know is that the Japanese, for psychological reasons, have got to hit back. They've got to save both their faces....

Don't throw away your gas masks. Don't cancel your Mainland booking. Don't neglect your defense duties. Don't be stupid.

The Japs *might* come tomorrow.

DON'T LET 'EM KID YOU, JOE
[July 15, 1942]

(Ed replied to a statement by Representative Andrew J. May [D., Ky.] Chairman of the House Military Affairs Committee, who had been quoted as predicting an early United Nations victory in the war—which would make it unnecessary, May said, to draft eighteen and nineteen-year-old youths.)

I do not impugn the loyalty or patriotism of the Gentleman from Kentucky when I assert that [his] statement might have been dictated word by word by Goebbels. It is an outstanding example of unconscious morale sabotage, tending to lull millions of Americans into a false sense of security. Hitler and Hirohito must have loved it....

There is not the slightest reason to believe that the war will be won by the U.S. this year or next. But there is a hell of a lot of reasons to believe it could be won by the Axis this year....

I don't know what sinister shadow darkened Mr. May's mind. It may have been Publicity. It may have been Votes. But a mind that can see harm in drafting youths of 18 and 19 at this time was darkened by something—it is the type of mind which multiplied by millions, could cause us to lose the war.* Or, if we are victorious, to lose the peace....

NOT FOR MICE
[SEPT. 22, 1942]

This is a call for men....

There are some 25,000 adult male citizens of Hawaiian, part Hawaiian and Caucasian blood living here in the city of Honolulu. Perhaps many of them do not know how badly they are needed, nor where and how to offer their services. This article will tell them how.

The BMTC needs men. The BMTC needs YOU.

If you are anywhere between 21 and the grave, have all your arms and legs, a little endurance, and a lot of guts....

(The column listed addresses and phone numbers where those interested in joining the BMTC could get further information.)

WANTED: 1,000 MEN
[Sept. 24, 1942]

Our boys are fighting and dying on the beaches of the green little Islands of the South Pacific ... over the waters of the Pacific, the Atlantic, the North Sea and the Mediterranean. In China, in Europe, in Africa, in Asia. It is quite probable that one day they will be fighting and dying here again, as they did on December 7.

...the army wants a strong, well-trained BMTC for certain definite purposes of defense and to help maintain law and order.

...the Government will arm and equip you. You will give a few hours of your time each week. That is not too much to give.... Honolulu needs you. It may need you damn bad some cloudy morning.

BMTCERS CAN SHOOT
[Sept. 30, 1942]

(An ex–master sergeant, in a letter to the *Advertiser*, questioned the wisdom of placing arms in the hands of men not qualified to use them. ERB answered the letter by telling of the training procedures and weapon instructions which were part of the BMTC course, and he added:)

...There are many old-time Army men in the BMTC. Mr. Pinchon should be in it. We need all the experienced men we can get, regardless of age. From the date of his service, 1898, I judge that Mr. Pinchon is about the same vintage as I, although probably

---

*Many Congressmen (and prominent citizens) were strongly opposed to the bill extending the draft when it came up for vote only four months before Pearl Harbor. The House passed it 203–202.

younger. I was discharged from the 7th Cavalry in 1896.*

I can still hobble. If he can, he should join up.

WHATSOEVER A MAN SOWETH
[Oct. 21, 1942]

Russia reproaches us for the paucity of aid we have given her.† ... She forgets that against her 2,000-mile front, we have a 25,000-mile front....

We admire Russia as a great and powerful ally [but] if Russia forgets, we do not. We do not forget that for more than a quarter of a century Russia has been trying to undermine and overthrow our government....

Before one plane or one bullet was sent to the aid of Russia, we should have demanded this assurance from Russia.... Perhaps, if we were convinced that Russia would always be an ally and would never again attempt to interfere in our politics, we could and would redouble our efforts to aid her now. But deep in the fiber of our being is suspicion and distrust of the Government of Russia ... sowing deep for a quarter of a century, planted it there.

Whatsoever a Man Soweth, he Reapeth.

SATURDAY NIGHT IN HONOLULU DULL
[Nov. 11, 1942]

Bernard Clayton, *Life* magazine representative in Hawaii, and I accompanied Brig. Gen. Thomas H. Green, executive to the Military Governor, on a tour of Honolulu front line civilian defenses Saturday night.

However, there was absolutely no activity in the front line trenches, the enemy "Demon Rum" having practically run out of ammunition.

(The trio toured the city from 7:30 to 11:30 P.M., visiting the Red Cross stations, first aid units, telephone censors, auxiliary police — all hard at work.)

And so to bed, taking with me an increased admiration for my fellow Americans — God bless 'em.

ERB broke up his regular commentaries to report on a field trip with an artillery outfit working on the defenses of Hawaii. It was released in the *Los Angeles Times* (and perhaps carried to other papers via the U.P. wire).

[Dec. 1, 1942]

Our battery left its position at 7:02 P.M. The range section and each of the big guns was hauled by an enormous, brutal-looking truck called a prime mover....

Captain Philip Bird of Oklahoma City, an observer, and I, of Tarzana, Cal., an innocent bystander, rode in the jeep at the head of the column with Capt. Robert Jaap of Canton, [Ohio] the battery commander. The convoy trailed out behind us like the tail of a comet — a 15 miles-per-hour comet....

A range section consists of several units, including heavy, extremely delicate, precision instruments.... In 15 minutes the first unit, in the range section, was set up and ready to function....

There was another snappy section that ran [the first unit] a close second. We saw them huddled on their knees in a circle, laboring in the dim rays of a single flashlight even before the first gun was rolling to its position. This was the craps section....

What most impresses one is the assurance and confidence with which these boys handle an intricate job so remote, for most of them, from the peacetime work which they did a few months ago.

(Ed managed to get closer to the war at the tail end of 1942. What probably pleased him most was the front-page space the newspaper gave to his story, plus the byline: "United Press Staff Correspondent." Unfortunately, the headline was the most interesting part of the article.)

---

*Actually March 23, 1897, after ten months' service.
†On October 1, 1941, a little more than three months after the German invasion of Russia, the U.S. granted the Soviets credit for $1 billion in materièl and other lend-lease aid. A new agreement went into effect July 1, 1942.

TARZAN'S CREATOR,
NOW COVERING WAR,
FINDS AUSSIE CUSTOMS ODD
[JAN. 4, 1943]

I have no business by being here and shall probably lose my job and have to go back to writing Tarzan and Martian stories and other factual and scientific works but when the opportunity presented itself, I couldn't resist the temptation. So here I am "down under" on Christmas, 1942, and glad of it....

ERB further reported that he was routed out of bed at 3:30 A.M. and loaded onto a truck with a dozen other men ... but not much was happening so he told of finding Aussie customs odd. Such as: "Streetcars are calls trams, cars are driven on the wrong side of the street, cops are called constables and whiskey means scotch."

(Ed got within shooting range when he reported from a South Pacific base, most likely in southern New Guinea or Guadalcanal.)

[Feb. 14, 1943]

I have just returned from a couple of days in the field with a tank outfit. Sure I had plenty of fun; but then I didn't have to camp out for the duration, I hope....

Standing on the summit of a hill, I watched the tanks move into position to attack. It was interesting. It was thrilling. I should like to describe it to you. But I have a hunch it won't get by [the censors].

What I hope does get by is this brief description of how your men are living and working way down here to-hellengone from home. They are cheerful, their health is excellent on the Island. They want letters ... cheerful letters....

Honeys, write your boy friends. When you don't, their buddies tell them you have fallen for some rejectee.

(ERB had more thoughts about "mail," and the result was this editorial in the *Advertiser*.)

[March 20, 1943]

There is food for solemn thought in the observation of Edgar Rice Burroughs upon mail for the men in the fighting fronts. His suggestion that free mail be discontinued to discourage indiscriminate letter writing may not meet general approval, but his pleas that letters to the fighting men be put on a more personal plane is sound....

(After his brief stint "up front" with the army, ERB made plans to join the Air Corps but, first, he had a few words to say about Hirohito and the murder of Doolittle's fliers.)*

BOMB HIRIHITO
[April 24, 1943]

...the purpose of these murders and the public announcement was obviously intended to intimidate us and deter us from further bombings of industrial Japan. Another example of Japanese stupidity. They have only advanced the day of the next bombing ... and multiplied the number of bombers that will reign death and destruction upon them.

In the first raid on Tokyo, we purposely refrained from bombing the palace of the syphilitic, near-imbecile god whom they worship. The Japanese mind could attribute this humanitarian decency only to fear. The next raid should disabuse their mind of this false conception.

---

*Commanded by Major General James H. Doolittle, carrier-based army (B-25) bombers raided Tokyo on April 18, 1942. The airmen who had been forced down and captured by the Japanese were publicly beheaded.

Appendix D

Proposal for a National Reserve Army

Several months prior to the end of World War I, Edgar Rice Burroughs, Captain,* 1st Battalion, 2d Infantry, Illinois Reserve Militia, proposed a National Reserve Army, in a letter to the editor of the *Army and Navy Journal* (August 31, 1918):

> Marching in the Memorial Day parade in Chicago there were, I understand, some eleven thousand uniformed men of the Illinois Reserve Militia and the Illinois Volunteer Training Corps from Cook county. About half of these men are equipped with rifles, and all of them have received more or less training during the past year. They are typical of several hundred thousand other men throughout the country who belong to similar organizations. They are volunteers for military training—active exponents of a sincere belief in the necessity for further preparation for whatever military service the Government may require of them in the future. They represent, however, only a small proportion of the available men between the ages of eighteen and forty-five who should be receiving military training and now that the draft age limits may be extended these men and their organization naturally assume a greater importance to the Government than ever before. The question arises as to how these trained units may be utilized to the best advantage.
>
> One of the inherent weaknesses of the present Reserve Militia and Volunteer Training Corps is due to the fact that they are volunteer organizations. Will we never, even in the face of all the sad experience of our own

---

*ERB enlisted in the reserve militia May 28, 1917, was appointed a captain January 1, 1918, and a major on October 15.

times backed by the historic calamities of past centuries, get once and for all away from all connection with voluntary military service? No man should be allowed to wear the cloth until he is ordered to do so by competent authority—no man should be permitted to enlist; but every man should be compelled to serve in the same capacity.

A National Reserve Army suggests a plan of service and preparatory training that would meet the military requirements of each state for protection against internal disorders, and at the same time furnish trained recruits for the National Army, instead of unloading upon it enormous batches of raw material at each call. A law could be enacted providing for a preliminary draft of men between eighteen and forty-nine who should be required to serve in local units until such time as they might be drafted into the National Army.

Their duties would be such as not to interfere with their present occupations, including drills two nights a week and Sunday mornings. Their active service might be limited to service within their respective states at the discretion of the Governors. By this plan no more would be required of any man than is being voluntarily given by many thousands today. The expense to the Government would be comparatively small—consisting only in uniforms and equipment, all of which might be transferred to the National Army, if necessary, as the men were drafted for the latter service.

We should give men preliminary training before placing them in the National Army. That this is worth while is evidenced by the fact that the large majority of Reserve Militia men are made squad leaders and non-commissioned officers immediately after reaching National Army training camps, although, in Illinois, at least only two hours drill a week is required. In a year we are required to attend drill for a total period of training that aggregates less than two weeks of average working days. If it is worth while under such conditions how much greater would be the benefits to Government, state and individual if these units could drill three times a week under a compulsory law that would insure maximum instead of minimum attendance?

If this sort of preliminary training served to eliminate two weeks' elementary training at the National Army cantonments, then saving to the Government would be well worth while. The actual saving in subsistence and pay would more than cover the cost of equipping these men for the Reserve Army, while the saving in time might easily prove far beyond possible estimate were we able at the end of six months to place an additional man in France two weeks earlier than under present conditions. Nor is this all—the longer the war continues the more proficient would the men of the National Reserve Army become and the shorter the course of training required at National Army cantonments.

The greatest difficulty which presents itself is the efficient offering of such a Reserve Army; but even this may be overcome by a system of examinations and by establishing training camps for those officers where they would receive instruction for short periods and at such intervals during the year that their means of livelihood might not be seriously interfered with.

It is, of course, a great undertaking; but it is worth the effort and most assuredly warrants serious discussion. From an intimate knowledge of conditions affecting the Reserve Militia and the Volunteer Training Corps gained by actual experience since the first unit was formed, I am convinced that such a plan would meet with wide approval, not only among men already affiliated with these organizations, but with those who have not yet enlisted in one or the other. At present a few men in each community bear the expense and make the sacrifices to a thankless service which they believe a necessary service. With Federal backing and the consequent standing it would give these organizations, one of the greatest present discouragements to the work would be eliminated—I refer to the national endency to ridicule the "Home Guard."

The nucleus of a new Army is already trained—a sincere, intelligent, patriotic nucleus of men who are not only contributing voluntarily and by taxation to the support of the Government's war policy; but who for over a year have been training themselves practically without recognition or support against the time the President might need them as fighting men. Let us use these men—let us have a law that will build around them a National Reserve Army.

Appendix E

Novels of Edgar Rice Burroughs

Tarzan Series	Book Publication	Magazine Publication	Year Written
Tarzan of the Apes	1914	1912	1911–12
The Return of Tarzan	1915	1913	1912–13
The Beasts of Tarzan	1916	1914	1914
The Son of Tarzan	1917	1915–16	1915
Tarzan and the Jewels of Opar	1918	1916	1915
Jungle Tales of Tarzan	1919	1916–17	1916–17
Tarzan the Untamed	1920	1919–20	1918–19
Tarzan the Terrible	1921	1921	1920
Tarzan and the Golden Lion	1923	1922–23	1922
Tarzan and the Ant Men	1924	1924	1923
The Tarzan Twins	1927	never	1926–27
Tarzan, Lord of the Jungle	1928	1927–28	1927
Tarzan and the Lost Empire	1929	1928–29	1928
Tarzan at the Earth's Core	1930	1929–30	1928–29
Tarzan the Invincible	1931	1930–31	1930
Tarzan Triumphant	1932	1931–32	1931

Tarzan and the City of Gold	1933	1932	1931–32
Tarzan and the Lion Man	1934	1933–34	1933
Tarzan and the Leopard Men	1935	1932–33	1931
Tarzan and the Tarzan Twins with Jad-bal-ja, the Golden Lion	1936	never	1928
Tarzan's Quest	1936	1935–36	1934–35
Tarzan and the Forbidden City	1938	1938	1937
Tarzan the Magnificent	1939	1936–38	1935–37
Tarzan and "The Foreign Legion"	1947	never	1944
Tarzan and the Madman	1964	never	1940
Tarzan and the Castaways	1964	1940–41	1939–40

Martian Series	*Book Publication*	*Magazine Publication*	*Year Written*
A Princess of Mars	1917	1912	1911
The Gods of Mars	1918	1913	1912
The Warlord of Mars	1919	1913–14	1913
Thuvia, Maid of Mars	1920	1916	1914
The Chessmen of Mars	1922	1922	1921
The Master Mind of Mars	1928	1927	1925
A Fighting Man of Mars	1931	1930	1929
Swords of Mars	1936	1934–35	1933
Synthetic Men of Mars	1940	1939	1938
Llana of Gathol	1948	1941	1940
John Carter of Mars	1964	1941, 1943	1940, 1941

Venus Series			
Pirates of Venus	1934	1932	1931
Lost on Venus	1935	1933	1932
Carson of Venus	1939	1938	1937
Escape on Venus	1946	1941–42	1940
The Wizard of Venus	*	never	1941

Inner-World (Pellucidar) Series			
At the Earth's Core	1922	1914	1913
Pellucidar	1923	1915	1914–15
Tanar of Pellucidar	1930	1929	1928
Tarzan at the Earth's Core†	1930	1929–30	1928–29

The Wizard of Venus, a novelette, was published in book form in 1964 as part of the book *Tales of Three Planets*, which also included:
    Beyond the Farthest Star (Part 1)
    Tangor Returns (Part 2)
    The Resurrection of Jimber-Jaw
†Also listed in the Tarzan series.

Back to the Stone Age	1937	1937	1935
Land of Terror	1944	never	1938–39
Savage Pellucidar	1963	1942, 1963,	1940, 1944

Apache Series

The War Chief	1927	1927	1926
Apache Devil	1933	1928	1927

Other Stories	Book Publication	Magazine Publication	Year Written
The Mucker	1921	1914, 1916,	1913, 1916
The Girl from Hollywood	1923	1922	1921–22
The Land That Time Forgot	1924	1918	1917–18
The Cave Girl	1925	1913, 1917	1913, 1914
The Bandit of Hell's Bend	1925	1924	1923
The Eternal Lover	1925	1914, 1915	1913, 1914
The Moon Maid	1926	1923, 1925	1919, 1922, 1925
The Mad King	1926	1914, 1915	1913, 1914
The Outlaw of Torn	1927	1914	1911–12
The Monster Men	1929	1913	1913
Jungle Girl	1932	1931	1929
The Oakdale Affair and The Rider	1937	1918	1917, 1915
The Lad and the Lion	1938	1917	1914, 1937
The Deputy Sheriff of Comanche County	1940	1940	1930
Beyond Thirty and The Man-Eater	1957	1916, 1915	1915
I Am a Barbarian	1967	never	1941

Compiled with the help of Henry Hardy Heins.

Appendix F

Edgar Rice Burroughs Ape-English Dictionary

A light
ab boy
abalu brother
abu knee (kneel)
adu lose
ala rise
amba fall
ara lightning
arad spear
argo fire
aro shoot, throw, cast
at tail
atan male
bal golden
balu baby
balu-den stick, branch, limb
band elbow
bar battle
ben great

bo flat
bolgani gorilla
bu he
bund dead
bundolo kill
bur cold
busso fly
buto rhinoceros
b'wang hand
b'yat head
b'zan hair
b'zee foot
dak fat
dak-lul lake
dako thick
dako-zan meat, flesh
dan rock, stone
dan-do stop
dango hyena

dan-lul ice
dano bone
dan-sopu nut
den tree
dum-dum tom-tom, drum, gathering
duro hippopotamus
eho much
eho-dan hard
eho-kut hollow
eho-lul wet
eho-nala top
es rough
eta little
eta-gogo whisper
eta-koho warm
eta-nala low
etarad arrow
ga red
galul blood
gando win
gash tooth, fang
gimla crocodile
go black
gogo talk (buffalo)
gom run
gomangani Negro
gom-lul river
gor growl
gorgo buffalo (moon)
goro moon
gree-ah like, love
gu stomach, belly
gugu front
gumado sick
gund chief
histah (hista) snake
ho many
hoden forest
hohotan tribe
horta boar
hotan clan
ho-wala village
ho-wa-usha leaves
hul star
jabo shield
jar strange
kagoda? Do you surrender?

kagoda! I do surrender!
kal milk
kalan female
kalo cow
kalu mother
kambo jungle
kando ant
karpo middle, center
kas jump
klu hen
klu-kal egg
ko mighty
kob hit
koho hot
kor walk
korak killer
kordo dance
ko-sabor mighty lioness
kota tortoise
kreeg-ah beware, danger
kree-gor scream
kudu sun
kut hole
lan right
lana sting
lano mosquito
lat nose
litu sharp
lob kick
lot face
lu fierce
lufo side
lul waer
lul-kor swim
lus tongue
mado lame
mal yellow
mangani great apes
manu monkey
meeta rain
mo short
mu she
m'wa blue
nala up
neeta bird
nene beetle
nesen grasshopper

no brook
numa lion
nur lie (untruth)
olo wrestle
om long
omtag giraffe
pacco zebra
pal country (tribe's hunting grounds)
pamba rat
pan soft
pand thunder
panda noise
pandar loud
pand-balu-den rifle
pan-lul weep
pan-vo weak
pastar father
pele valley
pisah (pisa) fish
po hungry
popo eat (also "so")
por mate
por-atan husband
por-kalan wife
rak yes (also "huh")
rala snare
ramba lie down
rand back
rea word
rem catch
rep truth
ro flower
rota laugh
ry crooked
ry-balu-den bow
sabor lioness
sato kind
sheeta panther, leopard
skree wild-cat
so eat (also "popo")
sopu fruit
sord bad
ta high, tall
tag neck
tan warrior
tand no, not
tanda dark

tandak thin
tand-ho few
tandlan left
tand-litu dull, blunt
tand-lul dry
tand-nala down
tand-panda silent, silence
tand-popo starve
tand-ramba get up
tand-unk stay
tand-utor brave
tand-vulp empty
tan-klu rooster
tantor elephant
ta-pal hill
tar white
tar-bur snow
tarmangani white men
tho mouth
thub heart
tongani (tongoni) baboon
tor beast
tro straight
tu bright
tub broken
ubor thirsty
ud drink
ug bottom
ugh okay
ugla hate
ungo (unga) jackal
unk go
unk-nala climb
usha wind
ut corn
utor fear, afraid
van well
vando good
ved mountain
vo muscle
voo-dum dance
voo-voo sing
vulp full
wa green
wala nest, hut, home, house
wang arm
wappi antelope

wa-usha	leaf	*yuto*	cut
whuff	smoke	*za*	girl
wo	this	*za-balu*	sister
wob	that	*zan*	skin
yad	ear	*zee*	leg
yang	swing	*zor*	in
yat	eye	*zu*	big
yato	look, see	*zu-dak-lul (za-dak-lul)*	ocean
yel	here	*zugor*	roar
yeland	there	*zu-kut*	cave
yo	friend	*zut*	out
yud	come	*zu-vo*	strong
yut	stab, gore		

Compiled by Thomas McGeehan, and published in *ERB-dom*, October 1962. Reprinted by permission of editor-publisher Camille Cazedessus Jr. (Dictionary has been revised from ERB's original list to include additional words used in Tarzan comic books and various reprints.)

Index

Ace Books 12
The Adventures of Tarzan (film serial) 105
The Adventures of the Black Girl in Her Search for God (Shaw) 47n
Alger, R.A. 25
All-Story — Cavalier Weekly 24, 64, 65, 82–83, 95n
All-Story magazine 17, 17n, 38, 39, 42, 64n, 65n, 100n
All-Story Weekly 20n, 65n, 82, 83, 96n
American Battery Company 22, 23, 29, 30, 35, 41
American Civil War 17, 21, 23, 94
American Film Company 66
Apache Kid 25
Ape-English Dictionary 205–208
Arbuckle, Fatty 99
Argosy All-Story Weekly 24n, 88n, 96n
Argosy magazine 13n, 100n, 128n, 163n, 165n, 168n
Armed Services Editions, Inc. 157
At the Earth's Core (Burroughs) 49, 188
Author's League of America 50
Author's Photo-Play Agency 64

Ballantine Books Inc. 11–13, 157
Bancroft, Cecil F.P. 20
Bantam Books, Inc. 157–158
Barker, Lex 108, 182
Barney Custer of Beatrice (Burroughs) 66n
Bean, Normal (Norman) 39, 42, 60
The Beast of Tarzan (Burroughs) 64, 66, 69, 201; foreign editions of 51, 81, 111; reprint rights to 56
Berlin Film Control Board 81, 86
Berlin *Lokal Anzeiger* 85
Berliner Tageblatt 85, 86
Beyond Thirty (Burroughs) 68n, 203
Biblo, Jack 11
"Bloody 7th" 24–26
Blue Book Magazine 13n, 79n, 117n, 118n, 119n, 120n, 131n, 161n, 163n, 168n
BMTC (Business Men's Training Corps) 193–94
Boston Advertiser 52
Bray, Joseph E. 51, 153–155
Brix, Herman 36, 145
Brown School (Chicago) 17

Burroughs, Abner T. (grandfather) 16
Burroughs, Edgar Rice: ancestry of 6–19; business 28–29, 30–33, 35–37; death of 182; education of 17, 19–20; initiation into writing 37–39; Kipling compared to 56–61; listed 41–42; marriages of 18, 23, 28, 29, 56, 131, 137, 149, 154, 169, 172, 176; military 22–28, 77; mining 31, 32; novels of, listed 201–203; railway police 32–33; ranching 113–114; war correspondent 175–179, 193–197; *see also* specific works
Burroughs, Edna McCoy (sister-in-law) 29
Burroughs, Ella Oldham (sister-in-law) 29, 31
Burroughs, Emma Hulbert (1st wife) 18, 23, 29, 38n, 67; death of 151; marriage of 120, 131–132; returns to Chicago 32– 33; in West 32–33
Burroughs, Evelyn *see* McKenzie, Evelyn Burroughs
Burroughs, Florence Dearhold (2nd wife) 131–132, 148, 151,

209

166, 167, 169, 181; divorces Burroughs 172
Burroughs, Frank Coleman (brother) 17, 19, 22, 31; as businessman 33, 38; marriage of 28
Burroughs, George T. (father) 16, 17–18, 25, 28, 32, 35; business career of 22; character of 44; death of 49
Burroughs, Grace Moss (sister-in-law) 28
Burroughs, Henry S. (Harry) (brother) 17–18, 28, 44; as businessman 35–39; marriage of 29; as miner 20, 31–32
Burroughs, Hulbert (son) 10, 11, 13, 74, 120, 156, 170; birth of 37
Burroughs, Joan see Pierce, Joan Burroughs
Burroughs, John Coleman (Jack) (son) 10, 74, 156, 182; birth of 49; as illustrator 125
Burroughs, Mary Rice (grandmother) 16
Burroughs, Mary Zieger (mother) 16–17, 35, 79
Burroughs, Studley (nephew) 31
Burroughs Bibliophiles 61
Burroughs (Edgar Rice), Inc. 10, 12, 140, 143, 155, 185; formation of 114; reprint rights of 156
Burt (A.L.) & Company 53n
Business Men's Training Corps (BMTC) 193

California 63, 181; first residence in 67, 68; safari to 66, 67, 181; second residence in see Rancho Tarzana
Canaveral Press 12–13
The Capture of Tarzan (Burroughs) 68n
Carson of Venus (Burroughs) 171, 202
The Cave Girl (Burroughs) 49, 65, 155, 203
Champlin-Yardley Company 38
Chapman, William G. 51–52, 64
Charlton Publications, Inc. 184
Chicago, Illinois 17, 23–24, 32, 64–66, 68; 1893 World's Fair in 22
Chicago Daily News 115–116
Chicago Journal 73
Chicago Post 52
Chicago Tribune 61n
Civil War 17, 29, 79
Cleveland, Grover 20–22, 25n
The Climate and the View (Burroughs) 60
"*The Contribs of Yesteryear*" (Burroughs) 60
Coriell, Vernell 11, 182
Crabbe, Buster 138–139

Davis, Robert H. 44 50, 170
Dearholt, Florence see Burroughs, Florence Dearholt
Debs, Eugene V. 17
The Deputy Sheriff of Comanche County (Burroughs) 167n, 168n, 203
Dieck (Charles) and Company 84
Dover Publications 12
Duranty, Walter 110
Durling, E.V. 70, 73

The Efficiency Expert (Burroughs) 36n, 97
Elser, Maximillian, Jr. 124
The End of Bukawai (Burroughs) 68n
Escape on Venus (Burroughs) 15, 170–171, 202

Famous Books and Plays, Inc. 123–124
Fantastic Adventures 15n, 16n, 171n
Fielder, Brig. Gen. Kendall 176–178
The Fight for the Balu (Burroughs) 68n
Fort Grant, Arizona 24
Foster, Harold (Hal) 124
Frankfurter Zeitung 84–85
Franklin, Oliver R. 175, 177

Galveston News 52
Germany 81, 82–86, 172, 173
Geronimo 24
The Girl from Farris's (Burroughs) 68n, 95
The Girl from Hollywood 36n, 95, 98, 100–102, 161, 203
The God of Tarzan (Burroughs) 68n
The Gods of Mars (Burroughs) 49, 75, 155, 202
Gould, Herbert A. 51
"Grandma Burroughs' Cook Book" (Burroughs) 30
Greeley, Evelyn 79
Gridley Wave (fanzine) 11, 61n
Griffith, D. W. 66, 67, 71n
Griffith, Gordon 71, 72, 105
Grosset & Dunlap, Inc. 11–13, 53n, 153; reprint rights of 155–159

Haggard, H. Rider 56–57
Hagenbeck Wild Animal Show 22
Harding, Warren G. 91, 91n
Harvard School (Chicago) 17
Harwood, John 11
Haymarket Square riot 17
Heins, Henry H. 11n, 203
Hitler, Adolf 84, 86, 194
Hollywood 63, 95, 130–131, 133; sin and scandal in 98–100; in

Tarzan and the Lion Men 143–146
Holmes, Oliver Wendell 19, 20
Honolulu Advertiser 168–170, 176, 179, 193–197
Hopper, Hedda 60, 60n
Hulbert, Emma see Burroughs, Emma Hulbert

Idaho 13, 22, 28, 31–33, 38
Indianapolis News 101
Indians, American 24–25

Jensen, Mildren 116, 136, 149, 150
Jungle Tales of Tarzan (Burroughs) 43, 74, 77, 84, 128, 158, 161

Kalivoda, R. 159
Kelly, Kitty 73
Ketchum, Tom 24
King, Capt. Charles 21, 37
Kipling, Rudyard 22, 55, 57, 96, 188; *The Jungle Book* 55, 57
Kipling Society 61
Kreuzer, James R. 183

The Lad and the Lion (Burroughs) 203; film of 65, 68, 69
The Land That Time Forgot (Burroughs) 75, 155, 203
Lay, Robert D. 67
Lesser, Sol 136, 139, 167, 168, 178, 182
Liberty Magazine 143n, 144
Lincoln, Elmo 71–73, 75, 105
Llana of Gathol (Burroughs) 172, 202
London, Jack 44
Los Angeles Examiner 90
Los Angeles Times 56, 169, 176, 190, 196

McClurg, A.C., & Co. 12, 39, 44, 50–51, 53–54, 60, 64, 69, 75, 78, 82, 84n, 95; publishes *Tarzan of the Apes* 50–53, 64, 82; reprint rights of 187
McCoy, Edna (sister-in-law) 29
McKenzie, Evelyn Burroughs (niece) 28, 44; on her uncle 28
McKinley, William 29
Macmillan's Magazine 59
The Mad King (Burroughs) 49, 66n, 203
Maine (battleship) 27
The Man-Eater (Burroughs) 66n, 203
Markey, Enid 72, 73, 75
Maxon, Rex 124–125
Merrill, Frank 107
Metcalf, Thomas N. 38, 39, 50
Methuen and Company Ltd. 69, 75, 100, 155
Metro-Goldwyn-Mayer 107, 136

Metropolitan Newspaper Service 124, 125
Miller, Fred 71, 73
Milwaukee Journal 52
Minter, Mary Miles 99
The Monster Men (Burroughs) 49, 155, 203
Moss, Grace (sister-in-law) 29
Motion Picture News 104, 106, 189
"Mowgli" 55–59
The Mucker (Burroughs) 44, 66n, 155, 203

Nada the Lily (Haggard) 56–57
National Film Corporation of American 70, 106
Neebe, Joseph H. 123–124
The New Adventures of Tarzan (film serial) 148, 167
The New Stories of Tarzan (Burroughs) 43, 68n, 73
New Story magazine 49, 50
New York Evening World 51, 64n
New York Herald 101
New York Post 101
New York Sunday World 28n, 187–188
The New York Times 13, 53, 72, 101, 189–190; reviews *Tarzan of the Apes* 53, 72, 73
New York Tribune 52
Normand, Mabel 99
Numa-Goldwyn Productions 103

The Oakdale Affair (Burroughs) 75, 125n, 203; film of 79
O'Connor, John 158
Oldham, Ella (sister-in-law) 29, 31
Omaha World-Herald 52
Orchard Lake Michigan Military Academy 21
O'Sullivan, Maureen 136, 139
Out of Time's Abyss (Burroughs) 75
The Outlaw of Torn (Burroughs) 39, 43, 49, 66n, 155, 203

Parry, Albert 126
Parsons, William 66, 74, 75
Passaic Herald 102
Pellucidar (Burroughs) 66n, 202
The People That Time Forgot (Burroughs) 75
Pershing, Gen. John J. 68
Phillips Academy (Mass.) 19–20
Pickford, Jack 98
Pierce, James 10, 137; as "Tarzan" 107, 128, 138, 167
Pierce, Joan Burroughs (daughter) 10, 16, 21, 74; birth of 36, 42, 181–182; on her father 30, 47, 61, 68, 74, 78, 82, 115, 116, 140, 150, 181

Pollar, Gene 104
Portland Oregonian 101
A Princess of Mars (Burroughs) 75, 203
"Proposal for a National Reserve Army" (Burroughs) 199–200

The Quest of Tarzan 168n

Rancho Tarzana 10, 115–116; artist's colony on 113–114; described 78–79, 115; sale of 150–151
Rappe, Virginia 99
Red Book magazine 50, 59
Reed, Vivian 69
Reichenbach, Harry 71, 104
Reid, Wallace 100
The Return of Tarzan (Burroughs) 11, 12, 56, 59, 188, 201; as comic strip 124; critique of 82, 130; film of 102, 105; pessimism in 37; reprint rights 69, 159
The Return of the Mucker (Burroughs) 68n
Rogers, Brevet Maj. J.S. 21, 23
Romance of Tarzan (film) 59
Roosevelt, Franklin D. 21, 65, 127, 138, 154n, 172–173
Ross, Nellie Taylor 90–91
Rothman, Ralph 10, 155; on Burroughs 136; reprint rights 150, 157
Rough Riders 28
Russia 126, 173, 184, 196

Sacramento Bee 101
St. Paul Pioneer 52
Salt Lake City, Utah 32
San Francisco Argonaut 52
Schramm, Karla 104–105
Schroeder, Elise 64
Scopes "Monkey Trial" 92
Searle, Kamuela C. 105
Sears, Roebuck and Company 36, 169
Selig, William, N. 65–66, 68
Selig Polyscope Company of Chicago 65
Shaw, George Bernard 47n
Shaw (A.W.) Company 43–44
Sidney, Scott 78
Slaves of the Fish Men (Burroughs) 16, 202; film serial of 103–105; foreign editions of 86; reprint rights to 156
Sorel, Stefan 84
Spanish American War 27–28
Sparks, D. H. 159
Stace, Burroughs and Company 37, 38
Stern (Joseph W.) & Co. 64
Sweetheart Primeval (Burroughs) 66n

Sweetser, Lewis H. 18, 18n, 31
Sweetser-Burroughs Mining Company 31
The Synthetic Men of Mars (Burroughs) 168, 202

Tannen, Jack 11–12
Tarzan and His Mate (film) 139
Tarzan and the Ant Men (Burroughs) 41, 88, 153, 201; critique of 89–92
Tarzan and the Black Boy (Burroughs) 68n
Tarzan and the Castaways (Burroughs) 113, 128–131, 163, 202
Tarzan and the Champion (Burroughs) 168n
Tarzan and the City of Gold (Burroughs) 35, 113, 128–131, 163, 202
Tarzan and the Forbidden City (Burroughs) 165–166, 202
Tarzan and "The Foreign Legion" (Burroughs) 10, 164, 175, 178, 202
Tarzan and the Golden Lion (Burroughs) 35, 88, 201; on civilization 37; film of 11, 106, 136; reprint rights to 159
Tarzan and the Green Goddess (film) 147n, 167
Tarzan and the Jewels of Opar (Burroughs) 68n, 75, 107, 201; foreign editions of 84; reprint rights to 158
Tarzan and the Jungle Murders (Burroughs) 168n
Tarzan and the Leopard Men (Burroughs) 131–133, 202
Tarzan and the Lion Man (Burroughs) 163, 103, 161, 202; critique of 143–146
Tarzan and the Lost Empire (Burroughs) 12, 13, 117, 201, 202
Tarzan and the Slave Girl (film) 11n, 182n
Tarzan and the Tarzan Twins with Jad-bal-ja, the Golden Lion 168n, 202
Tarzan at the Earth's Core (Burroughs) 12, 57n, 118–119, 127, 201, 202
Tarzan Clans of America 168
Tarzan Escapes (film) 150
Tarzan, Lord of the Jungle (Burroughs) 116–117, 128, 201; reprint rights to 158
Tarzan of the Apes (Burroughs), 10, 12, 21, 55, 92, 93, 163, 165, 182, 183, 185, 188, 201; as comic strip 124–125; critique of 44–47, 52–53, 130; film of 64–65, 66, 69–73, 75, 78, 82, 86, 107; foreign editions of 86, 172; publication of 51-2, 59; reprint

rights to 69, 84, 156, 159, 163; sales of 153; writing of 44–46
"Tarzan Special" cocktail 128
Tarzan the Ape Man (film) 148
Tarzan the Fearless (film) 138, 144
Tarzan the Invincible (Burroughs) 120, 135, 144, 201
Tarzan the Mighty (film serial) 107
Tarzan the Terrible (Burroughs) 49, 158, 188, 201
Tarzan the Tiger (film serial) 107, 136
Tarzan the Untamed (Burroughs) 82, 84–85, 87, 88, 159, 181, 201
Tarzan Triumphant (Burroughs) 120, 201
Tarzan Triumphs (film) 120
The Tarzan Twins (Burroughs) 10, 168n, 201
Tarzan's Quest (Burroughs) 109, 123, 130, 161–164, 167–168, 202
Tarzan's Revenge (film) 60n, 83

Taylor, William Desmond 99
Tennant, J. H. 51
The Terrible Tenderfoot (Burroughs) 168n
Thomas, Olive 98
Thrilling Adventures 13n, 168n
Thuvia, Maid of Maris (Burroughs) 68n, 155, 202
Todd, Thelma 137
Toronto Globe 53

Under the Moons of Mars (Burroughs) 39; publication of 69; writing of 60
United Features Syndicate 125–126
Universal Films 66

Variety (newspaper) 137, 148n
Vienna *Neue Freie Presse* 85

The War Chief (Burroughs) 24, 155, 203

The Warlord of Mars (Burroughs) 49, 155, 202
Weissmuller, Johnny 135, 139, 140, 168
West Point (U.S. Military Academy) 22–23
Wilkening, Cora C. 64–65
Williams, Edna 64
Wilson, Winslow 71
Wilson, Woodrow 63, 68, 68n, 75
Winslow (T. J.) Company 36
The Witch-Doctor Seeks Vengeance (Burroughs) 68n
World Columbian Exposition (Chicago) 22
World War I 68
World War II 126, 140, 173, 178

Yale University 18, 19, 31

Zieger, Mary (mother) *see* Burroughs, Mary Zieger

www.ingramcontent.com/pod-product-compliance
Ingram Content Group UK Ltd.
Pitfield, Milton Keynes, MK11 3LW, UK
UKHW050535150426
5217IPUK00026B/1941